More Cadillac V-16s
Lost and Found

Also by Christopher W. Cummings

Cadillac V-16s Lost and Found: Tracing the Histories of the 1930s Classics
(McFarland, 2014)

The Cadillac That Followed Me Home: Memoir of a V-16 Dream Realized
(McFarland, 2006)

More Cadillac V-16s Lost and Found

67 New Histories

CHRISTOPHER W. CUMMINGS

McFarland & Company, Inc., Publishers
Jefferson, North Carolina

Photographs are from the author's collection unless otherwise stated.

LIBRARY OF CONGRESS CATALOGUING-IN-PUBLICATION DATA

Names: Cummings, Christopher W., 1952– author.
Title: More Cadillac V-16s lost and found : 67 new histories / Christopher W. Cummings.
Description: Jefferson, North Carolina : McFarland & Company, Inc.,
Publishers, 2021 | Includes bibliographical references and index.
Identifiers: LCCN 2020054463 | ISBN 9781476681061 (paperback : acid free paper) ∞
ISBN 9781476641034 (ebook)
Subjects: LCSH: Cadillac automobile—History—20th century. | Antique and
classic cars—Collectors and collecting—United States.
Classification: LCC TL215.C27 C863 2021 | DDC 629.222—dc23
LC record available at https://lccn.loc.gov/2020054463

BRITISH LIBRARY CATALOGUING DATA ARE AVAILABLE

ISBN (print) 978-1-4766-8106-1
ISBN (ebook) 978-1-4766-4103-4

Front cover: Cadillac V-16 at the AutoMuseum Volkswagen (Autostadt Zeithaus) in Wolfsburg, Germany, with a modern reproduction of an original Fleetwood roadster body (courtesy of Fred Bausch)

Printed in the United States of America

McFarland & Company, Inc., Publishers
Box 611, Jefferson, North Carolina 28640
www.mcfarlandpub.com

Table of Contents

Introduction

HISTORY IS PERISHABLE. PEOPLE FORGET what happened, and those who remember pass away, not always leaving oral or written records. And the documents and things left behind often waste away or are repurposed and lost. In the course of gathering the biographies of Cadillac V-16 motor cars, more than once the trail has led to someone who can no longer reveal who owned a car before he did, or what interesting adventures may have occurred. Or a state's motor vehicle records or those of an old Cadillac dealership are found to have been discarded. And the most poignant moments have been on hearing that a friendship that began because of shared interest in these automobiles has been cut short by the friend's passing.

The Cadillac V-16 cars of the 1930s were a *tour de force* in terms of technology as well as elegance and glamour. From an engineering standpoint, they presented a new standard of quiet, powerful propulsion, and from a comfort and indulgence perspective, they rivaled even the most opulent bespoke motor cars. The V-16s (and their sibling V-12s) secured for Cadillac a position of preeminence in the American luxury car market that lasted for decades. Each one of the cars has a unique and intriguing tale to tell, if one can find the clues, and if the leads are fruitful.

Since the publication of *Cadillac V-16s Lost and Found*, additional cars have permitted their stories to be teased out of documents, photographs, interviews, and even the cars themselves. And because those stories are ephemeral, nothing will do but to put them into words and commit them to print, so that others may know how fascinating were (and are) the cars, their owners, and the others whose lives they have touched through the years.

This book is not a history of Cadillac or General Motors, although you will find bits of that history woven in. Nor is it a technical work or treatise. It is a virtual car collection that means to take the reader back through the lives of each of the Cadillac V-16s in the exhibition. Please enjoy yourself, and enjoy the cars.

Background

IN THE MID–1920S, THE AUTOMOBILE market saw Cadillac as a very well-designed and well-engineered car that was dependable and admirable, but that was not on the same level as Packard, Pierce-Arrow, or Peerless, or other respected high-end makes. To change that perception, a plan was hatched to move Cadillac into the top tier of luxury motor car manufacturers. They would build and market a sixteen-cylinder car that was every bit as elegant and finely finished as the fanciest custom-built motorcars of the day.

The development of the Cadillac V-16 proceeded in secrecy. During the second half of the 1920s, Cadillac let slip, as though it were unintentional, the rumor that a V-12 engine was in the works. This was a cover story—it was true, but not the whole truth. And when technical drawings had to leave the tight confines of the actual working group, they were labeled "Truck" or "Bus." When the V-16 was finally announced, it took the automotive world by complete surprise.

The new Cadillac engine was a work of art in more ways than one. It was essentially two straight eight engines working a common crankshaft and using a single cam. From the gas tank forward, there was a separate fuel system for each bank of cylinders, with separate manifolds, vacuum tanks, and carburetion. A separate coil fired the plugs on each side of the engine through a single distributor.

Silent operation of the overhead valves was achieved by innovative hydraulic dashpots that worked eccentric bushings to automatically take up any lash in the valve mechanism. Horsepower was conservatively rated at 175–185, but the enormous pulling power from low speed was what truly impressed. The car would move out smoothly and without complaint in third gear from 5 or 6 miles per hour. Engine designer Owen Nacker saw to it that the engine was a delight to the eye, as well, concealing tubes and wiring, and using porcelain, enamel, chromium and polished aluminum to dazzling effect.

Fleetwood designed and offered literally dozens of body styles for the V-16, many of which were unavailable on other Cadillac chassis. The car could be finished in any available paint color, although the company urged customers not to use some colors that might fade or deteriorate quickly. Upholstery and fitments were of the highest quality, and here again, customers could request their own choices of fabrics and trim.

Cadillac V-16s sold furiously for about the first half of 1930, and then began to taper off as the reality and likely duration of the Depression became evident to the public. Although Cadillac would continue to offer and sell V-16 motor cars through the 1940 model year, annual sales fell rapidly from nearly 3,000 cars in the first year. Subsequent years saw triple digit sales at best, and in several cases, fewer than 100 cars were sold in a particular year.

Cadillac V-16 Production by Year	
1930–31—3248	1936—52
1932—299	1937—50
1933—125	1938—310
1934—56	1939—133
1935—50	1940—50

A totally new, side-valve engine was introduced for 1938, and that briefly boosted annual sales above 300. The new engine had half the number of moving parts, less weight, and lower displacement, but produced the same power as its predecessor. It sat lower in the car, accommodating the new lower body designs, and it could be installed on the same chassis as the Cadillac V-8 cars. The 1938 through 1940 Series 75 V-8s and Series 90 V-16s shared the same body shells, with different decorative trim and finer appointments on the V-16s.

But by the late 1930s, manufacturers had discovered how to make a V-8 that was every bit as powerful and smooth as the V-16, and that was simpler and less expensive to produce. People debate whether Cadillac ever made money on the sale of its V-16 cars. But profitable or not, the V-16 cars did their job—from 1930 onward, Cadillac was taken quite seriously as a force to be reckoned with in the field of high-end luxury automobiles.

The Cars

1

One of the Very First

Mr. Lorin Tryon was born in San Francisco in 1927. From 1972 until his death in 1999, he co-chaired the illustrious Pebble Beach Concours d'Elegance, and was instrumental in bringing it from a local car show to the world-renowned annual event that it is today. He was also president of the Blackhawk Automotive Museum. When he was 25 years old, he purchased a V-16 Cadillac for $600. "It was a tossup," he said, "between the V-16 and Duesenberg." It wasn't just any V-16, however. It was one of the very first. It was also one of the first "Madame X" V-16 cars built by Cadillac.

The Fleetwood bodies designed and fitted out for the V-16s were magnificent examples of the coachbuilder's art. But the styles that were given the "Madame X" sobriquet were a cut above even those. Designers had long wished to slim down the substantial pillars holding up the roofs of closed sedan bodies, but for reasons of structural soundness, that was not possible. By 1930, however, new developments in metallurgy and casting techniques allowed Fleetwood to incorporate startlingly narrow windshield and door window pillars that added an extra measure of visual grace to the car (and not incidentally, improved outward sightlines for the driver). The new slender pillars were used in the 4100 Series V-16 body styles along with thin chrome reveal moldings for the door windows, and simple body moldings. Inside, the trimming was restrained, with painted wood garnish moldings surrounding the windows and smooth seating surfaces without pleats or tufting.

The later Madame X cars boasted one-piece windshields tipped back at what was then a rather racy angle of 18 degrees from vertical. But the earlier examples had a nearly upright, two-pane windshield that was split vertically at the center of the car. Each pane was hinged at the top corners and could be pushed out at the bottom to allow ventilation.

The origin of the name and concept of the "Madame X" Cadillacs was disclosed in a 1954 interview that General Motors styling chief Harley Earl gave to an author who was planning to write Mr. Earl's biography (unfortunately that biography was never done). In the interview, Mr. Earl related a conversation he'd had with Cadillac President Lawrence P. Fisher about Mr. Earl's desire to personally design and build a custom automobile body "to keep my hand in it" and show the rest of the design staff that he could build a body from start to finish. Mr. Fisher asked what chassis he wanted to work with, and Mr. Earl asked for a LaSalle. He intended the car to be for Mr. Fisher, who used a driver. So the car was designed as a four-door model. The chassis was dropped several inches, and the windshield and door window pillars were made extremely thin for that time—so thin that people in the building fretted that Mr. Fisher would be crushed if the car ever tipped over. So Mr. Earl had the pillars constructed out of milled steel to be "stronger than hell." The body was trimmed and painted as beautifully as possible, and the car was

A deluxe prototype. **Here is one of two experimental Madame X bodies that were mounted on 1929 Cadillac V-8 chassis at the behest of Cadillac President Lawrence P. Fisher. It is likely that the body from one of these prototypes was moved to a new V-16 chassis to become one of the debut cars in that new line, and one of the display cars at the New York unveiling in early January 1930 (courtesy Jim Schild).**

presented to Larry Fisher, who used it for two years before giving it to a friend. Mr. Earl went on to tell his interviewer that at the same time as the project to design the car was being undertaken with Mr. Fisher, actress Pauline Frederick was performing in the stage play *Madame X* at a small theater not far from the GM Building. Mr. Earl said:

> I told Pauline that I had built the car. I had been down to see her the night before. I went backstage and we had dinner that night together and I said, "We'll call it Madame X."[1]

In addition to the car that Harley Earl built for Lawrence Fisher on a 1929 LaSalle chassis a second LaSalle chassis was fitted out and officially designated a non-production 7-passenger Imperial, "Madame X." Like the former car, this one was also charged to the account of Lawrence Fisher.[2] Two 1929 Cadillac cars were built with the instruction "non-production Cadillac 7-passenger Imperial Madame X to be mounted on this chassis." As can be seen in a surviving factory photograph, it was a style popularly known as a landaulette, a limousine in which the rear quarter of the passenger compartment roof was

1. Earl, Harley, quoted by Holls, David, Letter to the Editor, *The Self-Starter*, Cadillac-LaSalle Club, Inc., Detroit, MI, Vol. 34, No. 7, July 1991: pp. 11.
2. Schild, James, *Fleetwood—The Company & the Coachcraft*, Columbia, IL: The Auto Review, 2001. Revised second edition published June 2011: p. 163.

collapsible and could be lowered to give the passengers the open-air experience of a convertible, while retaining the elegant fitments and formality of a limousine. This landaulette body was practically identical to the body that Cadillac would mount on the V-16 chassis and ship to the New York auto show in January 1930, and some believe that one of these bodies was used for that show car. What became of the second car is not known.[3] The "Madame X" car that Harley Earl built for Lawrence Fisher served as the styling exercise for the 1930 and '31 V-16 4100-series cars that would share the theatrical nickname. In common with the LaSalle prototype, all of those cars shared very thin windshield and window posts, a horizontal belt molding extending from the radiator to the rear of the car, thin chrome window reveals with sharp corners, and plain hood and cowl. As previously noted, the early Madame X V-16s also shared the upright, "V" windshield (later models would switch to a sharply raked, one-piece windshield).

From the available evidence (and there's not much that survives) the launch of the Cadillac V-16 at the beginning of 1930 (like most introductions of new car models) was a pretty hectic affair. A December 10, 1929, letter from Lawrence Fisher to the dealership network announced that the new car would be exhibited at the New York Automobile Show in the Grand Central Palace commencing January 4, 1930, and simultaneously at the General Motors Salon to be held at the Hotel Astor on Broadway between 44th and 45th Streets. And yet when the time came, Cadillac was able to field only two (or three) completed cars for those shows. One was a Series 4264-B cane-bodied town car (engine number 700002, or the second in the official series of V-16 engine numbers). Another was a Series 4108-C "Madame X" imperial landaulette sedan (engine number 700004).

A formal catalog for the V-16 cars had not been produced in time for the introduction, and instead a 10" by 14" brochure was quickly prepared (16 pages including the covers). It illustrated eleven of the body styles, and in an envelope glued to the inside back cover, presented designers' drawings of thirty or more of the offered designs inked on tracing paper. A prospective customer could place one of the translucent images over a colored surface and visualize the finished car in that hue.

A shipping ledger for the 1930 and '31 V-16 cars has survived, and it shows next to each engine number the body style of the car, the date on which it was shipped from the factory, and the destination (distributor or dealership). The first six engine numbers (700001 through 700006) indicate "Factory" as the shipping destination. That designation usually indicates an intermediate stop such as to the factory showroom, before shipment to a final destination (although it was also used when a car was intended for promotional purposes or for the use of company personnel). The first engine number that shows a destination other than "Factory" is 700007, which was shipped to Cleveland on January 29, 1930 (although 700005 and 700006 were each subsequently shipped to Chicago before 700007 went to Cleveland). For several of the cars that were shipped to "Factory" there is an additional notation that the car was "returned for credit" and the body was remounted on another chassis and shipped elsewhere, or was otherwise disposed of.

It's possible that the first half-dozen engine numbers correspond to promotional vehicles, cars to be displayed at the salons and shows in the major cities, such as New York, Chicago, Los Angeles, San Francisco. Once the show season had passed, the cars

3. *Id.*

1930 V-16 Series 4108-C Imperial Landaulette. **This was one of the first Cadillac V-16 cars unveiled to the public. Designed as a chauffeur-driven limousine, the roof behind the rear doors is collapsible for open-air touring (courtesy Roy Schneider).**

would have been available for sale to customers. Assuming that most real-world customers would be looking for something short of the absolutely most ostentatious model, there would be a certain incentive to remove the show car body and store it for later sale, so that the chassis could be fitted with a different body to fill a live customer order. In fact, the Series 4108-C imperial landaulette body from one of the New York show cars was later mounted on a different chassis with engine number 700821 and shipped to San Francisco in March of 1930.

The Madame X features had been worked out on the prototypes described earlier. With the display of the Series 4108-C landaulette in New York, they were now incorporated into the V-16 car—the upright split windshield, narrow pillars, and bright-metal reveals for the door windows gave just the right sparkle to the coachwork. The collapsible rear quarters echoed the carriages of Europe's royal families. The spacious passenger compartment (with a window to divide it from the driver's area) had two fold-down "opera seats" for occasional guests. But the most unusual feature was probably the instrument panel. On most of the 1930 and 1931 V-16s that Cadillac built, the instruments are grouped at the center of the panel in a cluster shaped like a trapezoid with a bowed lower edge, flanked by decorative engine-turned panels. On the Series 4108-C (and some of the other early Madame X cars) the instruments are spread across the instrument board from door to door, in a pair of engine-turned panels that form a semicircle with the straight edge as its base. The whole affair is vee-d slightly at the center to conform to the windshield angle. Next to this display, the elaborate instrument panel of the Duesenberg J looks positively restrained.

As mentioned, after the New York shows, the landaulette body was removed from its chassis and placed on another one (with engine number 700821). There may have been need for a chassis to satisfy a pressing customer order, or there may have been a problem with the original chassis—an early production glitch, a bad engine, who can say? But the reconstituted car was shipped to the Don Lee dealership in San Francisco and sold, reportedly for the very impressive sum (for the time) of $9,988. James Schild's book *Fleetwood—The Company & the Coachcraft* names the buyer as M.A. Astredo of San Francisco. Lorin Tryon, in an article in *The Self-Starter*, also says that "Mr. M.A. Astredo" was the original owner.[4] According to the research of subsequent owner Steven Nannini, a Mr. Charles C. Howard was reported to have been the initial purchaser. (That person would appear to have been a different person than Charles Stewart Howard, the West Coast distributor for Buick cars who owned the legendary race horse Seabiscuit. Charles S. Howard would own another 1930 Cadillac V-16, with a custom convertible sedan body that he commissioned from the Murphy Company of Pasadena, California.) The factory build sheet for engine number 700821 calls for Series 4108-C body number 3 "to be dismounted and placed on a new chassis to fill this order" and the build sheet carries the instruction "TAG MRS. C.C. HOWARD." There was a real estate contractor in the bay area named C.C. Howard in the late 1920s and early '30s,[5] and perhaps this car was ordered for his wife (the build sheet also calls for delivery of a lap robe with the car). We don't seem to have a provable chain of title, however, so the matter remains open to some conjecture. Also uncertain is what the original purchase price was, although subsequent owner Dave Towell and early V-16 restoration expert Wayne Merriman believed that it had been $10,500 (at a time when a fully-optioned Chevrolet could have been bought for around $675).

In any event, the car seems to have stayed in California, and in 1952, it came into Mr. Tryon's hands. He owned and cared for it until 1965, when Toledo, Ohio, Cadillac dealer Dave Towell bought it. Mr. Towell and his wife picked up the stately Cadillac in San Francisco and drove it south to Los Angeles and, via Route 66, eastward through Arizona and New Mexico, and then northeast to Kansas City, Kansas. There they turned the car over to Wayne Merriman, who would give the engine its first complete overhaul. They kept a journal of the road trip and the couple composed a hugely entertaining article for the July 1966 issue of *The Self-Starter* with photographs and descriptions of their challenges—including push-starts, jump-starts, on-the-road carburetor rebuilds, cracked wheel lock rings, and biting cold weather.[6] But they made it to their destination and kept their sense of humor and adventure intact.

In the 1980s, Steven Nannini of Tucson, Arizona, heard about the landaulette from Wayne Merriman. He bought the car from the Towells, and began a thorough restoration.

---

4. Uhlir, Agnes, "WOW! V-16 452 Cadillac Landaulet," *The Self-Starter*, Cadillac-LaSalle Club, Inc., Detroit, MI, Vol. VIII, No. 2, Nov.-Dec. 1965: pg. 10.

5. C.C. Howard the contractor was responsible for developing the Stonehenge and Stoneleigh residential neighborhoods on Santa Clara Avenue in Alemeda, California.

6. Towell, Ann, "—Moving East," *The Self-Starter*, Cadillac-LaSalle Club, Inc., Bloomfield Hills, MI, Vol. VIII, No. 9, July 1966: pp. 7–13.

***Returned to regal glory.* This 1930 V-16 Madame X landaulette was lovingly restored by Steve Nannini when he owned it. Intricate interior trimming fabrics were faithfully reproduced (courtesy Joseph Scott).**

Instead of staying with the original black exterior color, he chose a two-tone gray color scheme. He had the original fabrics carefully analyzed and proceeded to obtain and have installed exact duplicates. For example, the windlacing around the body openings used five different diamond weave patterns that Mr. Nannini was able to have re-loomed by hand and worked into the restored interior. Wayne Merriman rebuilt the engine and transmission. Al Kruger trimmed the interior, and Tom Sparks restored the woodwork and painted the car. After the work was finished, Mr. Nannini entered the car in the Pebble Beach Concours d'Elegance. Although it was in the running for "Best of Show," it was ultimately awarded the prestigious "Most Elegant" title. That certainly describes the design, and the flawlessly renewed execution.

At Pebble Beach, Nevada collector Robert M. Lee admired the Cadillac and expressed his desire to buy it. Mr. Nannini was agreeable, and now one of the first V-16 Cadillacs ever seen by the public graces Mr. Lee's collection and remains a witness to the conquest by Cadillac of the 1930s luxury car world.

2

Cadillac Odyssey

On May 9, 1930, a new Cadillac V-16, Series 4335 convertible coupe with engine number 701081 was purchased. Series 4335 was the more conservative of the two convertible coupe styles offered in the V-16 line for 1930 and 1931. The windshield was nearly upright, with two panes that joined at the center and angled rearward in a gentle "V" shape, viewed from above. When raised, the convertible top was a bit more squared off than that of the sportier Series 4235 cars, and when lowered, the frame and folded material formed a significant, if orderly, stack around the rim of the passenger compartment.

This particular Series 4335 car was finished in Stygian Blue and Tokio Ivory. The rear deck, body moldings, chassis and fenders were blue, while the body sides, door panels, wheels, cowl, and hood were ivory. The pin-striping on the body and fenders used the same blue and ivory hues. Upholstery was leather, and Burbank cloth covered the top. The only optional equipment ordered from the factory consisted of wire wheels (in place of the standard wooden wheels) and two fender-mounted spare tires (instead of the standard single, rear-mounted spare).

The car was sold new by the Don Lee dealership in San Francisco, though no record exists of the name of the original owner. During the course of the 1930s, the car travelled 19,000 miles, but no one around today knows how that happened or what adventures the big Cadillac experienced.

In 1941 a gentleman in Oakland, California, took title to the convertible coupe and kept it into the 1960s. Somewhere toward the end of that tenure, the car was set upon by vandals while it was parked next to the owner's cabin on a wooded hilltop in the Oakland area. The vandals stripped what they could from the car (instruments, engine parts, wheels, doors, hood and radiator), and tossed the cabin's furnishings over a nearby cliff. What was left of car and cabin kept a lonely vigil while the owner avoided them and the painful disappointment of his loss.

In 1964 the fellow was walking down a road near Brookdale, when Cadillac collector Russell Lloyd stopped and offered him a lift. The men's conversation turned to old cars and the passenger announced that he had a 1930 Cadillac V-16 convertible coupe in Oakland. He described how to find the car, and Mr. Lloyd subsequently located it with some difficulty and took some photographs. He returned to the owner and purchased the car, receiving a 1941 title and a bill of sale.

In the early 60s, the big Classics of the 1930s were starting to be appreciated, but they had not begun the meteoric price rise that subsequent decades would witness. It was still possible to locate parts in some salvage yards and from other enthusiasts, for manageable amounts of money. And materials and labor for painting, plating and upholstery were much less expensive then. Nevertheless, Russell Lloyd felt that this particular classic convertible had too many missing parts, and would be too difficult for him to restore on his own.

So Mr. Lloyd approached fellow California Cadillac enthusiast Paul Schinnerer of Long Beach, and asked him if he would be interested in buying the somewhat incomplete 1930 Cadillac convertible coupe. Paul is (and was already then) no stranger to Cadillac V-16s and the details of their construction and function. He had started around 1950 with a 1930 all-weather phaeton that his brother Al had rescued from a farmer's field, where it had languished after having been rolled. Paul literally learned by doing, restoring that car over a period of years to like-new condition. Looking over the photos of the convertible coupe that Russell Lloyd showed him, he concluded that the only potentially serious unknown was the condition of the structural wood pieces, since he knew that the car had been sitting outside for a considerable length of time.

In spite of having just purchased a house, on May 30, 1964, Paul bought the car for $275 and promptly had the title transferred to his name. He had accumulated a variety of V-16 parts (including wheels and instruments) and knew where he could get additional parts from a Series 4380 all-weather phaeton to fill in some of the missing items on the car he'd just bought. He checked with the owner of a complete Series 4335 car and confirmed that the front doors from an all-weather phaeton would fit as replacements for the missing doors he needed for his convertible coupe (although the hinges are different—the all-weather phaeton door has two "barrel" hinges, while the door for the convertible coupe uses three butt hinges). Norm Taunton in Galt, California, was enlisted to locate Paul's newly-acquired car, and the all-weather phaeton parts.

Norm took Paul to the derelict gas station in a village north of Oakland. Many old Cadillac parts were lying around, but the place was locked and there was a prominent "NO TRESPASSING" sign. The two men adjourned to a bar across the street and asked after the owner of the gas station. Informed that he was likely at home, they drove back a few miles to the man's house and rang the bell. A man in his sixties answered the door and chatted with Norm in a thick accent. Norm told him they were interested in the Cadillac parts, and the trio drove back to the old gas station. In, around, and underneath the building, they examined a trove of parts that included rust-free fenders and doors, a complete hood, top frame, a set of headlights, rear axle gears, and four nineteen-inch wheels. Paul agreed on a price and shook hands with the gas station owner, promising to pick up the parts in a few weeks.

Continuing on to Oakland, Paul and Norm set about locating the V-16 convertible coupe. They had some difficulty reaching the location, even with the map that Russell Lloyd had drawn. When they arrived at the old shack and searched through the trees and bushes, an old seat cushion was the only trace of a car they could find. Inquiring at a nearby (occupied) cabin, the lady inside told them that someone had removed the car a couple of weeks earlier.

Returning home, Paul called Russell Lloyd, and neither he nor the man Russell bought the car from could shed any light on its disappearance. Nor could the local police provide any information or resolve the matter. Several months later, when Paul had nearly lost hope, a fellow Cadillac enthusiast called to say he knew who had the car, and a second source chimed in the next day. Armed with the young man's name and address (still in the Oakland area), Paul flew to San Francisco and met with Norm to work out a plan. The two men had some difficulty locating the address, but with the help of a neighbor, they found it. The V-16 was there, but it had been taken apart.

The man who answered the door said that his son was restoring the Cadillac, which he had thought was abandoned. Paul showed him the title, and he readily agreed that Paul should take the car. Stepping outside, Paul examined for the first time the V-16 convertible coupe he had purchased, lost, and then found again.

The fenders had little rust and were straight. The rumble seat lid, golf bag doors, and two good running boards were present. The frame had been stripped bare and was ready to be cleaned and painted. The front suspension parts and the rear axle and springs were lying near the disassembled engine. The engine number on the crankcase matched the number on Paul's title. The next hurdle would be getting all of this material back home to Long Beach.

Back home, Paul was contemplating the expense of renting a suitable truck and hauling the parts back to his house. Then Norm called and offered the use of the truck he used in his lumber business. Paul offered to pay for Norm's trouble and expense, and they arranged a day to go to Oakland. The day before, Norm called to say he'd already loaded the car and would be picking up the extra all-weather phaeton parts the next morning.

The neighborhood was agog when Norm's big Mack diesel truck pulled up loaded with old car parts. After several hours of heavy lifting and creative unloading techniques, Paul's entire back yard was covered with almost enough parts to assemble two cars. He said it was a beautiful sight. He had the car. He had the parts he needed. And the all-weather phaeton doors fit the convertible coupe body perfectly.

***Partially reassembled for sale.* This is how the convertible coupe looked at the time David Blake sold it to a gentleman from the Czech Republic. Most of the chassis, body and drivetrain are there, and the major body parts are straight and solid. But many parts have yet to be acquired and attached (courtesy David Blake).**

Sixteen pistons. Cadillac achieved increased engine displacement, torque and horsepower by using smaller and more numerous pistons. Three inches across and moving through a four-inch stroke, eight power pulses per crankshaft revolution resulted in unheard of smoothness (courtesy Jaroslav Koniček).

***Nearing completion.* In short order this car was transformed from a rough project car into a potential show winner, needing only minor finishing touches to bring it back to the eye-catching blue and ivory masterpiece that left the factory (courtesy Jaroslav Koniček).**

As it happened, Paul didn't complete the restoration of the convertible coupe. He sold it in 1966 to a fellow named Roger May in Arizona, and it was subsequently acquired by Bob Blake of Phoenix. Bob was a collector of performance cars of all types and vintages. He was an admirer of any car with an exotic engine built to perform. In the early 1950s, he and a friend had bought a home-built hot rod that had been constructed around a 1932 Cadillac V-16 engine. Bob had been restoring that hot rod with his son Dave when he passed away in 2004.

The 1930 Series 4335 convertible coupe joined several other Cadillac V-16s that Bob Blake owned, including a rumble seat coupe (Series 4376), a five-passenger limousine (Series 4330), a five-passenger closed coupe (Series 4381) and another Series 4335 convertible coupe that was a good deal more complete and unmolested. The convertible coupe that we are concerned with spent most of the ensuing years in storage, waiting its turn for attention and refurbishment.

About ten years after Bob Blake's death, his son offered both of the Series 4335 convertible coupes for sale as a package deal. The photos taken at that time show one car still wearing most of its original paint and upholstery, and even traces of its convertible top,

***Opposite: Freshening the interior.* Restored gauges, controls, and instrument panel promise a worthy final product. Temporary driver's seat permits guiding the car around the shop. Pipes on the inside of the firewall are part of the vacuum system that operates the fuel pumps, windshield wipers, and brake assist unit (courtesy Jaroslav Koniček).**

***Restored from little more than a parts car.* This beautifully rehabilitated engine once again displays the painstaking attention to detail that characterized the spectacular 1930 V-16 Cadillac powerplant. Designer Owen Milton Nacker crafted this engine to be seen and appreciated as a work of art (courtesy of Jaroslav Koniček).**

looking like a well-worn used car and capable of being driven (as was proven by a YouTube video of a test run through the Phoenix neighborhood around Dave Blake's business, Blake Machine Company). By contrast, the car Paul Schinnerer once tracked down and owned was in need of a lot of assistance. There was a very straight, rust-free, and pretty complete body and drive train. But a good many "little parts" were missing—some engine accessories and fittings, instruments, gear shift mechanism, spare tires, body trim pieces, as well as the entire interior and convertible top. A good foundation was there for a restoration project, but a lot of work would need to be done.

In 2014, the cars were purchased, and each went to a collector in the Czech Republic. It is pleasing to report that the blue and ivory car that left the Cadillac factory with engine number 701081 is being treated to a worthy restoration, and will one day return to its original dignified beauty. At this writing it is reported that the engine is once again running.

3

A Swiss Fire Chief's Car

ONCE THE NEWNESS WORE OFF, and huge luxury automobiles of the early 1930s became a "drug on the market" as the Great Depression settled in, many early Cadillac V-16 motor cars were conscripted into uses for which their designers and marketers had no conception. After all, the chassis were robust and nearly indestructible, the engines and drivetrains had incredible pulling power, and in an age when gasoline cost pennies per gallon, fuel economy was not an over-riding concern. We know of an ambulance, still extant, that was constructed in the mid–'30s upon a 1930 Series 4375-S sedan.[7] And tales abound of cars shorn of much of their bodywork to serve as utility trucks or tractors. One convertible coupe had its frame shortened and lost its bodywork aft of the windshield in order to be put to work pulling gang mowers on a golf course. At least two V-16 cars went to work with fire-fighting organizations. One of these has been reincarnated as a roadster and resides in Russia. The other served with the fire department of the community of Illnau in Switzerland, was partially restored, and was most recently seen in Germany, before being re-imported to the U.S.

On August 13, 1930, a Series 4155-C Madame X five-passenger imperial cabriolet was shipped to Antwerp, Belgium. The 4155-C body style number described a five-passenger sedan with a roll-up window to divide the driver's and passenger compartments, and a collapsible rear quarter (partial convertible top) over the back half of the passenger compartment. Only five examples of this body style were built. The coachbuilder's term for that style was "landaulette," and such a car was a limousine with an added fresh-air feature for the passengers. The "41" prefix in the style number (as well as the "Madame X" sobriquet) denotes a series of advanced styling features, including a raked windshield (dramatically raked for the time), roof pillars that were thinner than those on the standard V-16 Cadillac models, and slender chrome reveals around the door windows. Madame X styles sold new for approximately $1,000 more than corresponding standard-bodied cars. The collapsible rear quarter feature added a further $750 to the initial purchase price. This was a very special variation of an already-exclusive line of Cadillac vehicles.

The finish and trimming specifications for this particular car called for a symphony of maroons. The beltline molding and the window frames above it were painted Viceroy Maroon, as were the fenders and the chassis. The body and doors below the beltline (including the hood and cowl) were Coromandel Maroon. The wheels were Janus Maroon, and the body pinstriping was Casino Red. On the inside, the side trim panels, door panels and headliner were maroon taupe broadcloth (#2970 in the catalog of

7. That car has recently been returned to its original passenger car configuration.

***Open rear quarter.* The distinguishing feature of a landaulette is that the portion of the roof directly above the rear seat passengers and behind their heads is collapsible like a regular convertible top (courtesy Yann Saunders).**

Cadillac's supplier William Wiese & Company), and the seat cushions and backs were trimmed in whipcord fabric of the same color. The instrumentation was modified by Cadillac for the destination market. The fuel gauge is calibrated in liters, and the speedometer reads in kilometers per hour. The steering is left-hand drive, consistent with requirements in continental Europe.

As was typical for cars going to Europe, lower-compression heads were installed on the engine to accommodate the lower octane fuels common there. And a power tire pump was ordered for the car. That tire pump would have been a unit that mounted in place of a small steel plate on the left side of the transmission housing. A control shaft protruding through the driver's floorboard could be twisted to engage the pump's drive gear with the transmission's reverse idler gear to turn the pump "on." With the wide variations in road surfaces at that time, and the tires of the day, it's not surprising that so many cars carried two spare tires, and some had their own compressed air pumps.

While it is not known who ordered this landaulette and purchased it new, how it survived the depredations of World War II, or how it came to Switzerland, a Swiss registration card documents its ownership and use during the 1950s by the Illnau fire brigade. The same card describes the car as pulling a fire fighting trailer (perhaps carrying ladders or hose?). Maybe it was the chief's car? Or maybe it and its trailer comprised the village's sole fire engine?

Around 1960, this Cadillac was acquired by Mr. Walter Grell of Rheinfelden (also in Switzerland). Mr. Grell did the best he could restoring the car, and he drove and used it, still with heavy truck tires as were probably used in its fire-fighting days. In 1985, Mr. Yann Saunders saw the car at an international Cadillac meet in Zurich, took photos and was able to speak with the owner's son. A subsequent letter from Mr. Saunders to Mr. Grell, seeking information and pre-restoration photos of the car, went unanswered.

In 2014, the V-16 landaulette showed up on the Internet offered for sale by a firm in Germany, E. Thiesen Berlin GmbH. On the company's website, the car sported new wide whitewall tires and it no longer bore the add-on "trafficator" turn signals that earlier photos revealed. The asking price was €200,000 (about $253,000).

Madame X features. **In this view of the 4155-C ("C" for collapsible rear quarter) it is easy to see some of the distinctive features of the "Madame X" series cars. The windshield is tipped back at a dramatic angle, and the window openings are framed in bright-metal reveals. The item attached to the driver's windshield pillar is a trafficator (turn signal semaphore) to comply with European regulations (courtesy Yann Saunders).**

In terms of rarity, this car appears to be the lone survivor of the five like it that Cadillac built. In terms of condition, there are some issues. The taillights are from a 1932 Reo Royale, itself an impressive and rare car, and the outside door handles do not match. The engine is fitted with Solex carburetors in place of the original Cadillac-Johnson units, and the cylinder blocks and heads should be painted black. The vacuum tanks on the firewall are mismatched—one is a chrome-plated unit from an early 1930 V-16 (later cars such as this one were equipped with painted vacuum tanks), and the other is missing the chrome-plated top cover.

The cast and chrome-plated embellishment piece that outlines the instrument panel and the gauge cluster is missing. The original pop-out ignition switch and transmission lock has been replaced with an aftermarket item. On this body style one would expect to find a pair of small folding auxiliary seats in the rear compartment. They may have been lost when the car was serving as a fire-fighting vehicle. Overall, this Cadillac is very presentable, although in spite of the restoration, the patina of age shows through in places like the instrument cluster and the engine compartment. The maroon and black color scheme is consistent with the original combination, although the light tan broadcloth interior differs from the maroon originally called for.

***Folded top.* The rear portion of the roof stacks neatly behind the rear seat. The tail lights are from a 1932 Reo Royale (courtesy Yann Suanders).**

In late 2016, having been shipped back to the United States, the V-16 landaulette was offered by Dragone Auctions as lot number 122 to their Boston Cup Auction. The pre-sale estimate was $350,000 to $375,000. In early 2017, new owner Charles Lemaitre of Hardwick Massachusetts, offered the car for sale at $374,900. On August 15, 2019, it was offered at Worldwide Auctioneers' Pacific Grove [California] Auction, and the selling price as reported by *Hemmings Motor News* was $176,000.[8] Apparently, however, a sale was not consummated and the car, at this writing, remains with Mr. LeMaitre.

8. Litwin, Matthew, and Conwill, David, "Worldwide Auctioneers, Pacific Grove," *Hemmings Motor News*, Bennington, VT, Vol. 66, No. 11, November 2019, pp. 78–83, 82.

4

A YouTube Star

Rides with Chuck is a series of videos posted on the Internet venue YouTube.com. In each of the videos, the narrator interviews and rides with the owner of an interesting automobile, with cameras rolling for the viewing benefit and vicarious pleasure of whoever may choose to watch. One of the videos begins with a quick once-over of a recent Cadillac concept car, the "Ciel," on its stand at the 2012 Chicago Auto Show.[9] Soon the real subject of the episode comes into view—a 1931 Cadillac V-16 Series 4361-S five-passenger town sedan.[10] The narrator introduces the car's owner, Dennis Sobieski of Downers Grove, Illinois, who climbs in, fires up the engine and sets out on a peaceful tour of the neighborhood. The viewer gets to hear the engine run, look down the long hood as the car moves down the road, and ride along as a passenger. The camera focuses on close-up details of the driver's compartment, and watches from beside the road, and from another car, as the sleek Classic Cadillac glides serenely by. Meanwhile, Mr. Sobieski describes his car, its characteristics, and its historical context. The audio picks up the singing of the gears as the car accelerates and slows (it wasn't until 1932 that Cadillac transmissions were equipped with silent helical gears for first and second). The video ends in Mr. Sobieski's driveway, where we get to see the engine and watch it start and run.

Best foot forward. **This Series 4361-S town sedan is unrestored except for the front seat fabric. Placed in a museum in 1941, it passed to a succession of collectors in the early 1980s. A YouTube video can be accessed that takes the viewer on a ride in this car while the owner talks about it.**

A town sedan (or club sedan as it was also known) was a family car, with seating for five and a built-in trunk behind the passenger compartment for vacation trips ("touring" as it was called). Behind the standard trunk was a folding rack

9. https://www.youtube.com/watch?v=wXzepgUoXhA. Accessed March 28, 2018.

10. In the video, the car is described as a 1931 model, but this car, with engine number 702710, was shipped during 1930, and most sources use 702887 as the last 1930 engine number, with numbers from 702888 through 703251 designated 1931 cars. The 1930 and 1931 V-16 models were identical (with the exception of some minor running changes introduced at various points during what was effectively a 24-month model year).

***A 1930 V-16 family sedan.* The 4361-S town sedan is a car for a family of five, with a built-in trunk for their belongings, and a folding rack for an additional accessory trunk, if needed. It was perfect for touring (the contemporary term for taking a vacation trip) in comfort, even on the sometimes-sketchy roads of the time (courtesy Richard DiFiglia).**

on which could be mounted an additional trunk for more luggage, if needed. Unlike the larger five- and seven-passenger sedans, a town sedan placed the back seat far enough from the front seat to allow adequate foot room, but not far enough to leave room for opera seats or full-width jump seats. The profile of the car was less formal than the larger sedans, but a V-16 town sedan was still an impressive motor car.

The car in the video is engine number 702710 with body number 254. The town sedan body style was the fourth most popular among buyers of 1930–'31 V-16s, with 258 built. This one was shipped new to San Antonio, Texas, in September of 1930. The build sheet for this car calls for an all-black car, with the exception of chrome-plated hood and cowl vent doors, Romany Red brake drums, chrome-plated wheel spokes, and an argent pinstripe on the body moldings.[11] At this point the identity of the original owner is a mystery, although the build sheet bears the instruction "TAG BLEDSOE." That sort of notation on the build sheet generally indicates the name of the original buyer, but who Mr. Bledsoe was is not apparent so many years later.

Liston Emmanuel Zander was born in 1897 in Lexington, Texas, and lived almost 90 years. He made a career in finance and did well enough to begin collecting old cars, and he became one of the pioneers of the hobby in Texas. He is credited with owning the first car museum in that state. About 1941, he acquired this Cadillac V-16 Series 4361-S town

11. There was more information on the back of the original build sheet, but the copy that has survived is missing that second page.

sedan in excellent condition. He didn't drive the car, but kept it in his museum for years, and around 1980, sold it to a friend. The friend wanted to give the stately old Cadillac to his son as a graduation present. The son accepted the gift, but was intimidated by the car and never started or drove it. Dennis Sobieski acquired the car from Urbana, Illinois, collector and restorer Allen Strong. When Mr. Strong got the car it hadn't been run or driven since before World War II.

Allen Strong cleaned the fuel system, checked out the engine electricals, installed a new battery and started the car with a minimum of fuss. He says it was a very solid, good-running car. When a Series 4260 V-16 sport phaeton became available, however, Mr. Strong put an advertisement in *Hemmings Motor News* and sold the town sedan to make the purchase. He bought and continues to own the sport phaeton.

In the YouTube video, Mr. Sobieski described the V-16 town sedan as unrestored except for the front seat upholstery. The original paint and chrome trim gleam quite respectably as one watches the car drive past the camera. In an interior shot of Mr. Sobieski's foot pressing the starter pedal, a few small moth holes can be seen in the front carpet, but overall the interior seems to be quite good for a car over eighty years old. Special touches include stainless steel spokes on the wire wheels, and chrome plated vent doors on the hood side panels and the sides of the cowl. A pair of "Pilot Ray" driving lights swivels to aim where the front wheels are pointed ("Pilot Ray Lights the Winding Way" was the advertising slogan).

Not long after the YouTube video was made, Dennis Sobieski sold the town sedan and it is now registered in New Hampshire.

5

A Roadster Rebuilt from Rust

The Great Depression of the 1930s caused many Americans to leave their homes and travel elsewhere to find employment, in order to escape the depredations of the "Dust Bowl," or just to try to start over again after financial setbacks. In 1939 a newlywed couple left the suburbs of New York City and moved to rural Goochland County, Virginia. Wendell Phillips Bowman Flynn, then 23 years old, and his wife Verna, 19, would have and raise a son (Wendell Bowman Flynn II, born in 1940) and two daughters.[12] In 1951 they would also acquire "Howard's Neck" a pre–Civil War farm near Pemberton, Virginia, that in 1972 would be added to the National Register of Historic Places.

Also in 1939, Mr. Flynn purchased a 1930 Cadillac V-16 Series 4302 roadster, engine number 702137, from a Ford dealer in Hopewell, New Jersey, where the car had been traded in for a newer vehicle.[13] It is reputed to have been purchased new by Arthur Atwater Kent, Sr., manufacturer of quality home radios during the 1920s and 1930s.[14] The V-16 roadster had been outfitted with one of the first car radios installed in a Cadillac (1930 was the first year that Cadillac cars were wired to accept radios). Mr. Flynn brought the roadster to Virginia.

Wendell Flynn was the type of man who would buy a car and then put the old one "on the back 40" and leave it there. Over the years a number of cars would be set aside on Mr. Flynn's land. Among them were five Cadillacs: the 1930 V-16 Series 4302 roadster; a 1931 V-16 Series 4130-S "Madame X" sedan; a 1934 V-12 formal limousine; a 1933 Cadillac of unknown model; and a 1935 V-16 Series 5876 coupe. There was at least one non–Cadillac as well, a 1931 Oldsmobile convertible coupe.

At first the cars were stored indoors, but after some time they were moved outside and were left exposed to the weather. Not surprisingly, their condition deteriorated over the years. Local people would tell folks passing through about the old Cadillacs in the woods, and some curious souls crept up on the derelict cars and left with parts, whether as mementos or as items to sell.

The 1930 roadster was especially forlorn. While Mr. Flynn was away with the U.S. Navy during World War II (he reached the rank of chief motor machinist's mate), his brother decided that the roadster could be converted into a useful tractor. He removed the body and set about shortening the frame, which he thought was too long. But he

---

12. It is possible that Mr. Flynn was named for Major General Wendell Phillips Bowman (1847–1928), who participated as a teenager in the Battle of Gettysburg and served as commander of the 28th Infantry Division of the Pennsylvania National Guard before retiring in 1910.

13. Mr. Flynn told Bob McGinnis that he thought the Ford dealer's name was Lampson.

14. In 1925, the Atwater Kent Manufacturing Company was the largest maker of radios in the United States. Unwilling to build cheaper radio sets, Mr. Atwater Kent chose to close his factory in 1936 and retire.

couldn't figure out how to go about making the driveshaft and other components conform to the new frame dimensions. Discouraged, he abandoned the tractor project and the roadster was left in pieces at the mercy of the elements.

In 1960, William Meffert, a student at the University of Virginia, found out about the eccentric family and their automotive trove. By that time, Mr. Flynn (Sr.)'s mother-in-law was living alone in the house, with the cars spread across the property in varying states of disassembly and deterioration. If anyone came around investigating or prospecting for cars or parts, she would call her son, who lived at Howard's Neck, not far away. He would invite the visitors to leave or summon the authorities. Mr. Meffert got to know the senior Mr. Flynn over a period of time, and together with Dick Terhune, the owner of the restoration shop where Mr. Meffert worked part-time, they put together a deal with the son to buy the roadster and the Madame X sedan.

Mr. Meffert found a buyer for the roadster in the person of California attorney Robert E. McGinnis. By that time, the car was in a sorry state of decomposition. Someone had removed and made off with the cowl section of the body, including the instrument panel, firewall, and windshield. The back section of the body with the rumble seat cover was lying separate from the rest of the car. The front fenders and radiator were still mounted to the frame, and the engine and drive train were there (if missing some notable parts like carburetors, distributor, oil filler caps and valley cover). The technical term for a car in that condition is "basket case" and most collectors shy away from such projects.

Not much to look at. **This was the scene that greeted William Meffert and Dick Terhune when they first saw the 1930 V-16 roadster on the Flynn property in Virginia. The cowl portion of the body was missing, along with the hood and an assortment of engine and trim parts. Here, the fuel tank can be seen lying where the driver's feet would rest (courtesy Robert McGinnis).**

Unfazed by the magnitude of the challenge, Mr. McGinnis bought the V-16 roadster in 1976 or '77 and had all the remaining pieces hauled out to San Diego. A neighbor allowed him the use of a garage to store the newly-bought car, and for fifteen years, Mr. McGinnis worked steadily at restoring it, doing a little every day. He has described the process of bringing this roadster back from the forlorn state in which he found it as "thirty-one years of restoration."

A lot of parts were missing when Mr. McGinnis got it, but the car is complete today. Everything on the car was made in 1930 for a V-16 Cadillac (except for a latching mechanism inside one of the doors that was sourced from a truck manufacturer in San Francisco). One of the headlights came from a V-16 that one of Mr. McGinnis's friends spotted while travelling in Mexico. The other came from a fellow in the Chicago area who advertises regularly in *Hemmings Motor News*.

Robert McGinnis obtained, and freely acknowledges, the help of many people. A body man named Red Tweit in West Los Angeles restored the fenders and body panels. Mr. McGinnis would go up there once a month and pay him some money. Richard Messick in Tarzana, California, was able to provide some parts, including the Pilot Ray driving lights. Penn Lenson an experienced restorer in Temecula, California, with the assistance of Barney Smiley (a former board member of John Brown University in

Test drive. **Restorer Penn Lenson is at the wheel as the 1930 roadster is taken for its first drive. The next stop would be Howard McKee's upholstery shop in Lakeside, California. Above the running board the battery is visible. The 1930–31 V-16 cars used a long, narrow 6-volt battery with the three cells joined end to end, instead of side by side. New white tire sidewalls still have the blue protective film (courtesy Penn Lenson).**

Arkansas now living in Lakeside, California), oversaw the process of assembling the body, having the upholstery and top installed, painting the car and seeing to the finishing touches. After the restoration was completed, Mr. Smiley talked the car up to people, and at a Cadillac-LaSalle Club meet it was awarded "best of show." Mr. McGinnis has not taken it to other car shows.

There are four photographs of the V-16 roadster as it looked years ago, weathered and scattered about the field in Virginia. For fifteen years the pictures hung in Mr. McGinnis's law office, where one visitor examining the images of the car's rusted parts advised, "Give it up, Bob." Today, those four photos are framed together with the certificate of title and bill of sale that Mr. McGinnis received when he bought the car, and are all displayed adjacent to the restored Cadillac in the San Diego Automotive Museum where it is on loan.

Mr. Flynn's Madame X sedan would have been at the other end of the price list from the roadster when the cars were new. The Series 4302 roadster was the least expensive body style among the V-16 offerings in 1930 and '31. By 1930, closed cars were generally considered more comfortable, more luxurious, and more dignified. The "Madame X" cars were closed cars with advanced features of styling and construction. Advanced metallurgy and casting techniques allowed for unusually slim pillars supporting the roof and separating the side windows and windshield. The windshield itself (on all but the earliest Madame X cars) was tilted back at an angle of 18 degrees from vertical, a very rakish angle for the time. And the interior appointments were more restrained than on the

Fully restored. **The former basket case now resides in sparkling splendor at the San Diego Automotive Museum (courtesy Robert McGinnis).**

non–Madame X body styles. Purchased new, a Madame X style (say, a Series 4130-S five passenger sedan) would cost approximately $1,000 more than its regular counterpart (a 4330-S sedan).

The sedan that Mr. Meffert and Mr. Terhune acquired bore only passing resemblance to the magnificent motor car it had been when new. All of the structural wood in the body was rotted and useless. Mr. Terhune removed the body from the chassis, having in mind some sort of project involving the chassis and drivetrain, but he decided that the chassis was too rough and sold the remains to Mr. Meffert. The rear portion of the body was just the thing to complete California restorer Bob Hoffman's Series 4155 Madame X sedan that had been cut down into a farm truck. Or Mr. Meffert could purchase the front part of the body on Mr. Hoffman's car and restore the car he had. They settled the matter with Bob Hoffman completing his Series 4155 (which now resides in a museum in England). The chassis of the Madame X sedan from the Goochland County cache was sold to Vignero Molari, an Italian enthusiast who visited Mr. Terhune's shop with some frequency. What he has done with it, and what body work may now grace it, remains to be discovered.

And what became of the rest of the cars that settled on the Flynns' property? The 1935 Cadillac V-16 coupe was sold to an enthusiast in New York. The 1933 Cadillac had been reduced to some assorted accessories and parts by the time Mr. Meffert came on the scene. Dick Terhune bought the 1934 V-12 formal limousine and sold it to someone else. It's not known what became of the 1931 Oldsmobile. Such are the unpredictable destinies of automobiles.

6

Allan Singer's Limousine

One of the fifty Series 4330 five-passenger imperial sedans that Cadillac built during the 1930–1931 model run was shipped to the company's Philadelphia branch on Shackamaxon Street on February 21, 1930. This one bore engine number 700251 and body number 11. The name of the first owner is a bit of history that is lost to us at this point. But he is reported to have been an executive with the Anaconda Copper Mining Company who lived in Philadelphia. He is also reported to have bought the car off the floor of the Philadelphia auto show, where it was being shown as part of the Cadillac display. He died in late 1931 or early 1932, and the V-16 Cadillac passed to his brother. Shortly after that, the brother, who owned a marine construction firm, moved to Toms River, New Jersey, and drove the car there, where he put it in storage. At that point, there were 6 or 7 thousand miles on the odometer.

The V-16 limousine slept quietly in a commercial building, next to an old Mack truck, for a good quarter century. About 1957, a seventeen-year-old car enthusiast named Tommy Ackerman found out about the Cadillac. A lot of local car guys were aware that there was a Cadillac V-16 being kept there, but they all knew that the owner was not at all interested in selling it. He didn't need money, and the car represented an emotional tie to his deceased brother. Tommy Ackerman persuaded one of the owner's employees to let him into the building to look at the car (which was half-buried under rope, carpet scraps and bits of lumber) and he was smitten. He really wanted to have and enjoy that car.

With the innocent impulsiveness of youth, Tommy approached the owner, but the man was furious that his employee had allowed Tommy into the building, and he told Tommy to stay away from the building or face legal action. Not deterred by the refusal, Tommy returned to visit the man, not once, but many times. He didn't have much money, but in those days you could pick up exceptional and fascinating old cars for next to nothing. Tommy was always buying and trading unusual cars, and he would often bring his latest acquisition by to show the older man and they would sit and chat. He never visited the V-16—just the man at his home.

As the man aged and grew ill, he also grew fond of Tommy Ackerman and realized that Tommy was interested in the Cadillac V-16 for the car itself, and not to "flip" it or trade it for something else. Eventually, Tommy was able to persuade the man to sell him the car. The price was $500, but Tommy Ackerman needed time to come up with the cash. While he worked out a loan with his grandmother (the lady who had helped him get the cars he loved to drive and work on) other auto enthusiasts took the opportunity to try to outbid him.

When he came back with the purchase price, the owner of the car said he had decided not to sell it after all. Tommy returned home crestfallen, and his father suggested he call the owner back and explain how much the car meant to him. The owner felt badly for Tommy and said that he would pay Tommy a hundred or two just to make things right. Tommy turned him down and said it was the Cadillac he wanted. Then Tommy and his dad went together to see the owner and plead their case. Satisfied that Tommy was the right person to sell the big Cadillac to, the owner finally agreed and Tommy and his father bought the V-16 Cadillac and the Mack truck.

***As found.* After years of storage in a New Jersey commercial building, a majestic Cadillac hides beneath rope, rugs, and lumber. This is how Tommy Ackerman first saw the car when he talked his way into the building (courtesy Allan Singer).**

They towed the Cadillac to their home in Waretown, New Jersey. Tommy got a lot of help from his brother Bob, but it took months of rehabilitative work to get the Cadillac running again after its long hibernation. Once it was back on the road, Tommy wanted to show it to the former owner. He went to the man's house, but his secretary said he was seriously ill and could not come to the door. A pounding noise from above turned out to be the old man beating on the window, trying to get their attention. So they carried him down the stairs in a chair, helped him into the back seat of the car, and drove him around town in regal splendor, visiting friends and familiar places.

It was not long after that drive that the old man passed away, and Tommy made a point of attending the funeral. Afterwards, the secretary told Tommy that the man had left something for him, and he should come back to the house. There he was handed a box containing the jewel-like Jaeger clock (with Fleetwood logo) for the Cadillac's rear seat vanity case, and some of the paperwork that belonged to the car. The clock must have been held back as a remembrance of the man's brother, once the Cadillac had found a new home. When he knew he was dying, he left instructions to give it to Tommy.

Sometime in the 1960s, Tommy Ackerman posed for a photo with the car in front of the Jefferson Memorial in Washington, D.C. In the photo, the car sports American flags on thin staffs mounted to the side-mount spare tires, and a trunk has been installed on the luggage rack over the rear bumper. Tommy strikes a playful pose by the driver's door. The short sleeves and the flags hint that the occasion might have been an Independence Day visit to the Nation's Capital. But it could have been any time in the ample part of the year during which Washington weather is warm.

Tommy Ackerman had heard that the original owner of his car, the copper company executive, had been working on a deal with the Soviet government to establish copper

***As proud as the day it was made.* The 1930 V-16 imperial sedan wears its patina well and commands respect (courtesy Allan Singer).**

mining operations in that part of the world. While he was on a trip to Siberia, the story had it that he had been killed and the government had asserted that White Russian anti–Soviet forces had been responsible. Only years later would he hear a much different tale.

During the 1970s when he was working on the car, someone told him about a man who had worked for Cadillac years before at the Philadelphia branch. Tommy contacted the fellow and he claimed to remember Tommy's car. He told Tommy about a modification he had made to the cooling system, and Tommy was able to confirm that claim. The man told Tommy that the original owner's chauffeur was still living, and told him how to get in touch. When Tommy mentioned the story about the original owner's demise in the Soviet Union, the man laughed and said that was just like Philadelphia society types—construct a really good story to hide a scandal. The chauffeur told him that the real story was that the car's original owner had been killed by a mobster in South Philly because the fellow had been messing around with the mobster's girlfriend. Apparently, it was his habit to frequent brothels and questionable establishments, and fatal consequences had ensued.

Tommy Ackerman thoroughly enjoyed the V-16 limousine and drove it regularly. When he served in the U.S. Navy, he drove back and forth in it to Norfolk. His commanding officer even allowed him to keep it on the base, which was highly unusual. It seems the commander liked to drive the old Cadillac himself. Over the years, the car that had been in great shape in the 1960s began to show wear, and in the days when everything was about restoring old cars to like-new (or better-than-new) condition, examples

In Washington, D.C. **Parked in front of the Jefferson Memorial, likely in the early 1960s, and with American flags fastened to the spare tires, Tommy Ackerman enjoys a warm day with his car in the nation's capital (courtesy Allan Singer).**

of true originality were dismissed as potential restorations rather than welcomed onto show fields. Tommy Ackerman ultimately relegated the V-16 limousine to the corner of a storage building.

In 2006, the Concours d'Elegance of the Eastern United States (sponsored by the Burn Prevention Foundation) featured V-16 motor cars. One of the people gathering cars and owners to participate in the show contacted Tommy Ackerman and invited him to bring his V-16 Cadillac limousine. He explained to Tommy that times had changed, and now an unrestored original car from the classic era would be highly esteemed at any show. With coaxing and persuasion he convinced Tommy to let him get the car cleaned up and to show it. Sure enough, the elegant sedan drew a constant stream of fascinated admirers.

Tommy had a young friend for whom he became something of an adopted father. That young man, Allan Singer, since grown, lived until recently with his family in Toms River. But years ago, he spent a lot of time with Tommy Ackerman and his 1930 Cadillac. After Tommy passed away, Allan Singer inherited the venerable motor car that he had been involved with since he was 15.

Today, this Cadillac presents a very original and very well cared-for example of the five-passenger limousine. There are one or two anomalies, though. The flying goddess radiator ornament was recast by Tom Ackerman's father for him, including a gold coin in the mix. The outside door handles and a couple of other exterior trim pieces were re-cast in brass by an Amish craftsman from Gordon, Pennsylvania. A few chrome items (such as the radiator shell) have been re-plated, but for the most part the car is in unrestored original condition.

The paint shows some dings and wear, but is a very handsome finish for an eighty-plus-year-old job. The body below the window frames and roof is a medium brown, and the rest of the car is a very dark brown, almost black. The build sheet called for "Beaverbrook Brown" on the lower body, and "Matisse Brown" everywhere else, with "Saxon Gray" for the wheels. The upholstery specification was "Wiese 2960" which was the number code for a maroon taupe wool "doeskin suede" broadcloth made for Fleetwood by William Wiese & Company.

Sadly, Allan Singer passed away in the summer of 2018. During the time he had owned it, Mr. Singer had shown his V-16 sparingly. More important to him was simply caring for and enjoying this beautiful survivor of a different era. He credited a good friend and fellow Cadillac enthusiast with convincing him to keep the venerable old Cadillac in as original a condition as possible. At this point in time, it's up to Allan's family to decide what's next for his remarkable Cadillac.

7

The Maharajah's Speedster

In the late 1920s and early 1930s, a popular automotive body style for playboys and extravagant motorists was the boat-tail speedster. A speedster was a two-seat car with minimal bodywork, that was meant to go fast on the road or (preferably) on a race track. Its forebears were early bare-bones experimental vehicles and race cars like Henry Ford's "Old 999." Early models had little more than a wheeled chassis, engine and drivetrain, cowl and firewall, two seats and a gas tank. In the early days, a riding mechanic was needed for repairs during road races, and to act as the rear view mirror (the first race car to mount an actual rear view mirror was the Marmon Wasp that won the first Indianapolis 500-mile race in 1911). More civilized speedsters like early Mercer Raceabouts and Stutz Bearcats, sported basic fenders and perhaps a monocle windshield to keep some of the bugs out of the driver's face.

Evolution of the style brought doors and rear bodywork, and attempts at streamlining the car. Enclosing the fuel tank behind the driver served to cut down on drag, and tapering the sides of the body to a rearward point produced a shape like an upside-down boat prow that prompted the name "boat-tail speedster." Some racecars even enclosed the driver completely, but most remained open like contemporary airplane cockpits.

One of the rare bare-chassis 1930 and 1931 Cadillac V-16 cars was shipped July 17, 1931, from the factory to Bombay, India, having been purchased by the Maharajah of Orchha. Geographically, Orchha is now a town in Tikamgarh district of Madhya Pradesh state, but once it was the seat of a state over which the Maharajah of Orchha ruled. The Maharajah who had ordered this Cadillac, Vir Singh II, had begun his reign March 4, 1930. In 1950 he would merge his state with the Union of India, and become the last ruler of Orchha. But in 1931, he wished to have a very special car.

The Maharajah sent his Cadillac chassis to the recently-formed firm of Carrozzeria Pinin Farina. Battista "Pinin" Farina had gone into business for himself in 1930, and this was one of his company's first major commissions. The chosen design resembled an aircraft fuselage, using the stock Cadillac radiator shell and hood in the front as a starting point, and taking those lines in gentle curves around the passenger compartment to converge on the sharp, vertical end point at the back. The opening for the front seat occupants was scooped out of the body like an early airplane cockpit, with a windscreen in the same spirit. The shape of the door openings was tipped rearward to inspire feelings of forward motion. Below the body, louvered panels covered the sides of the frame rails. Separate streamlined fenders covered each wheel, and in the absence of fender wells or running boards, the side-mounted spare tires appeared to float next to the cowl.

The rear compartment was impressive. The seat was positioned significantly higher than the driver's seat, and unlike a typical rumble seat, there was an entry door on each

"Boat tail." **The rear view of the Pininfarina-bodied Cadillac V-16 clearly shows where the expression "boat-tail" arises. Tail lights and bumpers are standard 1930 V-16 items (although a bar has been added to connect the bumpers). Visible door handles open doors on either side of the rumble seat compartment. Of course, the car is right-hand drive (photograph Yann Saunders collection, courtesy the late Dave Towell).**

side of the car. According to the lore that clings to it, the extra height was to permit the Maharajah to hunt tigers from the car. Given the state of most local roads at that time, and the low likelihood that such a car was taken off-road to any great extent, that story appears unlikely. It would seem more plausible that the Maharajah would simply prefer to see and be seen as he travelled.[15]

Although the car was fitted with a folding top (that disappeared under a body panel when not in use) it was not meant for rain or severe weather, but more as a sun shade for the driver and front seat passenger. It fit the windshield very loosely, and no provision was made for side curtains.

It is not certain when this unique motor car left royal ownership, but the Maharajah died in 1956, and in 1960 the car was purchased by Indian film star Sheikh Mukhtar (d. 1980). He had seen the unique back end of the car protruding from the door of a workshop, and had successfully negotiated its acquisition. At this point in its life, two of the whitewall tires that had adorned the car in its early days were still in service, but the rest had been replaced with truck tires. The headlights and parking lights had been detached from the front of the car, and Mr. Mukhtar and his staff pushed the big car home.

15. Cadillac and Pininfarina would maintain a relationship through the ensuing years, resulting in the limited production 1959 and 1960 Brougham sedans, the 1961 "Jacqueline" show car, and the 1987–1993 Allanté roadster.

***New and ready for delivery.* This picture was taken outside the Farina works. The crest and script of Pinin Farina can be seen just aft of the spare wheel. Note the early airplane-style cockpit and the separate, streamlined fenders. The sleek bodywork incorporates the Cadillac V-16 hood, radiator shell, lights and wire wheels, but transforms Cadillac's supercar into a wind-cheating shape that projects motion even when standing still (courtesy P. Canonica Torino-Yann Saunders Collection).**

Sheikh Mukhtar reassembled the Cadillac and painted the body a cheerful fuchsia, with black for the fenders, wheels, louvered panels covering the frame, and top of the rear deck extending around the rim of the passenger compartment and down the top of the hood. There is a 1965 photograph of the car with Sheikh Mukhtar and the renowned and tragic Indian actress Meena Kumari, taken on the set of *Noor Jehan*, a 1967 film that Mukhtar produced and in which he also performed.[16]

In the early 1960s, Akron, Ohio, Cadillac dealer Dave Towell began trying to purchase the boat-tailed V-16. He corresponded with Sheikh Mukhtar, but it was not until April 1976 that he acquired the car. An offer of $90,000 had been made by another interested American, and Mr. Towell was determined to beat that. He offered $105,000 and the deal was done. Sheikh Mukhtar had emigrated to Pakistan and had taken the car with him, avoiding seizure by the Indian government. It was shipped out of the Sub-Continent in a crate purporting to enclose farm equipment, reportedly with a stop-over in Dubai before entering the United States at the port of Baltimore. From there it was transported by truck to Mr. Towell's home, where it arrived in early July. Mr. Towell would subsequently sell the speedster to Tom Barrett III (co-founder of the Barrett-Jackson Auction Company). In the early 1980s, Mr. Barrett sold it to restorers Francis Roxas and Jack Fredrich for what was then the astonishing sum of $225,000.

---

16. At Mr. Mukhtar's request, this photo became the cover image of the June 1980 issue of *The Classic Car*, the magazine of the Classic Car Club of America.

***As repatriated to the U.S.* This is how the 1930 Pininfarina-bodied V-16 appeared when Ohio Cadillac dealer and enthusiast Dave Towell acquired it. The fuchsia-and-black color scheme was chosen by previous owner Sheikh Mukhtar, after he acquired the car from Vir Singh II, Maharajah of Orccha (in what is now Pakistan) (photograph Yann Saunders collection, courtesy the late Dave Towell).**

In the course of its subsequent restoration, the car received a repaint that largely reversed the previous body colors—the body was now black with red around the rim of the passenger compartment and on the blaze atop the cowl and hood. The wheels and the hood vent doors were chrome-plated, and the seats were trimmed with tufted, deep red velour. A removable windshield, patterned after the one for the passenger compartment, was fabricated and installed in front of the rear seat, giving the car the appearance of what it functionally was—a dual-cowl phaeton. A set of Pilot Ray driving lights were mounted in front of the radiator, rear-view mirrors were attached to the brackets holding the spare tires, and twin spotlights were installed at the windshield pillars. The mechanical restoration of this low-mileage Cadillac resulted in a car so whisper-quiet that at a show in California, Mr. Roxas was asked to start the engine when it was already running.

In a 1982 article in *Automobile Quarterly* author Nick Cole related some of the history of the Maharajah's V-16 and presented ten stunning photographs by Roy D. Query of the restored car.[17] One of the photos shows the velvet-lined compartments next to the rear seat that probably accommodated the Maharajah's hunting guns when he owned the car. In 1987, the car was the main subject of the poster for the 20th annual Palo Alto Concours d'Elegance.

A later refreshing of the car, in time for it to appear at the 1993 Pebble Beach Concours d'Elegance, returned the wheels to painted (red) and the hood vent doors to the

17. Cole, Nick, "The Pursuit of Elegance, The Elegance of Pursuit: 1931 Cadillac V-16 Roadster by Pininfarina," *Automobile Quarterly*, Vol. 20, No. 4, 1982, Kutztown, PA, pp. 418–425.

same black as the hood. The Pilot Ray lights and spotlights were removed, and the interior was returned to light brown leather. The poster for that concours, and the front cover of the program, featured a painting of the speedster done by artist Nicola Wood.

The few extant black-and-white photographs from the early 1930s show a car with light-colored body panels and frame valances, and a medium color for the fenders, deck, and hood blaze. Following its ownership by Sheikh Mukhtar, subsequent owners have encountered difficulty in determining the original color scheme, and reports are that the Pininfarina[18] company has no record of the colors they used on the car. However, Cadillac historian Yann Saunders received a November 24, 1990, letter from the brother of the current titular Prince of Barwani, telling of having seen the car when the Maharajah visited the boarding school that he attended, at which time it was "painted in its original colour of sky blue fenders and pale cream body." When the late Robert M. Lee showed the car at the 2005 Pebble Beach Concours d'Elegance, the body was once again cream-colored. The rear deck, passenger compartment rim, and hood blaze were a medium-light blue, along with the fenders. The wheels were a darker blue and the interior was light brown leather.

***At the 2005 Pebble Beach Concours.* This cream and blue color combination is believed to be the way the car left the Farina works. Note the coachbuilder's badge affixed to the body just aft of the spare tire. The open cockpit evokes early aeronautical design (courtesy Ronald Verschoor).**

18. In 1961 the President of the Italian Republic authorized the change of Signore Farina's last name to "Pininfarina."

***First in class.* The 1930 Cadillac V-16 Pininfarina-bodied speedster crosses the reviewing stand at the 2018 Pebble Beach Concours d'Elegance, having taken first in Class F-2, Motor Cars of the Raj (copyright Kimball Studios, courtesy Pebble Beach Concours d'Elegance).**

When the car was shown at the 2018 Pebble Beach Concours by the Anne Brockinton Lee/Robert M. Lee Automobile Collection, it took First Place in Class F-2, Motor Cars of the Raj. In the years since 2005, the exuberant cream and light blue color scheme had been returned to black with red wheels and red on the rim of the passenger compartment into the widow's peak on the top of the hood. The light brown leather upholstery remains. This magnificent automobile continues to exemplify at once the astonishing opulence of the maharajahs, the artistry of Pininfarina, and the apex of Cadillac engineering.

8

A Convertible Coupe from the Case Collection

ALBRO CASE (D. 1971) OF Windsor, Connecticut, was a member of the family that founded and ran J.I. Case and Company, pioneering manufacturer of farm tractors. Albro Case had a fondness for restoring and preserving old houses and old cars, and he had a collection of V-16 Cadillacs before collecting big old classics of the 1930s was fashionable. In 1966, he sold one of his V-16 cars to a young man named William Meffert.

Albro Case would not sell you a car if he didn't know and like you. Mr. Meffert had gotten to know him, and Mr. Case must have liked Mr. Meffert, because in 1966 he sold him a 1930 Cadillac V-16 convertible coupe. The car was a Series 4335, the model with a nearly-upright v-windshield, and straight lower edges for the doors. Series 4335 cars were still built at the original Fleetwood facility in Pennsylvania. The other V-16 convertible coupe style that was offered, the Series 4235, had a one-piece, slanted windshield, and the lower edges of the doors were gently curved to form what was called a "carriage sill." Series 4235 cars were built in Detroit, where many of the Fleetwood craftsmen had been transferred after General Motors began acquiring the company.

Not much is known about the prior history of this Series 4335 car, with engine number 700898 and body number 47, except that it was shipped new to New York City on the

Fleetwood design rendering. **This is the Fleetwood drawing of the Series 4335 convertible coupe. The split vee windshield and the rear of the top are near vertical. The straight body sill and window sill combine to give the car a formal presence, despite its promise of open-air motoring for two. The sportier Series 4235 convertible coupe had more relaxed and curved body lines (courtesy Z. Taylor Vinson Collection).**

4th of April, 1930. Cadillac sold the cars it produced to the dealer or the regional distributor, and such factory records as have survived rarely indicate the identity of the actual purchaser. Unfortunately, Mr. Case can no longer tell us from whom he acquired the car, and our trail goes cold.

At the time Mr. Case sold him the car, Mr. Meffert didn't have enough money to pay for it, even at mid–1960s prices. So Mr. Case just told him to pay $50 a month, and that's what he did. When the total he had paid reached the sum of $3,000, Mr. Case told him "The car is yours." Until that time Mr. Meffert hadn't known what the purchase price for the car would be.

The big Cadillac was enjoyed and worked on by Mr. Meffert, but in 1969, another car caught his eye. Mr. Meffert's heart had always been set on owning a Cadillac V-16 roadster. The roadster (Series 4302) was the lowest priced of the V-16s when they were new, but in recent years, it became one of the most desirable models for its jaunty, sporting look, and its relative quickness compared to the heavier larger convertibles and closed cars. Mr. Meffert was attending the University of Virginia in Charlottesville, and working part-time for a car restorer named Dick Terhune. On a trip to pick up a car for Mr. Terhune, Mr. Meffert had stopped for gas in Fairmont, North Carolina, and the attendant had shown him a V-16 roadster for sale in town. Mr. Meffert was smitten and began frantically working for ways to come up with $5,000 to purchase the roadster (see Chapter 9). It became clear that the convertible coupe would have to find a new owner.

Mr. Meffert sold the convertible coupe, sporting a coat of primer, to Doctor Donald

***Three different shades of red.* The seriously formal lines of the passenger compartment of the Series 4335 convertible coupe are apparent here—the nearly upright split windshield, the squared off convertible top. Just the thing if one wanted to relax, yet not be seen as frivolous or playful (courtesy Alan Merkel).**

Vesley, a collector of high-end Classics in Florida, and he borrowed the rest of the money for the roadster from his father. Subsequently, Dr. Vesley sold the convertible coupe to Heinz Prechter (founder of American Sunroof Corporation, a builder and installer of convertible roofs, trim packages and complete concept cars for auto manufacturers) in Michigan. In the 2000s, the car showed up on the auction circuit, wearing three shades of red, and a black cloth top. In January 2007, Canadian collector Brent Merrill was the lucky bidder at $236,500. The next year, he consigned the car and the hammer came down at $324,500. The buyer at that sale passed away not long afterwards, and his estate put the car back on the block. In 2010, the scarlet and maroon convertible coupe found a home with a collector on the East Coast, in whose discreet stable it remained for the next seven years. In 2017 the car reappeared, offered at the March 10–11 Amelia Island sale by RM Sotheby's. At that function it found a new owner at a purchase price of $368,500.

9

Graduation Gift

THE CADILLAC THAT RECEIVED V-16 engine number 701203 was a Series 4302 roadster. It was black with an apple green pinstripe (a color called "Winooski Green") and wheel spokes of the same color. The seats and interior panels were trimmed in black leather and the convertible top was beige cloth. The only optional equipment specified for the car were wire wheels (instead of the standard wood wheels), fender-mounted spare tires (instead of the single rear-mounted spare the car that would otherwise grace the car) and a faster rear axle ratio (4.07 to 1) than the stock gearing (4.39 to 1).

This particular roadster was shipped from the factory to Cadillac's Philadelphia Branch on Shackamaxon Street. It was destined to be a present for a young man on the occasion of his graduation from medical school, in the late Spring of 1930. Dr. Rayford Weinstein kept his V-16 roadster through the 1930s, '40s, and '50s, and through most of the 1960s. By 1969 he was retired and living in Fairmont, North Carolina.

A young doctor's graduation present. **This 1930 Cadillac V-16 Series 4302 roadster is the car that a newly-graduated medical student received new from his parents. Except for a crunched front fender and bent axle, the car suffered few indignities over the years. Now it is fully restored and carefully conserved. This is how the car appeared about 1970, black with apple-green wheels and a tan top (courtesy William Meffert).**

On New Year's Day, 1969, a graduate student at the University of Virginia named William Meffert was returning from a road trip to South Carolina. He worked part-time for Dick Terhune, an auto restorer, and he'd been sent in Mr. Terhune's old van to pick up a rare old car that the shop would be working on. Taking what he thought would be a short cut, Mr. Meffert found himself at Red Huggins's Gulf station in Fairmont, North Carolina. Mr. Huggins saw the lettering on the side of the van advertising the restoration of old cars, and he struck up a conversation with Mr. Meffert. What, he wanted to know, was inside the van?

Showing Red Huggins the 1925 Anderson phaeton in the van ("Only Car Built in Dixie") launched a long discussion, peppered with repeated offers by Mr. Huggins to show Mr. Meffert an old car in town that he thought Mr. Meffert would be interested in seeing. For his part, Mr. Meffert was interested in getting back on the road and back home, so he didn't bite. As the conversation continued, the "old car" became "a Cadillac." A bit later, it became "a Cadillac convertible." Then Mr. Huggins offered to close the station and take Mr. Meffert there himself. So off they went through side streets and byways until they came to a lone house at the end of a street, Spanish moss hanging from the trees and the blinds pulled shut on all the windows. Willie Meffert hung back cautiously as Mr. Huggins boldly strode onto the yard and up to the door. No one answered at the door, so they proceeded to the garage, and there inside was a 1930 Cadillac V-16 roadster.

Mr. Meffert had always wanted one car—a 1930 Cadillac V-16 roadster. He'd told Dick Terhune so, and Mr. Terhune had promised to look out for one. And suddenly here was one, in great shape, except that the right front fender was crunched and the solid I-beam axle was bent near the right front wheel. Other than that it was a lovely 18,000-mile original car. The two men knocked at the front door again before heading back to the Gulf station. On their return, they tried a phone call, and Dr. Weinstein answered. He had been home all that time, watching them through the blinds.

So Mr. Meffert headed back to the doctor's house (and Mr. Huggins went back to work). This time Mr. Meffert was invited in. Thus began a three-hour long conversation, during which Mr. Meffert heard all about the medical school graduation present and other stories. He heard that the doctor always suspected that his parents loved his brother more—they gave him a Murphy-bodied Duesenberg convertible. Ultimately, the talk led to an offer by Dr. Weinstein to sell the Cadillac to Mr. Meffert for $5,000. Mr. Meffert had nowhere near that amount of money, but he was determined to buy the car, and he returned home with that in mind.

Between a loan from his father and selling another car (see Chapter 8), Mr. Meffert assembled the requisite funds and returned to Fairmont. There with Dr. Weinstein was his lawyer, and once the money was paid and the car loaded up, nothing would do but that they all adjourn to celebrate with some fine moonshine. The lawyer confided to Mr. Meffert that his timing was remarkable. Dr. Weinstein's mother was away in California at the time, and if she had been home, she never would have permitted the doctor to sell the roadster.

Bill Meffert enjoyed the roadster and paid back the loan to his father. Then in 1971, he was trying to start a business, and his friend Bobby McGowan offered him "a lot of money" for the car. He sold it, and within a year it was in the hands of Warren, New Jersey, collector and restorer, Gifford Oborne, who would own the car until he died.

Mr. Oborne took the V-16 roadster to another restorer, Robert Rich, to have some work done on it. It was still with Mr. Rich when Mr. Oborne passed away in 1986, and by way of a mechanic's lien, accumulated storage fees, or other legal process, Mr. Rich ended up with title to the car. Subsequently, Mr. Rich sold it to the late collector and Classic car enthusiast Frank Ricciardelli.

Shortly after Mr. Ricciardelli acquired the roadster, it received a complete restoration, and he and his wife showed it successfully. Among the awards the car won were a National Award from the Antique Automobile Club of America (AACA) in 2002, and three awards at the 2011 Amelia Island Concours d'Elegance (Best in Class, Most Elegant Cadillac, and Barry Meguiar Award for Best Finish on an Automobile). The resplendent motor car is now in the care of an owner in Oklahoma.

10

Restaurant Rendezvous

Of the 3,248 Cadillac V-16 cars built in the combined 1930–31 model year, the most frequently-ordered were the large sedans: the Series 4375-S seven-passenger sedan (501 cars), Series 4375 imperial sedan (limousine) (439 cars) and Series 4330-S five passenger sedan (394). These elegantly built and appointed cars worked for a living, while the coupes and convertibles played along with their fortunate owners. The big sedans could be limousines for the rich and famous, corporate amenities for businessmen, high-class livery vehicles, or comfortable transportation for well-to-do families. The number of survivors of these particular V-16 styles has been disproportionately small, relative to their production numbers.

One chilly day in the early 1930s, a happy group from the San Francisco Bay area gathered in the parking lot of a Fat Boy restaurant for photographs with a 1930 or 1931 Cadillac V-16 sedan. Years later, three of the pictures taken that day turned up in a batch of photos purchased at a thrift store in Nevada.

Photo session at the barbecue. **In the parking lot of the Fat Boy Barbecue, a 1930 V-16 sedan becomes the context for family photographs. The car sports fender-mounted spare tires, aftermarket spare tire covers, Cadillac accessory wind wings, and a goddess hood ornament. Otherwise it is a stock Fleetwood sedan. Whether it was built for five or seven passengers is hard to tell from the viewing angle.**

Sisters? **Two ladies pose together before the Cadillac.**

In one shot, a lady in a cloth coat and hat is sitting demurely on the front bumper of the car, resting her forearm on the license plate, and smiling for the camera. On the back of the image is hand-written "The big Cadillac & me."

A second shot shows the same woman standing next to another in a fur coat with her arms around the first woman's shoulders. Penned on the reverse is "Vivian & I."

The third has a distinguished-looking gentleman in suit, overcoat, fedora and high-top laced shoes sitting on the end of the bumper next to an older woman. The two ladies from the other photos stand on either side of the seated couple. The description on the back reads "Ma & Don. Vivi & I." and is signed "Lee." Clippings in a scrapbook purchased along with the photographs indicate that "Lee" was Leila Stubbins, and about all that we know about her is that she performed in the late 1920s with a theatrical group, the Maylon Players in Spokane Washington.

The car with its goddess radiator ornament is centered in each image, and is either a seven-passenger or five-passenger sedan (the sight lines don't allow a good look at the shape of the rear quarter window, which would tell for sure). Most likely a family car, the hood, cowl and lower body panels are painted a light color, while the fenders, chassis, roof, and upper body are a contrasting darker hue. The fender-mounted spare tire sports an aftermarket, chrome-plated cover for its tread surface, and the left rear door is not quite closed. Two other cars can be seen in front of the restaurant, and although there's not much detail to identify them, they are clearly from the late '20s or very early 1930s.

Fat Boy Barbecue restaurants (or "Cabins" as they were known) were a chain that started in the early 1920s with a single location at 46th Avenue and Sloat Boulevard in San Francisco, and grew to include locations in the nearby communities of San Jose, Colma,

Left: Everyone smile! **The Cadillac gracefully accommodates the whole group for an ensemble shot.** ***Above: Art deco logo.*** **Fat Boy Barbecue was a chain of family restaurants in the San Francisco Bay area in the 1920s and '30s. Tableware at the restaurants was decorated with the likeness of the trademark winking fat boy.**

Milpitas, Palo Alto, Redwood City and San Mateo.

The distinctive art deco logo of a winking cartoon fat boy can be seen in a couple of the photographs. The Fat Boy location places the photo shoot in the San Francisco Bay area, and tends to indicate that the car was sold new by Don Lee's Cadillac dealership at 1000 Van Ness Street. Don Lee acted as Cadillac's West Coast distributor in the 1920s and early '30s, and operated several dealerships in Los Angeles and other cities.

There's no way to know from the photos what became of the Cadillac. In a very few years, automotive technology and streamline design would make the 1930 and '31 cars (Cadillacs included) seem dramatically out of date. Weather, critters, and neglect are always ready to convert a proud, shiny automobile into a literal piece of junk. And in the early 1940s and again in the early 1950s, wartime scrap drives would swallow untold thousands of older cars of all makes. The cars that survived the gauntlet of the years are the ones we see and enjoy today. We can only hope that the V-16 sedan that posed in front of the Fat Boy Cabin is one of those survivors.

11

A Buffalo Businessman's Convertible Coupe

LIKE ALL OF THE 1930–31 Cadillac V-16 cars, the Series 4235 convertible coupe is a big car, rolling three tons on a 148" wheelbase. But the lines and proportions of the car are such that it doesn't look at all ungainly or awkward. The two-place passenger compartment does not look lost on the long chassis, but fits perfectly between the engine compartment and the gracefully curved rear deck. The one-piece windshield slopes gently backward, and that angle is complemented by the sloping rear panel of the convertible top. The flourish of the slender landau irons is just enough flash to complete the theme of sporting elegance.

The convertible coupe with engine number 702381 was sold new to William G. Seville in 1930 for $7,100, and his monogram was painted on the doors. Mr. Seville owned Plastergon Wallboard Company and lived outside Buffalo, New York. Plastergon

Fleetwood design rendering. **This is a depiction by Fleetwood of the Series 4235 convertible coupe. The windshield has a marked rake, the lower edge of the body swoops down over the valence panel, and the convertible top has a forward lean to it, all of which distinguish this style from the more reserved Series 4335 convertible coupe seen elsewhere in these pages (courtesy Z. Taylor Vinson Collection).**

Up close and personal. **1930 V-16 convertible coupe sold new to Buffalo, NY, business executive William G. Seville. When it was restored in the early 1960s, replacement rubber treads for the running boards were not available, so polished wood strips were used. Josiah Lilly III and his Heritage Museums and Gardens have owned this car since the mid-1960s (courtesy Michael Milne).**

produced a wood fiber panel to replace traditional lath and plaster construction for interior walls of residential and commercial buildings. A predecessor of today's ubiquitous gypsum drywall, Plastergon's product was cutting edge in its day. Mr. Seville was doing well, and he owned two V-16s and a 300-acre horse farm outside of Buffalo. He kept the convertible coupe for nine years.

In 1939, Vincent Marchese of Buffalo bought the car for $850 and owned it for about a year.

The identity of the owner during the period 1940–1946 is not known. In 1947, Joseph Slattery paid $50 for the car and soon thereafter sold it to an unidentified buyer who lived on York Street in Buffalo. In 1954 that man sold it to Larry Weaver (also of Buffalo), who turned around and sold it to Mike Steffen (again of Buffalo). In 1958, Mr. Steffen sold the car to Dr. Robert Britt.

In 1961, Bud Tinney, son of the Cadillac dealer in Buffalo, purchased the V-16 convertible from Dr. Britt (along with an extra engine). He wasn't able to get the purchase price from his father (who had said "You make your money selling ***new*** cars!") so he went to GMAC[19] and borrowed the money. When he acquired the car, it was painted in its

19. GMAC (General Motors Acceptance Corporation) was for decades GM's captive finance entity to help customers buy GM cars on credit. In the aftermath of the government bailout of GM in 2008, GMAC became independent of GM, was renamed Ally Financial, and continued to finance purchases of GM products as well as other brands.

***On display at Heritage Museums and Gardens.* Seen from above, the pleasing proportions of the 1930 Series 4235 convertible coupe are readily apparent. Armrests for the rumble seat and golf bag compartment behind the driver's door are exemplary luxury touches. As rumble seats go, this one is fairly roomy (courtesy Michael Milne).**

original colors of maroon and black, and it was in beautiful shape (although it had 1929 Pierce-Arrow bumpers). Bud doesn't know what happened to the spare engine.

Dr. Britt had told Bud to bring along a mechanic when he came for the car. He brought along Lloyd Landel, the longtime service manager at the Tinney dealership. When Mr. Landel saw the car he said "Oh, Bill Seville's car! I knew that car when I was a boy. He had horses and I used to muck out his stables." He had the car running in 15 or 20 minutes. Then he pumped up the tires and Bud drove it home.

Bud called Jim Pearson in Kansas City, Kansas, for bumpers, and was able to buy a set for $150. In those days "Cadillac Jim" Pearson was the "go to" guy for parts (or service information) for the Cadillacs of the early 1930s. He had scoured the Cadillac dealerships in the Midwest and had bought up their obsolete parts inventories. These cars were his life.

Such restoration as was needed was performed by Mr. Landel. Bud had him repaint the car a light beige (a 1954 Cadillac color) and a dark brown for the fenders, moldings and rear deck. They couldn't get proper replacements for the rubber tread strips on the running boards, so they used wood strips instead (a solution that a number of V-16 owners employed in the days before the correct rubber parts were again available). Bud had obtained some Cadillac stationery from a friend who worked there, so he could make a realistic verification letter purporting to say that the car had been equipped that way at the factory. As it turned out, he never had occasion to show that letter to a car show judge.

Restored over fifty years ago. **Since 1966, this roadster has been in the collection of Josiah Lilly III. Though Mr. Lilly is deceased, the car is part of the Heritage Museums and Gardens that he founded in Sandwich, Massachusetts (courtesy Heritage Museums and Gardens, Sandwich, Massachusetts).**

Bud Tinney showed the convertible coupe at a 1964 Classic Car Club of America Grand Classic meet in Dearborn and it received a score of 100 points. It was the second 100-point car in a CCCA judged event. In 1965, about the time that he took over his father's dealership, Bud sold the V-16 to Cadillac dealer David J. Towell of Akron, Ohio. Mr. Towell didn't own it long—the next year he sold the Cadillac to Josiah Lilly III of West Falmouth, Massachusetts, heir to the pharmaceutical company family fortune. Mr. Lilly has since died, but the car is still owned by his Heritage Museums and Gardens in Sandwich, Massachusetts. For 50 years, the car has been conserved and cared for by the museum, and has been seen and enjoyed by countless visitors.

12

Eleanor

THE 1930 CADILLAC V-16 SERIES 4361-S town sedan with engine number 700537 was shipped new in March of 1930 to the Don Lee dealership in San Francisco, California. The car was black with Mulberry Maroon lower door and rear body panels, hood and cowl. A Gold Bronze pinstripe highlighted the body moldings and character lines. Aside from wire wheels and fender-mounted spare tires, the only factory-installed optional equipment indicated on the "build sheet" is a trunk. Since this particular body style came with a permanently mounted trunk, the build sheet item would mean an additional trunk to be placed on the folding luggage rack at the rear of the car.

The build sheet bears an instruction to "TAG FRANK GRACE." The few build sheets

The car. **The town sedan body style is a family car with room for five. The maroon and black color scheme is true to original specs, although the wheels were originally plain black and the pinstriping was gold-bronze (courtesy Wellington Morton).**

Equipped for touring. **The town sedan came with a permanently-mounted trunk and a folding rack on which an accessory trunk can be mounted, for extensive luggage capacity (courtesy Wellington Morton).**

have a "tag" instruction are the only indication in surviving Cadillac records of who the original purchasers of these cars were. As a rule, the cars were sold by the factory to the dealer or distributor, and the build sheet form has spaces on which to enter the dealer's or distributor's identity. Nowhere does it call for the purchaser's name. It seems that in only a few cases was it determined to be necessary to indicate who would be coming for the car once it reached the dealer. In those instances, a notation was typed in, wherever space permitted.

Although it has not been possible to definitively establish the identity of the Frank Grace referenced in the car's shipping order, there is a likely possibility. In 1897, Frank P. Grace and his brother J.T. Grace started a brewery in Santa Rosa, north of San Francisco in Sonoma County. Located where the city's Convention Center now stands, the Grace Brothers Brewery operated until 1966. Beginning with efforts to secure a steady supply of hops, the brothers also became involved in buying property and in real estate development. During Prohibition, a switch to carbonated beverages and ice cream kept the retail business alive until beer could once again be sold.

Frank P. Grace died in August 1930, so if he was the original owner, he was not able to enjoy the elegant Cadillac for long. He had five sons, however, including Frank Grace, Jr. If, in fact, the family that founded and operated the Grace Brothers Brewery owned this particular V-16 Cadillac, it is not clear when they disposed of it.

The car is reported to have been restored in Alabama in 1969. At some point subsequent, noted collector John McMullen of Lapeer, Michigan, acquired the 1930 Cadillac town sedan. In the November/December 1993 and January 1994 issues of the Cadillac-LaSalle Club's monthly magazine *The Self-Starter*, he offered it for sale for an asking price of $160,000. Eventually he traded the car to Joseph Morgan of Hampton, New Hampshire, for a 1931 Chrysler Imperial phaeton. On October 13, 1994, Mr. Morgan sold the Cadillac to a collector in Andover, Massachusetts, and on March 4, 2004, that man sold it to Gresham Roskamp of Dana Point, California.

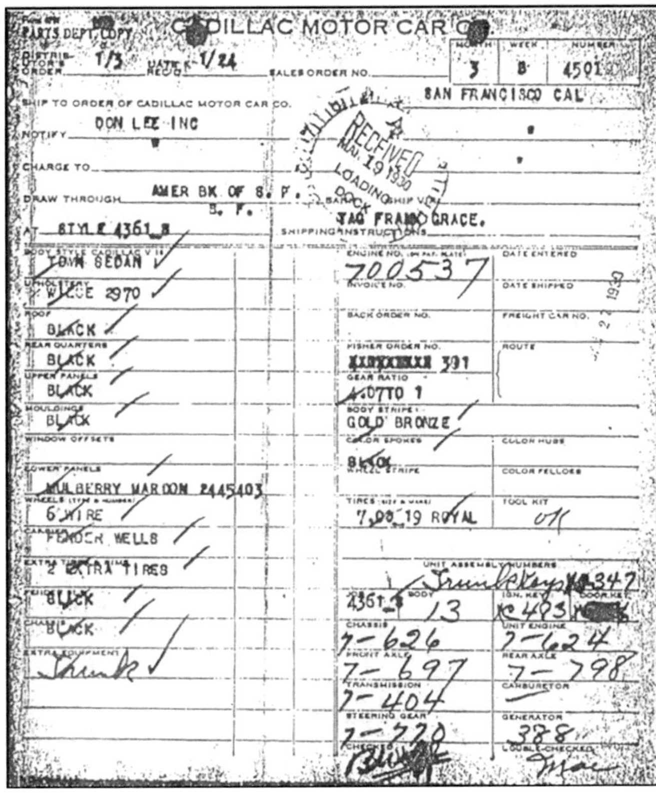

PARTS DEPT. COPY — CADILLAC MOTOR CAR CO.
DISTRIB. ORDER 1/3 DATE REC'D 1/24 SALES ORDER NO. 3 B 4501
SHIP TO ORDER OF CADILLAC MOTOR CAR CO. SAN FRANCISCO CAL
NOTIFY DON LEE INC
CHARGE TO
DRAW THROUGH AMER BK OF S. F. S. F.
STYLE 4361 B
TOWN SEDAN
SHIPPING INSTRUCTIONS: TAG FRANK GRACE.
RECEIVED ... 19 1930 LOADING DOCK
ENGINE NO. 700537
WHEELBASE 2970
BLACK / BLACK / BLACK / BLACK
FISHER ORDER NO. 391
GEAR RATIO 4.07 TO 1
BODY STRIPE GOLD BRONZE
COLOR SPOKES BLACK
MULBERRY MAROON 2445403
6 WIRE
TIRES 7.00-19 ROYAL
TOOL KIT O.K.
FENDER WELLS
2 EXTRA TIRES
BLACK
BLACK
EXTRA EQUIPMENT Trunk
UNIT ASSEMBLY NUMBERS: Trunk Keys
BODY 4361-B 13
CHASSIS 7-626 UNIT ENGINE 7-624
FRONT AXLE 7-697 REAR AXLE 7-798
TRANSMISSION 7-404
STEERING GEAR 7-720 GENERATOR 388

The build sheet. **The shipping order or "build sheet" for engine number 700537 bears the instruction "TAG FRANK GRACE." Mention of the actual purchaser on the build sheet was rare, and where found, it provides a helpful clue to the history of the car.**

Mr. Roskamp bought the car because he was curious about the mechanics and technology of the Cadillac V-16 motor cars, and he had it transported from Massachusetts to his home. He learned that in 1928 Cadillac started design engineering of a V-16 engine because less powerful engines were unable to power heavy cars (such as his 5,600-pound town sedan) up steep hills. Unfortunately, a recession took hold the year that the V-16 cars went into production (1930) and Cadillac never recovered the actual development costs. By Mr. Roskamp's own account he's not one for taking a car to a show and standing around with it for hours. When he did drive or show his V-16, though, people were always impressed by its elegance. He and his family nicknamed the car "Eleanor" after President Roosevelt's wife, and he always carried a jar of Grey Poupon mustard in the glove box. He told the author that he put about $15,000 into the car doing various incidental things—such as servicing brakes and suspension, having the door and window handles machined so that they turned smoothly, sorting out the carburetors, and replacing the carpets in the front and rear compartments. It was difficult getting "Eleanor" into and out of his garage, so after three years and putting five or six hundred miles on the vehicle, he offered it for sale.

Mr. Roskamp sold the Cadillac to Kenneth E. Guthrie of Everett, Washington. Sometime subsequently, it was sold as part of an estate by the Imperial Palace Collection in Las Vegas Nevada. The purchaser and new caretaker of the car was Wellington Morton of St. Johns, Florida. Among other things, Mr. Morton had the carburetors rebuilt, and

***The driver's seat.* Comfortable, adjustable front seat faces a full set of instruments and convenient controls. Fine inlaid wood appointments surround the occupants. Crank over the windshield raises the windshield glass for ventilation on warm days (courtesy Wellington Morton).**

the moth-damaged interior redone with correct wool broadcloth. Under his ownership, the elegant town sedan was shown at the 2014 Ault Park Concours d'Elegance in Cincinnati (where it took a class award), at the Lake Mirror Classic Auto Festival, at the Amelia Island Concours d'Elegance (as a display car), and at the 2015 Antique Automobile Club of America St. Augustine Fall Meet (where it won Best in Class).

In spring of 2017, Mr. Morton decided to sell his V-16 town sedan, and on April 1, 2017, Auctions America offered it at their Fort Lauderdale, Florida, event. A new owner took it away for a purchase price of $195,250.

13

In the Little Town of Dumfries

IN THE LITTLE TOWN OF Dumfries, Virginia, there still resides a salvage yard that was once known as "Skip's Used Auto Parts." Today it is part of a multi-state company known as LKQ, but in the middle of the last century it was run by a lively fellow named Medford Cosner, Sr., known to friends and customers as Skip. In the early 1960s, a very special used auto made its way to Skip's enterprise. It was a 1930 Cadillac V-16 Series 4376 closed coupe in surprisingly good condition. During the 1950s and into the early 1960s, the car had been owned by Mr. E.C. Moore, and he had kept it serviced at Capitol Cadillac in Washington, D.C. Somehow Mr. Moore found out that Skip had a 1930 V-16 sedan in his salvage yard, and over the course of ten or fifteen years he would drive his Cadillac coupe down from Washington and visit Skip's enterprise two or three times a year. Shortly before Mr. Moore passed away, he sold his Cadillac coupe to Skip, who was happy to put it to use as a push vehicle in his business.

The Series 4376 coupe was an impressive personal automobile, riding on the same 148-inch wheelbase as the other 1930 and 1931 V-16 Cadillacs. Accommodating the driver and a passenger in the enclosed compartment, the car had room for two more in the folding rumble seat. The nearly-upright split windshield consisted of two panes, each of which could be pushed open from the lower edge for ventilation. Behind the driver's head, the rear window could be rolled down into the body to provide even more air flow. The door windows were outlined with bright-metal exterior reveals, and the body had sweeping character lines from the top of the radiator shell arcing back along the top panels of the hood and curving down the sides of the cowl.

This particular car bears engine number 700827 and body number 16. When it was new, the car was shipped from the factory to the Madison Smith Cadillac Co. in Little Rock, Arkansas. It was all black except for sable lower door and body panels, and Persian Red pinstriping and wheel spokes. The only extra (optional) equipment indicated on the build sheet is two fender-mounted spare tires and wire spoke wheels.

There is a photograph of the big Cadillac with E.C. Moore holding the door handle and resting his right foot on the running board. The car sports two vertical bumper guards mounted near the ends of the front bumper, and a triangular bar is clamped to the center. In the picture, the car carries several accessory items with which V-16 owners often personalized their cars when new. Glass wind wings mounted adjacent to the windshield pillars permit comfortable motoring at speed with the door windows lowered. "Pilot Ray" driving lights work like modern cornering lights to help the driver see when turning at night. Painted metal covers trimmed with bright metal (and rear-view mirrors) dress up the fender-mounted spare tires. And the wire wheels, fender wells and second spare tire were all extra-cost options. The front license plate was issued by

E.C. Moore and his Cadillac coupe. Wearing District of Columbia plates, this Series 4376 V-16 coupe is one of 98 built in 1930–31. When a part was needed, Mr. Moore would drive the car to Skip's Used Auto Parts in Dumfries, Virginia (courtesy Skip Cosner).

the District of Columbia where Mr. Moore resided. The plate bears a date in the 1960s, and though it's difficult to establish the year with certainty, it looks like 1966. All of the chrome glistens, the paint is unblemished and glossy, and all of the bits and pieces are there. In the early 1960s, the big Classics were still largely disdained as clunky, obsolete used cars, and you could buy one in nearly new condition for a song.

Skip kept the V-16 coupe for five or six years, and drove it regularly. One day he had the urge to "see what it could do" and travelling through Dumfries (which was then a much smaller community) he put the accelerator down and held it. Crossing a little bridge, he saw the speedometer reach 100, and slowed back down. Afterwards, as he walked around the car, he noticed that the right front wheel had a serious crack in it, and a flash of total realization of the peril he had escaped prompted him to quickly replace the wheel (he had a spare in the yard). From then on he kept his driving speed between 25 and 35 miles per hour.

About 1964, restorer Dick Terhune (then living in Sanford, Florida) spotted the V-16 coupe parked on the side of a road. He later found Skip at a local bar and in the course of a round or two of refreshments, somehow persuaded him to part with the Cadillac. Mr. Terhune worked on the car extensively, and it was the first car that he restored. He wrote an extensive article about the car and its restoration that was published in the magazine of the Florida region of the Classic Car Club of America.

Today, the Cadillac coupe is black with a maroon top, and with maroon in the cove area, outlined by the character lines that sweep back from the radiator cap along the top

***Resplendent in red and black.* Warren Newton waves from the cockpit of his 1930 V-16 coupe. Upright split windshield is characteristic of the last Cadillac cars built at Fleetwood's factory in Fleetwood, Pennsylvania, before General Motors moved all Fleetwood operations to Detroit (courtesy Warren Newton).**

of the hood and down the sides of the cowl. A crimson pinstripe highlights the body moldings. The vent doors in the hood side panels and the sides of the cowl have been chrome-plated, as have the wheels. The spare tires no longer have the painted metal covers, though they do have rearview mirrors fastened to them.

By the time the car was offered for sale in early 2009 at the Internet web site of Hyman, Ltd., it had also been owned by Ohio Cadillac dealer Dave Towell, and by collector Warren Newton of Branford, Connecticut. Mr. Newton told the author he had purchased the Cadillac coupe from a Canadian collector, had kept it for about six years, and had sold it to a Midwesterner named Jim Miller. He said it was a good running car, but hard to start unless he primed the vacuum tanks beforehand.

The listing for the V-16 coupe on the Hyman, Ltd. website showed an asking price of $285,000. The next year it was offered at the Tulsa Auction of the Leake Auction Company, June 11–13. It drew a high bit of $240,000, but was not sold. It continued to be listed on the Hyman website, at $295,000.

In 2016, a video appeared on YouTube showing an interview with a couple in Turkey about their collector cars.[20] Prominent in the couple's immaculate display garage was the 1930 V-16 closed coupe, engine number 700827.

20. https://www.youtube.com/watch?v=9_sZTyk2JJE. Accessed December 10, 2019.

14

A Dressed Up Limousine

Bob Bahre was a dedicated collector of fine automobiles and was the creator and former owner of the New Hampshire International Speedway (now known as the New Hampshire Motor Speedway). In 1985 he owned a 1930 Cadillac V-16 seven-passenger imperial sedan, Series 4375, with engine number 702783 and body number 362. It had been shipped new to San Francisco on November 8, 1930. During the 1960s and 1970s, the car had been owned by Californian John S. Porter, who lived north of San Diego.

A total of 438 1930 or '31 V-16 cars were built in the 4375 body style, and only the Series 4375-S sedan (the same configuration without the partition between driver and passengers) was more strongly represented among the 3,248 V-16s produced in those first two years. Although the big sedans were the V-16 cars that worked the hardest (as transport for corporate executives or dignitaries, as high-end livery cars, or as private limousines for wealthy individuals) they were nevertheless exquisitely appointed, and heavily hand-crafted, luxury automobiles. From period photos, it's apparent that this one had survived quite well into the 1970s, retaining its handsome dark blue exterior finish and light tan broadcloth interior fitments. Even the umbrella that came with the car, with its amber-colored plastic handle, remained in its socket behind the front seat. Very little was noticeably missing—the glass sunshade over the windshield was gone, and the

***Fleetwood catalog drawing for the Series 4375-S.* The stately elegance of the lines on this car, while already somewhat dated in 1930, commands respect. A 4375 car would have been identical with the exception of an interior divider window (courtesy Yann Saunders and the Z. Taylor Vinson Collection).**

As originally built. This is the 1930 Cadillac Series 4375 with engine number 702783 when it was owned by John S. Porter of Poway, California. Except for a missing glass sunshade over the windshield, the car is as Cadillac shipped it new to San Francisco (courtesy Jeff Ordway).

Converted to a sedan cabriolet. Filled-in rear quarter windows, leather roof covering and decorative landau bars produce the style that Fleetwood called a sedan cabriolet. V-16 purchasers could order a five-passenger sedan cabriolet, but a seven-passenger job such as this one would have required a special order (courtesy Kirk Stevenson).

***Clean lines on the engine, too.* The early V-16s were designed to be seen and admired—enamel, polished aluminum, chrome and porcelain pleased the eye, and wiring was mostly concealed. What wasn't hidden was chromed or otherwise finished (courtesy Kirk Stevenson).**

right-hand taillight lens had been replaced with a different style. Otherwise the car was very much as Cadillac had built it.

Mr. Bahre's car was advertised for sale during 1985 in *Hemmings Motor News*, and it was displayed that October in the flea market at the annual AACA Eastern Division Fall Meet at Hershey. In 1987, the limousine was sold to Fred Weber's restoration business in St. Louis, Missouri. During the next three or four years, Marc Ohm undertook a series of modifications to the car, consistent with Fleetwood design practices on other body styles, that gave the car a more formal appearance and provided more privacy to the passengers. He filled in the rear quarter windows and applied a leather covering to the roof and upper rear quarters. After that, he fastened (decorative) landau irons where the rear quarter window openings had been. The finished product looked like a seven-passenger version of a Series 4355 imperial cabriolet.

Among the more than thirty body styles that were offered by Fleetwood on the 1930–31 V-16 chassis there was none that exactly matched the transformed Series 4375 that Marc Ohm had produced. There was a five-passenger closed sedan with closed rear quarters, leather roof and landau irons (the Series 4355). But officially there was no seven-passenger equivalent in that configuration.

However, the changes that were made to this particular car were well within the scope of the modifications that Cadillac and Fleetwood stood ready, even eager, to undertake if a customer requested them. In fact, according to surviving Fleetwood promotional material, for $300 additional to the purchase price (approximately 5 percent of the retail price of the car) and three weeks additional preparation time, Fleetwood would remove

Imperial division. **This partition makes the car an "imperial sedan." Hand crank raises and lowers the window for passenger privacy. Warm inlaid wood accents the top of the division and the windows, as well as the instrument panel (courtesy Kirk Stevenson).**

the rear quarter windows of a Series 4375 imperial sedan, replace them with solid quarters, apply a leather roof covering, and install decorative landau bows.[21] In all likelihood, the body style number would have been changed to 4375-LB. The goal of the V-16 program, after all, was to make available within the General Motors enterprise the full range of fine engineering and custom coachbuilding that prestige buyers were accustomed to seeking from multiple unrelated establishments.

In 1991 Marc Ohm told Cadillac V-16 owner and enthusiast Alan Merkel about the transformation, and disclosed that the car had been sold at the Auburn Auction that year to Peter Schlacter of Milan, Ohio. Mr. Schlacter also owned for some time the re-manufactured Series 4264-B cane-bodied brougham that David Holtzman and "Cadillac Jim" Pearson had caused to be built out of a Series 4291 V-16 town car. (That had been perhaps the most spectacular of the Fleetwood bodies offered on the V-16 chassis, and none of the originals had survived). Mr. Schlacter's family—wife Jane, son Andrew and daughter Jennifer—have always been actively involved with the Classic cars he has brought to their home.

The next owner of the transformed 4375 limousine was Alan Johnson of British Columbia, Canada. That would have been about 1996, and the car passed next to Alan's son Terry. Terry Johnson described the Cadillac to this author as "a wonderful driving car."

21. GM Heritage Center, Online Vehicle Information Kit for 1930 Cadillac V-16, pg. 118, accessed Aug. 8, 2016, at https://www.gmheritagecenter.com/docs/gm-heritage-archive/vehicle-information-kits/Cadillac/1930_Cadillac_V16_VVI.pdf.

In 2015, Alan Merkel received a phone call from Kirk Stevensen, also of British Columbia, who had recently bought the V-16 from Terry Johnson. Mr. Stevensen provided a set of photographs that show a car with deep red lower door panels and rear body section, deep red window reveals or offsets, black fenders, wheels, upper panels and leather roof covering. The hood side panels and the sweeping cove areas across the top hood panels and down the sides of the cowl are black as well. The upholstery in the passenger compartment is gray wool broadcloth, and the driver's compartment is trimmed in black leather.

This car, as restored, has a dramatic and elegant presence. The long V-16 hood balances the added length of the seven-passenger body in a satisfying way, and the car shows what could be done with a fairly straight-forward sedan design. The red and black color scheme is arresting without being overdone or busy. And the formal touches lend an exquisite dignity to an already impressive motor car

15

Poster Girl for a New Car Club

IN 1952, THE BIG LUXURY cars built in the late 1920s and through the decade of the '30s were largely disregarded by automobile aficionados and by the general public. Such cars were thought to be quaint, obsolete, and inconvenient used cars. There were, however, enough believers in their intrinsic historic, artistic, and aesthetic value to form the nucleus of a national club that would call itself the Classic Car Club of America. Today that club claims around 4,000 members, in the United States and abroad. Then, they were just a handful of enthusiasts trying to get their club organized and known. In March of 1952, comedian and TV and radio personality Herb Shriner invited the club to show 25 or 30 cars at the International Motor Sport Show at the Grand Central Palace in New York City. It was a splendid opportunity to gain public exposure and attract new members. But the club members were accustomed to using what would come to be known as Classic cars as everyday transportation, and each was reluctant to relinquish a daily driver for the week-and-a-half that the show would run. Two or three weeks before the show, someone spotted a 1931 Cadillac parked at a gas station. Inquiries as to the car's ownership elicited the name of Joseph F. Sulley, an accountant who lived in Brooklyn and worked at Rockefeller Center. Mr. Sulley was contacted, and the club offered to clean up the car if it could be exhibited at the car show. The owner agreed, joined the club, and served as its treasurer. Seventy-five new members were enrolled by the time the show ended, and on September 17, 1952, the Classic Car Club of America was incorporated in New York.

The car that was shown by the CCCA at that 1952 auto show was a 1931 Series 4380 V-16 convertible sedan, what was known as an "all-weather phaeton." In the early 1930s, a phaeton was usually a four-door convertible car with two rows of seating for five passengers (two in front and three in back). The body was generally shorter than that of a "touring car," which could have auxiliary seats for two more passengers. Phaetons and touring cars had folding tops but no side windows. Weather protection was dependent upon the prompt deployment of flexible side curtains (with transparent panels) that never quite seemed to form a water-tight seal. By 1930, a four-door convertible style had been developed with roll-up glass windows that securely kept out the wind and precipitation. The marketing name for these cars was "all-weather phaeton" but by the mid–1930s, they would be known simply as convertible sedans.

This particular all-weather phaeton, with engine number 703135 and body number 167, was shipped from the factory on June 30, 1931, to Cadillac's Philadelphia Branch. According to the shipping order or "build sheet," the body of the car and its wheels were painted an aqua color called Waterspray, while the fenders, chassis, and body moldings wore a forest green shade named "Crescendo Green." The only optional

***Venerable age, honestly worn.* This 4380 all-weather phaeton is the first car ever displayed at a Classic Car Club of America meet (in 1952). The convertible top has been replaced, but otherwise this car is unrestored. The chrome may be scuffed, and the paint nicked (with patches of the original green showing through the mid-century black re-paint). But the car is straight, complete, and running. The saying goes "They're only original once" (courtesy Alan Merkel).**

equipment specified is wire wheels and fender-mounted spare tires (the stock configuration would have been wood wheels and a single rear-mounted spare). As with most of the build sheets for these cars, there is no indication who the original purchaser was. Sometime between its original delivery and its appearance at the 1952 New York Auto Show, the car was repainted black. Joe Sulley, who became the CCCA's treasurer, owned the V-16 Cadillac for decades, and after his passing in August 1994, his family kept the car. Around 2012, CCCA members Charles LeMaitre of Massachusetts and Arthur Smith of Connecticut bought the car from the family. About twenty years ago, another CCCA member, Mark Smith of New Hampshire, had found out about the car from the McGowan brothers, a colorful band of siblings whose interests included performing together in a folk band with the name Farquar, as well as buying and selling and working on old cars. Recently, Mr. Smith bought this remarkable veteran motor car, and he owns it today.

Since acquiring his all-weather phaeton, Mark Smith has replaced the convertible top, the bottom cushions of the seats and the carpet. The rest of the car—body, chrome trim, remaining upholstery—he has chosen to leave in unrestored original condition. A fine dusting of rust can be seen on a few of the chrome trim items, and although the black paint retains its shine, there are lots of places where the original green hues show

Still running after 88 years. **This is true originality. This once-gleaming engine has lost the porcelain from the exhaust manifolds, and some of the enamel from intake, carburetor and air horn. The vacuum tanks should have black bodies, and the manifold vacuum line has been bent. Surface rust freckles the spare tire cover and the firewall. The owner reports that the engine runs just fine (courtesy Alan Merkel).**

through. Much of the black enamel on some of the engine parts and the porcelain coating for the exhaust manifolds have flaked off. The patina of age is borne lightly, but unmistakably. Mr. Smith reports that this 1931 V-16 runs really well, the way a Cadillac of the Classic Era should.

16

A Roadster with the Heart of a Madame X

For their 2018 auction on the occasion of the annual Eastern Meet of the Antique Automobile Club of America in Hershey, Pennsylvania (known to car buffs as simply "Hershey"), RM Sotheby's offered a 1930 Cadillac V-16 roadster with a very interesting history. The roadster body style has become the most sought-after of the "first generation" Cadillac V-16 cars and this one makes it easy to see why. The car in question was presented in two shades of green—a light olive for the body sides and the hood, and a forest green for the fenders, chassis, body moldings and deck lid. Upholstered in green leather to match the fender color, the car had a folding top in a light khaki shade, piped in the same green leather as the seats. Most every available accessory was fitted: fender-mounted spare tires with metal covers and mirrors; Pilot-Ray driving lights; dual spotlights and wind wings flanking the windshield; a goddess radiator ornament; and chrome-plated wheels and hood vent doors. Although some years had passed since the car was restored, everything still looked quite fresh.

Any motor vehicle that survives for eighty-plus years is bound to have some tales to tell and names to name, and this one is a good example of that. From the factory, the car was shipped to London, England, on July 26, 1930, bearing engine number 702414. But it wasn't a roadster. When built, the car bore a "Madame X" limousine body, Series 4175, specially fitted with right-hand drive. The car's body and hood were painted Cadet Blue, with Andalusite Blue moldings and an Andalusite Blue roof. The fenders and chassis were Andalusite Blue and the wheels were chromium plated. A gold bronze pin stripe completed the exterior theme. Inside the car, the chauffeur's compartment, instead of the customary black leather, was trimmed in pleated blue leather supplied by the Radel Leather Manufacturing Company. The upholstery for the passenger compartment was specified as pleated gray broadcloth (#2973 from the catalog of William Wiese & Company, a noted New York firm specializing in automotive textiles).

Madame X cars were all sedans, and they featured advanced design elements. They comprised a special sub-set of the V-16 cars, costing $1,000 more than their non–Madame X counterparts. The windshield was raked 18 degrees from vertical (as compared with only seven degrees for the non–Madame X cars). The "A" and "B" pillars (the windshield posts and the posts between the doors) were unusually thin, thanks to advanced metallurgy and casting techniques, and the door windows and backlight were outlined with thin bright-metal reveals. The interior trim was simpler and cleaner in design, with painted window frames and much more restrained use of inlaid wood trim pieces. This particular car bucked that theme somewhat, with its pleated upholstery fabric in front and rear compartments.

This Madame X limousine was reported to have been shown at the London International Motor Exhibition, held at the Olympia exhibition center from October 16–26, 1930. From there it was purchased on November 18 by Count Natale Labia (1877–1936). Count Labia was a member of the Italian Foreign Service who became Consul to Johannesburg in 1916. In 1929 he and his South African wife built an elegant home in Muizenberg to serve as their residence and to serve as the official residence of Italy's legation to South Africa. "Casa Labia" stands today and has been declared a national monument.

Count Labia gave his V-16 Cadillac to an Italian resident of Cape Town in return for services rendered. In turn, that fellow is reported to have sold the car to an Italian restaurant owned in Durban named L. Moero. In 1965, George Alexander Huddlestone (owner of the largest Ford dealership in Durban and founding member of the Veteran Car Club of South Africa) paid $600 to become the next owner, with the odometer showing all of 21,000 miles. Around St. Valentine's Day of 1977, the car arrived in the United States, sold by Mr. Huddlestone to The Vintage Car Store, a legendary dealership in exotic high-end old motor cars then located in Nyack, New York, run by the late Ed Jurist. The sale price was $42,500, and the mileage on the car at the time was 34,129.

Enthusiast Archie Meinerz of Franklin, Wisconsin, purchased the Cadillac from The Vintage Car Store, on October 16, 1978. Mr. Meinerz removed the blue Madame X body from the car and replaced it with a V-8 Cadillac roadster body that he had purchased from another enthusiast and collector, Dr. Art Burrichter (who was then living in Florida). He also sold the right-hand drive chassis, which was subsequently converted to left-hand drive and now undergirds a project car in Pennsylvania. Another V-16 chassis was procured, engine number 702414 was installed in it, and the V-8 roadster body was mounted. Substantial finish work would have been required in order to complete the transition, and Mr. Meinerz chose an attractive two-tone green color scheme that the car sports today.

Archie Meinerz sold the re-born roadster to Barnaby Brokaw of Solana Beach, California, and he later sold it to Robert F. Smith, an executive with General Electric and American Express. The car made its way to Dragone Classic Motorcars (then in Bridgeport, Connecticut), and that company ultimately sold it to Fred Weber.

Fred Weber and his son Dave ran a restoration shop in St. Louis, Missouri, through which passed a good number of the surviving V-16 Cadillacs. In 1992, the Webers showed the roadster at a Classic Car Club of America Grand Classic in Indiana, where it took a first-place award and won CCCA Senior Badge number 1742. In 1993, Fred Weber sold the car. Subsequently, it was acquired by collector and CCCA member Calvin High of Willow Street, Pennsylvania (who recalls buying it from a dealer in New Jersey). Mr. High did significant work on the car and installed a correct accessory luggage trunk, as well as metal spare tire covers. He sold the car in 1997 to a New Jersey collector, with whom it remained until 2005, when Tom Kowalski of Centennial, Colorado, acquired it.

Today the car is largely indistinguishable from a factory-built roadster. The few discrepancies are the kind that only a diligent enthusiast would look for. For example, the floor of the passenger compartment should be an uncarpeted metal plate with hard rubber treading. This was, after all, the least expensive of the V-16 models, and a body style considered relatively primitive even in 1930. And the inside of the joint between the cowl and the passenger compartment door should be painted body color, and not covered by a chrome-plated escutcheon.

***On its way to a new owner.* The newly completed V-16 roadster is being loaded at the home of Archie Meinerz in Franklin, Wisconsin, for the trip to new owner Barney Brokaw in California. Only a close examination by one who knows what to look for would disclose that the body is from a V-8 Cadillac roadster, and the engine was originally installed in a Madame X sedan that was shipped new to London (courtesy Barnaby Brokaw).**

The pre-auction estimate given by RM Sotheby's for the 1930 V16 we've been discussing was $400,000 to $450,000. That's considerably less than the recent sale prices of some V-16 cars that were originally built with roadster bodies and that still have their original engines. Nevertheless, at a sale price, including buyer's fee, of $495,000, the car found a new home.

17

The Groundskeeper

In some cases, the tribulations endured by particular Cadillac V-16 automobiles, and the unorthodox uses to which they were put, once the "new" wore off, make the fact of their survival (let alone restoration to like-new condition) genuinely miraculous. It's not surprising that a farmer on a tight budget might re-purpose a big old car with a robust chassis and powerful drivetrain to serve as a truck or tractor, cutting down the body, re-arranging the chassis, and doing whatever needed to be done to keep the vehicle running. What *is* astonishing is that some enterprising soul (or souls) would rescue such a transmogrified machine.

A Series 4335 V-16 Cadillac convertible coupe, engine number 701281, was shipped from the factory to the Don Lee dealership in San Francisco in early April 1930, only to be diverted to New York City. From the build sheet, it appears the car wasn't shipped to an owner until late May of 1931, over a year after it was built.

The car was painted in several shades of gray. The body was done in "Bellaire Gray," with "Gray Gull" moldings. The fenders and chassis were "Timberline Gray." "Cream Color Lt." was specified for the pinstriping, and the wheels were "Gray Gull" with chrome plated spokes. The side panels of the hood and the cove area on the car's cowl matched the "Timberline Gray" of the fenders and chassis. As a finishing touch, the hood vent doors and cowl vents were chrome plated. Inside, the seats and trim panels were covered with a "Mouse Gray" bedford cord and the Burbank cloth convertible top was lined with matching broadcloth.

Understated and dignified elegance characterized the presentation of this V-16 Cadillac. The subdued color palette would have worked well with the lines of the Fleetwood body. The Series 4335 cars like this one were relatively conservative in styling, with a nearly-upright, two-pane windshield, angled to a "V" at the center.[22] And the framing of the convertible top was rather squared-off. By contrast, Cadillac's other convertible coupe on the V-16 chassis, the Series 4235, was a sports model, with a gently raked, one-piece windshield and a top that was more rounded with a sloping rear panel.

We don't know who purchased this 4335 convertible coupe new, or what adventures it participated in, from the day it was sent to New York until some time in the 1980s, when the late Doug Anderson purchased it. By that time, this glorious motor car had been reduced to working as a tractor to pull gang mowers on a golf course. Only the cowl structure remained of the Fleetwood convertible coupe body, with the hood and

22. Cadillac V-16 bodies with this split windshield were produced at the Fleetwood plant in Pennsylvania and are some of the last Fleetwood bodies produced before that plant was closed and the transfer of Fleetwood operations to Detroit was completed.

radiator shell—no fenders, and no bodywork aft of the windshield. And the frame had been drastically shortened, such that the rear axle (without benefit of springs or shock absorbers) now sat directly below the point where the front seat would have been. Immediately behind the differential housing, a fabricated cross-member connected the stubs of the frame rails and formed the rear end of the vehicle. A heavy steel ring hung from the center of this cross piece, and that's where the mowing apparatus had been hitched. What was once a luxurious motor car had been cobbled into a crude lawn tractor.

As Doug Anderson purchased the car. **This 1930 V-16 convertible coupe had ended up stripped down and shortened, pulling gang lawn mowers on a golf course. The rear axle unit comes right up to the tail of the transmission and the frame has been drastically cut to accomplish this. Elegant engine-turned panels still flank the instrument cluster (courtesy Alan Merkel).**

Doug Anderson was able to secure a replacement frame from his friend Alan Merkel, who had purchased a distressed Series 4225 town car. The body of that other car had also been removed from the cowl rearward, but the chassis and frame remained intact and unmodified. Alan's town car had been most recently used as a truck in a Florida orange grove. Mr. Anderson removed the frame from Alan's car and incorporated it into his car. Then he had the missing parts of the convertible coupe body constructed for it by craftsmen in California.

Mr. Anderson became ill and passed away before his project could be completed. The car was sold to an enthusiast in Spain in 2004. That gentleman described his acquisition as a stalled project that he purchased out of an estate. In 2006, he treated the Cadillac to an extensive restoration. Today, the car wears silver for the body and chassis, with orange moldings, fenders, hood side panels, and wheels. The vent doors and wheel spokes are chrome plated, and the convertible top is gray cloth. The determination, effort, and expense involved in bringing this car back from its sorry fate are truly impressive. That it exists today, and was not parted out or junked, is truly remarkable.

***As restored in Spain.* The color scheme is certainly attention-getting. The car has 18-inch wheels (instead of the stock 19-inch wheels), and the handle for the golf bag compartment door is missing. The convertible coupe has been returned to the U.S., and the new owner has entrusted it to V-16 expert Sonny Elliott for sorting out (courtesy Yann Saunders).**

In 2014, the car was consigned to Significant Cars, Inc. and offered for sale on their website. It was also listed on eBay and other sale venues. Subsequently, collector and restorer Bruce Carey of Macedon, New York, purchased the convertible coupe and nicknamed it "Mean Tangerine." In 2017, he turned it over to renowned V-16 experts Sonny Elliott and Jeff Pearson to perfect the restoration and bring everything back to correct specifications.

18

Company Car

SOME OF THE EARLIEST CADILLAC V-16s were acquired and used by General Motors executives. Who could fault their judgment and taste in wanting to avail themselves of the very best that the company had to offer? And if the prerogatives of their position permitted it, why not? After all, the social strata they moved in were populated by just the sort of people the Cadillac Division wished to reach.

Lawrence P. Fisher (1888–1961) was essentially the father of the Cadillac V-16 program, having put into motion in the mid–1920s the secret project to catapult Cadillac into the top tier of luxury auto makers by designing, building and marketing a "Supercar" that would rival the elegant best of the established high-end marques (like Rolls-Royce, Hispano-Suiza, and the "three Ps"). He was one of six brothers who sold their family coachbuilding business (Fisher Body Corporation) to General Motors, and who became pivotal figures in GM's development and history. As Cadillac president from 1925 to 1934, Lawrence Fisher ably saw the V-16 project to fruition, and in spite of the tremendous headwinds of the Great Depression, Cadillac V-16s established the division at the top of the list of American fine car makers.

Early in 1930, Lawrence Fisher is reported to have acquired a Series 4330-S five-passenger sedan, engine number 700096, painted black with ivory pinstriping. Surviving Cadillac records show that the car was shipped new to Washington, D.C., on St. Valentine's Day. The upholstery was a medium tan broadcloth, and the driver's door bore the owner's initials in a diamond-shaped frame. For a modest charge, Cadillac would apply a monogram to the outside of the driver's door (for owner–driven cars), or the passenger compartment doors (for chauffeur-driven models). The 4330-S series was a regular sedan without a window between the driver's compartment and the rear passenger compartment, and it was not equipped with an intercom. So Mr. Fisher likely drove this particular 1930 V-16 sedan himself.

According to former owner Bud Tinney, Lawrence Fisher took delivery and used the car in Florida, where he had a cattle business. After some time, the car came into the possession of legendary collector and restorer Wayne Merriman of Shawnee, Kansas, who subsequently sold it to restorer Dick Terhune. Mr. Terhune later sold it to another noted restorer and enthusiast William Meffert of Charlottesville, Virginia. Mr. Meffert in turn sold the Cadillac to Hardwick, Massachusetts, classic car collector Charles LeMaitre. Sometime in the early 1970s, Buffalo, New York Cadillac dealership owner and collector Bud Tinney drove to Massachusetts with his restorer Bill Bettendorf. He paid Mr. LeMaitre $15,000 and, together with Mr. Bettendorf, drove the V-16 sedan back to Buffalo.

In 1978, Mr. Tinney sold the car, together with a V-16 roadster, to Dave Gano and his father, both of Salem, Ohio. Dave Gano remembers coming to the Tinney Cadillac

***Restoration almost complete.* The face of this 1930 Cadillac V-16 five-passenger sedan is a symphony of circles. From this viewpoint all that's missing is the glass sunshade that overhangs the top of the windshield. Dave Gano carried out a meticulous restoration of a solid original car in the late 1980s/early 1990s (courtesy Dave Gano).**

dealership in Buffalo. It had been the original Pierce-Arrow factory showroom, and the furniture still bore Pierce-Arrow emblems. The Ganos acquired a very original car, with most of the striping still evident, as well as Mr. Fisher's monogram. They repainted the car black, as the original (black) finish was crazed and had begun chipping off in places, and they overhauled the top end of the engine. Most of the chrome was in pretty good condition, but they had a new interior installed for the car by Sonny Crum of Chambersburg, Pennsylvania, using heavy broadcloth that very closely matched the original color.

In 1982 or '83, another Ohio resident, Frank Yonak, traded a new motorhome to the elder Mr. Gano in exchange for the V-16 sedan. Mr. Yonak brought the car to Hershey for the 1995 AACA Eastern Division Fall Meet and offered it for sale. In 1996, he sold it to John Asterino of Fairmont, West Virginia, and in June 2002, Charles LeMaitre again bought the car, along with a Duesenberg, from Mr. Asterino. Mr. LeMaitre sold the Cadillac to fellow Bay-Stater John Walsh.

In the November–December 2014 issue of the Cadillac-LaSalle Club's magazine *The Self-Starter*, Mr. Walsh placed an ad for the car, and shortly thereafter, Lawrence Fisher's V-16 sedan returned to Ohio, now under the care of Joe Crea.

19

Golf Cart

In the early part of the twentieth century, the game of golf became immensely popular in the United States. Buoyed by the formation of the United States Golf Association in 1894 and the Professional Golfers' Association in 1916, and supported by the proliferation of challenging courses across the country, by the time the "Roaring Twenties" began, the sport was all the rage.

One of the most beloved and accursed courses in the U.S. is the Oakmont Country Club, near Pittsburgh, that was designed and built in 1903 by steel and industry magnate Henry Clay Fownes. A frequent site of the U.S. Open tournament, it has earned the respect of players at all levels of the game. It doesn't give many opportunities to recover from a flubbed shot. H.C. Fownes's son William Clark Fownes, Jr. (who was named after an uncle and was generally known as "W.C.") is quoted as having said, "A shot poorly played should be a shot irrevocably lost."

H.C. Fownes ran the Oakmont Country Club with a firm hand until his death in 1935, at which point his son took over and continued holding the course and the club to the vision and tradition his father established. A talented golfer himself (he had won a number of amateur championships in the 1910s, and he was the playing captain of the first U.S. Walker Cup team in 1922), W.C. finally resigned and left the club in 1948 when he could no longer resist the need to add social activities and a swimming pool in order to retain membership.

On May 3, 1930, a Cadillac V-16 roadster was shipped from the factory to the Royston Cadillac Company in Pittsburgh. The shipping order bore the instruction "TAG W.C. FOWNES," a rare indication in surviving Cadillac records of the identity of the car's first purchaser. As a rule, it is not possible to discern the original owner of a Cadillac car from the shipping order or "build sheet." As far as Cadillac was concerned, the car was being purchased by (and shipped to) the dealer, factory branch, or distributor identified at the top of the build sheet. The actual sale of the car to an owner was between the dealer and his customer. Nevertheless, there are a few instances (typically where a special order is involved) in which a notation appears on the build sheet that gives away the name of the purchaser. This was such an instance, and indeed, the car had some interesting special features. This roadster, bearing engine number 701437, was painted black—body, fenders, chassis and wheels. The body stripe, the pinstriping that followed the moldings and character lines on all respectable motor cars of the time, was specified as a "hairline to match top" fabric. The rear axle ratio was the fast 3.47 to 1 gearing that was only offered for the first part of the 1930 model year, and then only in the lighter-weight open cars.

The Series 4302 V-16 roadsters were two-passenger vehicles with a rumble seat in back that could accommodate two additional passengers in pleasant weather. On the right-hand side of the body there was a square door that opened to the footwell of the rumble seat area, a feature popularly known as a "golf bag door." Mr. Fownes's car was ordered with two such doors, one on either side of the car. And the rear deck lid was specified to be hinged at the front to open as a deck lid, and not as a rumble seat. Just to complete the modification, the step plates on the right rear fender and the bumper that normally permitted a rumble seat passenger to climb in were ordered omitted.

So this would have been a no-nonsense roadster, a plain black car, a powerful and fast conveyance (the low axle ratio would permit easy cruising at today's highway speeds), with room to haul several golf bags and a good deal of luggage.

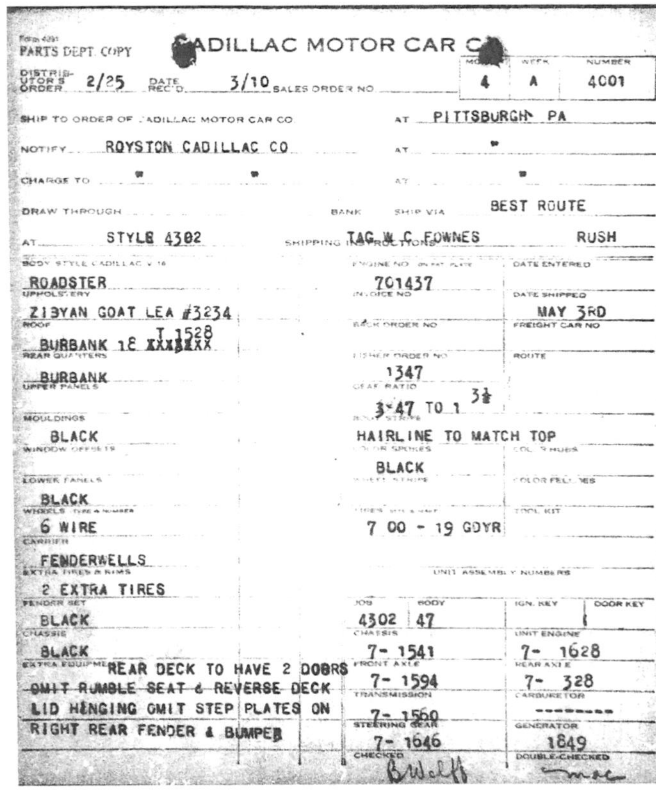

PARTS DEPT. COPY — CADILLAC MOTOR CAR CO.

Distributor's Order 2/25 — Date Rec'd 3/10 — Sales Order No. — 4 A 4001

Ship to order of Cadillac Motor Car Co. at PITTSBURGH PA

Notify ROYSTON CADILLAC CO

Draw through — Ship via BEST ROUTE

At STYLE 4302 — Shipping Instructions TAG W C FOWNES — RUSH

Body Style Cadillac V-16: ROADSTER — Engine No.: 701437

Upholstery: ZIBYAN GOAT LEA #3234 — Date Shipped: MAY 3RD

Roof: BURBANK 18 XXXXXXX T 1528

Rear Quarters: BURBANK — 1347

Gear Ratio: 3.47 TO 1 3½

Mouldings: BLACK — Stripe: HAIRLINE TO MATCH TOP

Color Spokes: BLACK

Lower Panels: BLACK

Wheels: 6 WIRE — Tires: 7 00 - 19 GDYR

Carrier: FENDERWELLS

Extra Tires & Rims: 2 EXTRA TIRES

Fender Set: BLACK — Job: 4302 — Body: 47

Chassis: BLACK — Chassis: 7- 1541 — Unit Engine: 7- 1628

Extra Equipment: REAR DECK TO HAVE 2 DOORS OMIT RUMBLE SEAT & REVERSE DECK LID HINGING OMIT STEP PLATES ON RIGHT REAR FENDER & BUMPER

Front Axle: 7- 1594 — Rear Axle: 7- 328

Transmission: 7- 1560 — Carburetor: --------

Steering Gear: 7- 1646 — Generator: 1849

Checked: B Wolff — Double-Checked: [illegible]

The tale told by the build sheet. **The shipping order for this roadster says "TAG W.C. FOWNES." The upholstery was to be Libyan goat leather, and the rear deck was to have a front-hinged lid, two side "golf bag" doors, and no rumble seat.**

It's not known what became of W.C. Fownes's V-16 roadster, or even how long he owned it, or what he did with it. But the telltale notations on the build sheet give an interesting idea of the type of person who ordered a V-16 Cadillac and how such a car could be personalized to accommodate the purchaser's needs and desires.

20

Hawkeye's X's

By any definition, John W. "Hawkeye" Hawkinson was an original. He was born in Hartford, Connecticut, September 13, 1932. Grandson of Amos Whitney (a co-founder of Pratt & Whitney, leading manufacturer of military and civilian aircraft, marine and industrial engines), he attended private boarding school, the University of Vermont, and Paul Smith's College. The nickname attached when a camp counselor admired his marksmanship. He largely ignored his family's fortune in favor of a simple life, alone in rustic nature. From his pre-teen years he was operating, working on, and collecting interesting old automobiles, and after college he bought a parcel of land in upstate New York near Saranac Lake, on which to build a restoration facility and structures to house the cars he was acquiring. He believed in cars that could go, and not necessarily "show." When he passed away July 15, 2016, he left forty-three vehicles and instructions that they be sold and the proceeds divided between the Adirondack Chapter of the Nature Conservancy and the New-York Historical Society.

1930 Cadillac V-16 speedster. **Originally a "Madame X" Series 4175 imperial sedan, this car (engine number 702200) had been converted into a speedster. Bodywork other than the cowl, top hood panels and radiator shell has been removed and a seat and steering wheel are the only accommodations for the driver. This is how the car appeared in 1957 (courtesy Alan Merkel).**

Hawkeye liked to drive his cars configured like the "speedsters" of the 1920s and early 1930s, with most of the body removed, and the driver and a passenger riding out in the open. Two cars that got this treatment were 1930 Cadillac V-16s. Each of them was an example of the Series 4175 "Madame X" seven passenger imperial sedan, a limousine that sported special design features including unusually slender windshield and door pillars, thin bright-metal reveals around the side windows, a windshield raked more steeply than other V-16 cars, a plain hood, and simpler interior trimming. Madame X cars averaged about $1,000 more in price than their regular counterparts.

The car with engine number 702200 had been shipped new from the Cadillac factory to New Haven, Connecticut, on June 28, 1930. Hawkeye had said that the car had been owned and used by the U.S. Navy, and that he had acquired it from the Sherman Construction Company. A photo he took in 1957 showed a huge vintage open-wheel race car, all wheels and engine. The body had been removed except for the cowl, the running boards, the top panels of the hood, the radiator shell and the enormous V-16 headlights. A leather-upholstered seat rests on a wood platform spanning the exposed frame rails, and the absence of a windshield means that the driver would need to wear goggles. By the time Alan Merkel saw the car in 1991, the cowl, hood and radiator had been removed and the engine and chassis had spent years in open storage, protected by corrugated metal and tarps held down by lumber and stones.

Hawkeye asked Alan if he could get a body for the car. Alan had a five-passenger sedan body (Series 4330-S, body number 24) that another enthusiast had sold him when the other fellow replaced his car's body with a town sedan body (Series 4361-S) that was

***As seen in 1991.* The bare chassis and engine are all that is left of the car bearing engine number 702200, and that has been covered by wood beams, corrugated metal, and tarps (courtesy Alan Merkel).**

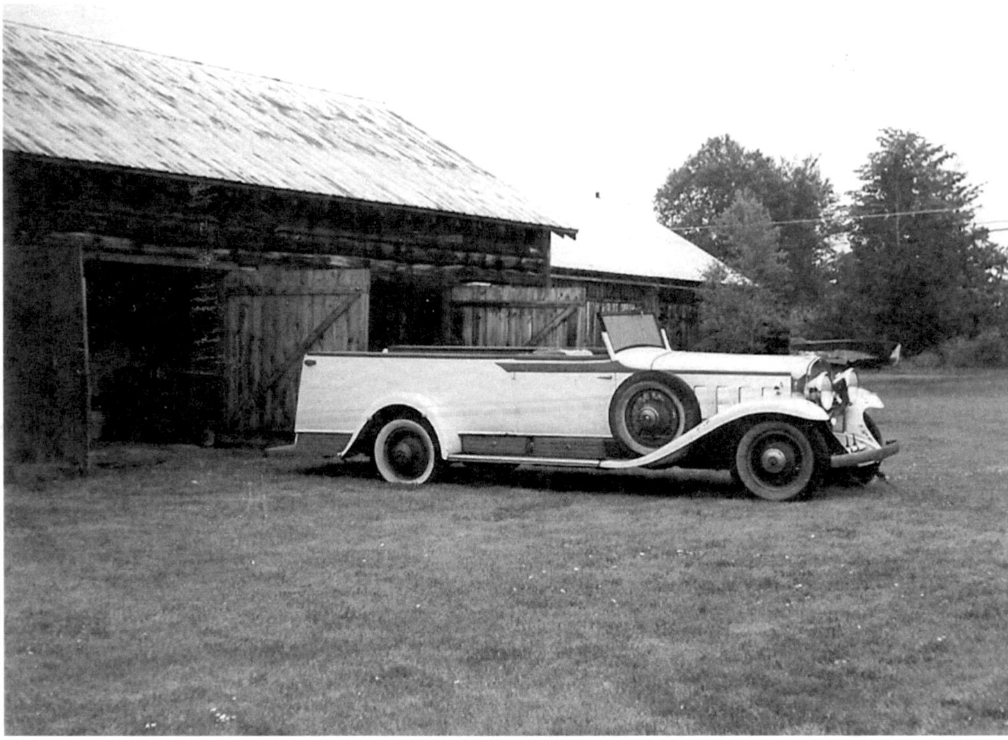

A custom-built fire hose wagon. **Another Madame X limousine, engine number 702390, was re-bodied by the Penn Yan Boat Company for use by an upstate New York fire brigade. The late John Hawkinson converted this vehicle into another speedster (courtesy Alan Merkel).**

in better condition and that he liked better. Alan sold Hawkeye the sedan body and traded a matching hood (with the sculpted character lines or "LeBaron sweep") for the plain hood from Hawkeye's car.

Mr. Hawkinson put the cowl from the 4330-S sedan body onto his chassis and once again had a V-16 speedster. (The rest of the sedan body, unfortunately, was left outside and neglected.)

Hawkeye's other Madame X car was the one that bore engine number 702390, and it had been shipped new to Syracuse, New York, on July 18, 1930. He bought it in 1955 from a fellow named Charles Sawyer in Cincinnatus, New York. The roof of this car and the body aft of the front doors had been removed and replaced with fabricated bodywork to convert it into a hose truck for a fire brigade. The custom work had been done by the now-defunct Penn Yan Boat Company (then located in the Finger Lakes area of upstate New York) and by the time Hawkeye acquired the vehicle, it was being used as a wrecker. He separated the added structure from the rest of the car and set it aside. At the time John Hawkinson passed away, the car was intact from the cowl forward, with the windshield supported by foreshortened "A" pillars, and nothing but a two-person seat on the chassis behind the rear edge of the cowl.

In the latter half of 2016, classic car collector and restorer Allen Strong of Urbana, Illinois, acquired both of the Hawkinson V-16 Cadillacs. He decided to sell engine number 702200 and its chassis with the transplanted cowl. At this writing, a dealer in Wisconsin is offering it for sale. Engine number 702390 and its chassis being more complete, Mr.

As it sits today. **With another cowl and hood mounted, 702200 once again looks like a vehicle. The engine is missing much, including manifolds and carburetors. A good deal of work would be needed to make it drivable (courtesy Allen Strong).**

Strong decided to keep it and work on it. Because there was so little left of the car's original Madame X limousine bodywork, restoring it to its original configuration was not a practical option. Mr. Strong chose to construct a roadster body for the car and otherwise to restore it to original Cadillac standards. Knowing Allen Strong's standards, the result will be beautiful.

21

Survivor of the War in the Pacific

On March 27, 1930, a Series 4361-S V-16 town sedan with engine number 700659 left the factory for the Greenlease Moore dealership in Oklahoma City. The car was arrayed in four different shades of blue. Boatswain Blue covered the door panels, the lower rear body, the cowl and the hood. The body from the wide belt molding up, the fenders, and the chassis were all Classic Blue, with Canterbury Blue for the pinstriping. Finally, the wheels were painted Antibes Blue. Sadly, we don't have paint chips to show exactly what those different hues were and how they worked together. But we know that someone put some thought into how this car would impress the viewer.

The 4361-S town sedan was what was commonly called a "close coupled" sedan, that is, one without extra floorspace in the rear passenger compartment for auxiliary seats. The seating arrangement is what we're most often accustomed to in modern sedans, where the back seat passengers' knees are close to the front seatbacks. Because the car used the same chassis as the longer sedans, there was room behind a town sedan body for a built-in trunk between the rear of the body structure and the folding luggage rack. If the owner added an accessory trunk, a town sedan could carry quite enough clothing changes and personal items for a long trip.

Sometime during the 1930s, this particular town sedan made its way to Japan, reportedly under the ownership of a wealthy industrialist. Somehow and for some reason, the Fleetwood body was replaced with a 1937 Packard 120 sedan body. The Packard body was grafted onto the Cadillac chassis and cowl with some evident skill, and the Cadillac fenders were extended and skirted in a nod to styling trends subsequent to 1930. But the upright radiator and rectilinear hood are visually somewhat jarring in the midst of the streamlined curves that make up the rest of the ensemble. This long automobile must have been a very imposing sight in a land where most cars were imported American and European models, most domestic autos were quite small, and car owners were generally limited to the nobility and corporate powerbrokers.

With the onset of military activity, the car was secreted in a cave to avoid its confiscation by the Imperial armed forces for wartime use. The owner is reported to have died in 1941, though whether he was killed in military service is not known. His grandson was born in 1947, and it was he who would eventually sell the car to New Zealander Duncan Fox.

In the early 2000s, Duncan Fox had been dealing with a vendor in Japan for rare Chevrolet parts he needed for the restoration of McLaren race cars from the last century. The vendor had their own racing enterprise and sold parts as a side business. About 2006,

Unusual modernization. **Sometime before the Second World War, the 1930 Fleetwood town sedan body was removed and replaced with the body from a 1937 Packard 120 sedan. The Cadillac fenders were extended and skirted, and in that altered configuration, the car waited out the hostilities hidden in a cave (courtesy Duncan Fox).**

Mr. Fox became aware that in the background in the vendor's storage facility there was a large old black sedan. Gradually he found out that it was a Cadillac V-16 from the early 1930s, and his interest was piqued. He was able to elicit only sketchy information—the deceased grandfather of the business's owner had hidden the car during the Pacific War and it wasn't in running condition. Mr. Fox remained interested, but for various reasons he was not able to initiate a purchase until late 2014.

As Duncan Fox began to work towards buying the Cadillac V-16, his inability to speak Japanese was compounded by the weak English of the Japanese owner. When he received more photographs, it became clear that the car bore a later (and non–Cadillac) body, and that the long storage (some of it outdoors) in a maritime environment had degraded surfaces and finishes to a noticeable extent. Mr. Fox experienced a range of different emotions—disappointment at the toll exacted by the elements over the years; confusion as to what one could do with this creature that was neither Packard nor Cadillac; but also a fascination with a truly unique motor car that had definite possibilities in spite of its condition.

The clearer picture he now had of the car's true state helped bring the asking price down to a more realistic level, and it freed Mr. Fox to consider replacing the hybrid bodywork with a new creation to his personal tastes. After all, if the original body is long gone, and the existing (deteriorated) body is from a lesser model of a different make, why

***Side view of the Cadillac-Packard hybrid.* Stock Cadillac features are the radiator shell and hood, part of the cowl, the spare tire bracket and the wire wheels. Chalk lines on the side of the car are Mr. Fox's preliminary sketching out of his speedster design (courtesy Duncan Fox).**

shouldn't the new owner be able to craft a new body, particularly if the design was consistent with what Fleetwood was offering when the car was new?

Duncan Fox began conferring with renowned automotive historian and fellow Kiwi Maurice Hendry as he worked up sketches of what the finished car might look like. The two men favored a boat-tailed speedster design—one of the sportiest and flashiest styles in the early 1930s—a two-seat configuration with a body faired from the radiator shell past the passenger compartment and gracefully tapered to a point or a sharp prow at the back. Fenders were typically separate, either as cycle-type or as teardrop-shaped pods or pontoons. Such designs were employed on Packard, Auburn and Duesenberg chassis, to name a few.

Meanwhile, the depth and intricacy of the administrative and logistical process for exporting an old car from Japan quickly became mind boggling. Time and patience were consumed but he finally obtained ownership of the car. Then, there was the challenge of getting the old beast shipped overseas to New Zealand and cleared for entry into the country, another set of hurdles.

When at long last the car arrived and he was able to take possession of it, the car was much as Mr. Fox had grown to expect. Some things like the radiator ornament had gone missing. But overall he was happy with his purchase and he began hands-on planning of the process for realizing his dream.

Unfortunately, a number of things have caused delays in Duncan Fox's project.

***Intact but weathered engine.* The 452 cubic-inch V-16 powerplant is largely correct and complete. The distributor cap is from 1932 or later, and the aftermarket coils are strapped to the radiator support rods, as they won't fit into the proper sockets in the radiator top tank. And there's an extra vacuum takeoff from the line attached to the intake manifold. Otherwise, everything is where it should be (courtesy Duncan Fox).**

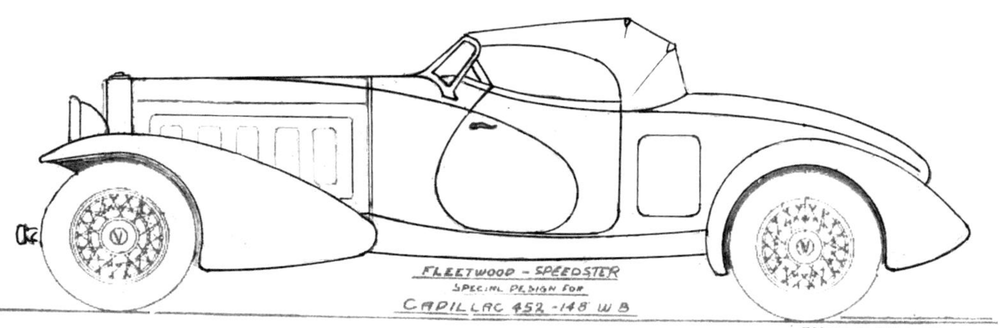

***Design for a Fleetwood Speedster.* Duncan Fox has revised a Fleetwood design drawing to reflect a streamlined two-place open car. He hopes to replace his car's grafted-on Packard body with a period-credible sporting design that he can enjoy (courtesy Duncan Fox).**

"McLarens keep getting in the way," he told the author, referring to his race car restoration business. But he's a determined man and there's no doubt he will give his V-16 a new life.

22

Jazz-Age Jalopy

Frank Sebastian was a restaurateur and impresario who owned and operated a number of establishments in southern California during the 1920s and '30s. In 1926, he opened "Frank Sebastian's Cotton Club" at the corner of National and Washington Boulevards in Culver City. The place was not related to the famous Cotton Club in Harlem but featured similar entertainment, presenting exclusively African American orchestras. Frank Sebastian's Cotton Club had formerly been known as the Green Mill, built in 1923. It was already an important entertainment venue when Mr. Sebastian took it over, and he would make it one of the Los Angeles area's major Prohibition-era nightspots. Later it would become "Casa Mañana," a major dance spot, then "Meadowbrook Gardens" and finally "Zucca's Opera House" before it burned to the ground in 1950.

Jazz greats like Duke Ellington and Cab Calloway played there. And there's a photograph from July 1930 on the Internet, posed outside of the front entrance to the club, with a large group of tuxedo-clad men lined up behind a 1930 Cadillac V-16 Series 4380 all-weather phaeton. Three gentlemen are standing in front of the car. On the left is soon-to-be world-renowned jazz trumpeter and singer Louis Armstrong. In the middle is Frank Sebastian holding a document of some sort (a contract? a program?). And on the right is Les Hite, the bandleader who conducted the orchestra for Louis Armstrong's gigs at the club over the period from July 1930 into March 1932. A prominent sign proclaims "HERE NOW—Frank Sebastian presents LOUIS ARMSTRONG King of the Trumpet and the New Cotton Club Orchestra." The fancy-dressed men behind the Cadillac are the members of the orchestra.

The car in the photograph is shiny and new, painted in a very light color (the photo is black-and-white, so we can't tell the exact hue). And it's been fitted with a spotlight mounted on a stanchion bolted to the left-hand running board. That's an accessory that was popular in the late 1920s, but was very rarely seen on cars in the 1930s. White sidewall tires, a single Pilot Ray driving light, and an unusual radiator ornament make this a car to be seen in. The big Cadillac has a shiny cover on the fender-mounted spare tire announcing "Frank Sebastian's New Cotton Club" so it's pretty safe to assume that it belonged to Mr. Sebastian, and he used it to promote his business.

Louis Armstrong went on to an illustrious career. The car he posed next to slipped into used car depreciation, and the next we know of it, Don Jackson, a Chevrolet dealer in Lindsay, California, picked it up in 1948 or '49. Soon after that, he sold the V-16 convertible sedan to a fellow in Porterville, California, for $175. That fellow did some work on the car (which reportedly included converting the hydraulic valve-silencing mechanism to mechanical), before he got tired of it. In 1950, he offered to sell the car to Don Jones, also of Porterville, for $250. Mr. Jones was a newlywed, and he had just purchased his father's

***Backdrop for a special occasion.* This 1930 V-16 all-weather phaeton graces a publicity still for an appearance by immortal jazz trumpeter Louis Armstrong at Frank Sebastian's New Cotton Club in July of 1930 when he was on the verge of stardom. By the driver's door (l. to r.) stand Louis Armstrong, Frank Sebastian, and orchestra leader Les Hite. The members of the New Cotton Club Orchestra are on the other side of the Cadillac. The spare tire cover reads "Frank Sebastian's New Cotton Club" (courtesy Albert Vollmer).**

cold storage and meatlocker business. Needless to say he did not have cash to spend. He declined the offer, but the fellow kept coming back and trying to convince him to buy the car. Finally, Mr. Jones offered him $250 worth of frozen meat, and a deal was struck.

Mr. Jones told the author a few years ago that the purchase of this Cadillac was as close as he ever came to being divorced by his wife. She thought it was a terrible idea. But by the time she passed away in 1990, she had fallen in love with the car. The car Mr. Jones bought still wore its original paint, with Alvarado Ivory for the body and Desert Sand for the fenders, chassis, and body moldings. He looked at a color chart and selected an Oldsmobile Holiday Red color for the body, and had the fenders and chassis painted a dark maroon.

The build sheet for Mr. Jones's car (engine number 700817 and body number 55) shows that the car was shipped new in February of 1930 to the Inglis Uppercu Cadillac dealership in New York City. The notation "TAG J.W. NOYES" likely indicates the original owner, or the person who picked up the car for the purchaser. As noted previously, the car was painted Alvarado Ivory with Desert Sand moldings, fenders and chassis. Pin striping was in the same colors, opposite of where the striping ran. The only extra equipment specified was a spotlight on a stanchion, to be mounted on the driver's side running board.

Don Jones still owned the V-16 all-weather phaeton when he passed away in 2012.

He drove it and used it the way it was meant to be enjoyed. In 1987, he and the car participated in the festivities celebrating the 50th anniversary of the opening of the San Francisco Bay Bridge. His car is probably the only Cadillac V-16 car ever fitted with a wolf whistle on the intake manifold. It's easy to imagine the fun of driving an elegant and imposing carriage past impressed bystanders, and then surprising them with a most incongruous sound effect.

In 2017, avid collector Bruce Carey acquired the 1930 Cadillac V-16 all-weather phaeton, engine number 700817, and added it to his stable (already including two other 1930 V-16s—a Series 4376 stationary coupe, and a Series 4335 convertible coupe).

23

Mr. Uppercu's Personal Roadster

The Series 4302 Cadillac V-16 roadster with engine number 700802 and body number 20 was shipped from Detroit to New York on April 2, 1930. Upon arrival it is reported to have been placed in a Spring auto show in the New York area. After that it became the personal car of Mr. Inglis M. Uppercu, the namesake of a network of Cadillac dealerships in the New York City and northern New Jersey area. Born in Evanston, Illinois, in 1877, Mr. Uppercu was an American success story. His family moved to New York City when he was 11 years old. After studying law at Columbia University, he worked for a couple of automobile manufacturers before starting his own auto sales company, and then branching out into aircraft manufacturing and even regional air line operations. In 1908 he bought out the sole New York City Cadillac dealer. In 1931, he would sell his dealership group to the Cadillac Division of General Motors and retire from the automobile business a wealthy man, but he would continue to be active in other pursuits until he retired fully in 1938.

Dealer tag. **Inglis M. Uppercu operated a network of Cadillac dealerships in the New York/New Jersey area in the late 1920s and early 1930s. His organization sold many of the 1930–1931 V-16 Cadillacs. This 1930 roadster was sold at the store in downtown Newark, New Jersey (courtesy RM Sotheby's).**

The life of Mr. Uppercu's roadster through its first decade is concealed from us by the fog of time, but by the mid–1940s, it had found its way across the country to a California salvage yard, largely complete but quite dilapidated. Later, an old car collector purchased the car, and it appeared in the 1957 movie *The Tarnished Angels* (starring Robert Stack, Dorothy Malone and Rock Hudson). Then in 1961, Decatur, Illinois, Cadillac dealer Jack Tallman bought the car, sight

***The sight that greeted Jack Tallman.* The Decatur, Illinois, Cadillac dealer bought his roadster, sight unseen, and set about returning it to its former glory. Parts were harder to come by in the early 1960s, but substantially less expensive than today, once you located them. Although missing various items (e.g., windshield, convertible top, headlights, horns and spare tire), the car is pretty straight and appears sound.**

unseen.[23] He had told his father that he had always wanted a V-16 Cadillac roadster, and when the transport truck arrived, he had one. He was not deterred by its condition, and embarked upon a thorough restoration.

In an April 1964 article by Agnes Uhlir, editor of the Cadillac-LaSalle Club's newsletter *The Self-Starter*, she describes the efforts Jack Tallman expended to bring his car to a condition "as near as possible like a brand new 1930 Cadillac V-16 Roadster."[24] He completely disassembled the car and rebuilt each of its components. Some parts served as patterns to fabricate new replacements. Others had to be hunted down from locations around the U.S. He brought silver coins to his dentist for casting, by the lost wax process, a reproduction of the small V-16 emblem that attaches to the gas tank cover.

In the early 1960s when Mr. Tallman was working on his roadster, he was able to consult the original color chips and sales literature at the Cadillac factory in his quest to duplicate the original colors for the exterior—red for the body, and black for the fenders, body molding, and rear deck. He covered the seats in black top-grain cowhide, and used black fabric for the convertible top, again following the original specifications. According to the article, Mr. Tallman described the restored car as "smooth as a turbine, and a

23. Jack Tallman was the third-generation owner of his family's Cadillac dealership.

24. Uhlir, Agnes, "1930 Cadillac V-16 'Fleetdowns' Roadster by Fleetwood,' *The Self-Starter*, Cadillac-LaSalle Club, Inc., Detroit, MI, Vol. VI, No. 6, April 1964, 111–14. The article is accompanied by numerous photographs and it quotes Mr. Tallman's description of the restoration process.

Down to the frame. The bare chassis rests, upside down, on the floor of Mr. Tallman's dealership service department.

Restoration progressing. The painted body and fenders are in place, and the engine has been installed and hooked up. The doors have yet to be hung, the windshield remains to be placed, and the open floor affords a view of the bell housing at the rear of the engine.

Looking good as new. Mr. Tallman's Series 4302 roadster is resplendent, totally transformed from the sad condition in which he received it.

Jack and Marilyn Tallman with their roadster. **Third-generation Cadillac dealer Jack Tallman poses with his wife and the 1930 V-16 roadster he restored. Mr. Tallman owned and enjoyed the car for fifty years (courtesy Brent Merrill).**

real joy and pleasure to drive." By 1964, the Cadillac had been awarded several prestigious awards by the Antique Automobile Club of America, including a National First.

Mr. Tallman and his wife used and enjoyed the roadster over the years, and accumulated 60,000 miles, while keeping the car in like-new condition. They would keep the car until 2011, four years after he retired, when it was offered at the Amelia Island sale held by RM Auctions. Sold there for $506,000, it is now in the care of Mr. Brent Merrill of Ontario, Canada. Sadly, Jack Tallman passed away several months after the auction.

Opposite: Spotless engine compartment. **Owen Nacker designed this engine to be seen and admired. Chrome-plated vacuum tanks on the firewall flank twin enameled valve covers that rise above porcelain and enamel manifolding. The shiny cylinder between the cylinder banks is the oil filter (vital to keep grit from fouling the hydraulic valve silencers).**

24

A Performance Coupe

In 1930 and 1931, Cadillac built 98 of the Series 4381 five-passenger coupes on the V-16 chassis, of which only a very meager handful have survived. The Series 4381 was an unusual-looking car—it stands out among the more than thirty other V-16 body styles offered by Cadillac, looking more like a family car than an exclusive luxury automobile. Two relatively wide doors, hinged at the back, opened onto a passenger compartment that included two separate front seats (driver's and passenger's) and a bench seat for three in back. The front passenger seat back folded forward onto the cushion, and then the entire seat tipped forward to provide easy access to the back seat area. A separate storage compartment was built into the rear of the body, with access by way of a hinged, external lid. A Series 4381 car has relatively large side windows, for a remarkably airy and open feel. Also, the windows have slender chrome-plated reveal moldings and the windshield and door pillars are narrow like those on the "Madame X" cars, all adding to an impression of lightness for this large motor car.

In modern automobile design, most cars that are described by their makers as coupes are constructed with the same configuration as the Series 4381 Cadillac—two doors, two rows of seats (front and back), and an enclosed trunk compartment behind the passenger area.[25] In the early 1930s, the term "coupe" by itself typically described an enclosed car with two doors with room inside for two people. It might have a rumble seat behind the enclosed passenger compartment to provide exposed accommodations for two more riders, or it might have only a luggage compartment beneath the deck lid. Today a car that carries only two people is either a sports car or another specialty design (like the first-generation Honda Insight, sold from 1999 through 2006).

Surviving records indicate that one Series 4381 coupe, bearing engine number 702106 and body number 2, was shipped to Cadillac's Detroit Branch office on June 20, 1930. Less than a month later (July 15) it was diverted to Cleveland, and more than a year after that, it was again diverted, this time to Canton, Ohio. The build sheet for the car shows a color scheme of black fenders, wheels, roof, upper rear quarters and body moldings, with the doors and the lower body panels painted "State Blue," and with "Cream Color Lt." for the pinstriping. In the block on the form for the color of the window reveals or "offsets" is typed "Chromium Plated," and the upholstery code (Wiese 2973) indicates a blue-gray wool broadcloth manufactured by William Wiese & Company. Although the build sheet indicates that the car was equipped with the "fast" rear axle gear ratio (4.07 to

25. It is true, however, that recently certain manufacturers (e.g., BMW and Mercedes) have used the term "coupe" to describe a sedan with a low roofline and other features that produce what the manufacturer sees as a "coupe-like" appearance.

1), from at least the early 1950s its rear axle gearing has been the standard 4.39 to 1 ratio. The only items of optional equipment indicated are two fender-mounted spare tires, wire wheels in place of the standard wood wheels, and some sales and service literature. The notations "Changing tires" and "Repainting wheels" appear under the extra equipment heading, likely indicating that a charge was made for those two tasks at some point before the car found its eventual purchaser.

According to the oral history that has followed this car, it was sold new to the manager of the Loew's State Theater in Cleveland. The original purchaser reportedly drove the car regularly until the death of his wife. When he remarried, his new bride told him she did not want to be seen in the car, and it was relegated to storage for years in a barn (a leaky one, as it happens). Ultimately, a fellow in Warren, Ohio, was able to purchase the coupe for use as a parts car for a V-16 phaeton he owned. In the process of restoring the phaeton, he took the coupe apart and (among other things) replaced its 19" wire wheels with 18" wheels from a V-8 or V-12 Cadillac. Not very long after he bought it, he sold the car to Bob Scofield, a master mechanic at GM's Packard Electric plant in Warren.

Mr. Scofield decided that he wanted to "soup up" the coupe, and he pestered the Cadillac Division engineering department until they provided him copies of the engine blueprints. He determined that he could shave a full .125 inch (⅛") off of the surface of the cylinder heads where they mate with the cylinder blocks, without weakening the heads or interfering with the integrity of the water jacket and passages. That modification decreased the volume of the combustion chambers, significantly raising the compression ratio. In addition, Mr. Scofield designed, engineered, and had built a set of

***Five-passenger coupe as Norm Uhlir was driving it in 1958.* Norm had bought the car in 1953 or '54, missing exhaust system parts. He found and installed the missing parts, and did extensive restoration of the structural wood in the car. He owned and drove the car regularly until 1973 (courtesy Norm Uhlir).**

adapters to permit the installation of two of the Stromberg carburetors used on early 1940s Buick Roadmasters (the two-barrel Model AAV-16). The result was a very responsive automobile.

Then Bob Scofield bought a new home in a development where he could not keep his Cadillac and remain in compliance with the residential covenants. So in 1953 or '54, he determined to sell the car to another GM engineer, a co-worker at the Packard Electric plant named Norm Uhlir. Mr. Scofield was very assertive in his campaign to have his friend buy the V-16 coupe. One evening he invited Norm over to see the car, which did not have the exhaust manifolds in place. While Mr. Uhlir was examining the engine, Mr. Scofield fired it up, and the earsplitting racket that ensued took Mr. Uhlir completely by surprise (and impressed him). When he finally consented to become the Cadillac's next caretaker, he traded a low-mileage 1941 Buick for it, and he had to tow his new acquisition home behind his 1941 Oldsmobile. He wasn't able to drive the V-16 coupe until he'd gotten the manifolds sorted out and had installed pipes and mufflers (for which he used two Chevrolet six-cylinder exhaust systems).

Sad condition of the coupe's structural wood. **Looking through the front door opening towards the driver's footwell, the wood post that normally stands behind the edge of the cowl (known as the "front door lock pillar") has been placed in the open to show the degree of deterioration of the wood before prior owner Norm Uhlir replaced it (courtesy Norm Uhlir).**

In 1957, Norm Uhlir received another promotion and was transferred to the General Motors Building in Detroit. By now, he was confident driving the big old car, and he set out on the trip from Warren, via the Ohio Turnpike. He made careful preparations for the journey, including taking the car to the local Cadillac dealer to have the brakes adjusted. Nevertheless, the trip had some interesting twists. For one thing, there were seven flat tires along the way—each time it was the left rear wheel. First he used the two fender-mounted spare tires, then the tires he'd fastened to the car's trunk rack, and then the extra tubes he had stashed in the luggage compartment. He stopped outside Toledo for one flat, and his wife (who had been following in a modern car) took the wounded tire, wheel and all, into the city to be fixed. By then it had become apparent that the Cadillac dealer back in Warren had adjusted the left rear brake too tight, and as the car drove along, the drag of the brake shoes against the drum heated that wheel enough to ruin the inner tube.

Not to be upstaged by the chassis, the engine played its own trick. For no apparent reason, one bank of eight cylinders ceased firing. That doesn't stop a Cadillac V-16 from running, or make it undriveable. But suddenly having half the power at highway speeds can be disconcerting and potentially dangerous. Norm couldn't figure out why the one bank had cut out, or what to do to convince it to resume running. But after limping along for a while the engine inexplicably returned to full power, and the difficulty disappeared. He could only speculate that there had been an intermittent break in one of the dual ignition circuits. Both car and driver finished the trip safely and in good shape.

With the Stromberg carburetors and the higher compression ratio Norm Uhlir was able to realize 12 miles per gallon, instead of the more typical 7 to 10 mpg for these powerful but thirsty beasts. Norm put many hours into restoring the car, and along the way he replaced the downdraft carburetors with the correct Cadillac-designed updraft units. He removed the body from the frame to work on the chassis, but before hoisting it up in the air, he had to replace a good deal of the structural wood framing, particularly in the cowl area and the roof. Over the years, water from the leaky roof of the barn in which it had

Downdraft carburetors for added performance. **Prior owner and GM master mechanic Bob Scofield designed and engineered the adaptors that permitted him to mount Stromberg AAV-16 carburetors in place of the original updraft units for this 1930 Series 4381 coupe. Small chrome air cleaners are temporary stand-ins while Norm Ingold completes the restoration process (courtesy Norm Ingold).**

been stored had invaded the car's body, and had largely rotted out the "A" pillars and the wooden cross brace behind the instrument panel.

Attention was paid to the mechanical systems as well, and that was more easily done with the body set aside. Among other tasks, the 18" wheels that had been installed on the car were replaced with correct 19" wire wheels sourced from some people in California, and Norm installed two electric fuel pumps in the back of the car where the fuel lines leave the tank.

Beginning in 1958, Norm Uhlir would spend years leading and serving the Cadillac-LaSalle Club. His five-passenger V-16 coupe became a familiar sight to CLC members. In the early 1970s, though, he was approached by Norm Ingold, a New Mexico resident, who was very interested in the venerable Cadillac. Eventually a deal was struck, and in 1973 Mr. Ingold became the next owner. He took delivery of a partially assembled vehicle, and he has done his share of work on it, including re-fitting the downdraft carburetors that Bob Scofield had so industriously installed. He relates that he was able to arrange a test of his car's wide-open-throttle performance, and that it reached 100 mph. He says that he intends to keep those Stromberg carburetors in place.

25

Criss Goad's Sedan Cabriolet

It seems that no matter how nice a restored Classic car seems, the new owner is always going to have to sort through some "issues" before the car and its caretaker get comfortable with each other. These are, after all, used cars. And some of the materials that were more than satisfactory eighty or even ninety years ago don't always age well (or resist the solvent properties of modern fuels). Moreover, unless a car is exercised regularly, it can forget that it's in running condition. It's probably just part of the fun (or the price) of enjoying fine automobiles from another era.

Tom Goad of Birmingham, Michigan, was a veteran member of the Classic Car Club of America, and had done great things for that organization (particularly for its Michigan Region). When he first encountered what would be his wife Criss's 1930 Cadillac V-16 Series 4355-S sedan cabriolet, it was on display at the CCCA's 1996 Annual Meeting in Colorado Springs, Colorado.[26] Tom and Criss Goad had travelled by train with several other couples to attend the meeting, and when they arrived at the historic Broadmoor Hotel, the display of Classic motor cars was truly impressive. One car in particular captivated Tom Goad, and he took several photographs. It was what Cadillac referred to in 1930 as a "sedan cabriolet," a four-door car with blind rear quarters (no quarter windows) and a padded fabric roof covering with decorative landau irons and a small rear window. Built without a divider window between the driver and passenger compartments, and upholstered in fine cloth throughout, this one would have been an owner-driven car when new. Clearly meant to provide formally elegant transportation for some lucky person at the tail end of the "jazz age," the Cadillac the Goads were looking at had been restored as a prominent part of the extensive collection of Zach Brinkerhoff, Jr. Particularly appealing to Mr. Goad was the two-tone paint scheme of a light green on the lower body panels, wheels, window offsets, and inner part of the hood side panels, and a darker green for the chassis, fenders, upper body, and the cove area outlined by the sweeping character line across the hood and down the cowl sides. Chrome-plated hood vent doors and stainless steel wheel spokes provided visual highlights.

This sedan cabriolet, with engine number 701413 and body number 59, was shipped from the factory to Philadelphia May 1, 1930. When new it had a much more subdued appearance. Originally, in Tom Goad's words "it was an all-black car," black paint, black

---

26. Tom Goad wrote a thorough account of their acquisition of, and experiences with, the 1930 V-16 sedan cabriolet for the Michigan Region CCCA magazine. See Goad, Tom, "1930 Cadillac, 16 Model 452 Cabriolet Sedan by Fleetwood," *Torque*, Michigan Region Classic Car Club of America, Ferndale, MI, No. 371, March-April 2004: pp. 5–11. This author has incorporated information from that article, as well as from personal conversations with Mr. Goad.

Resplendent on display. **At the 2016 Classic Car Club of America Annual Meeting the Series 4355 V-16 sedan cabriolet that Tom Goad purchased for his wife Criss cut a very dignified and majestic figure. The beige roof covering works nicely with the two-tone green paint scheme.**

sidewall tires and wheels, and black leather roof covering. The only bit of color was the bronze pinstriping. Early CCCA member and successful Philadelphia furrier Stanley Tarnopol had acquired the car still arrayed like that, and he had driven it and enjoyed it "as is." The car acquired its more ebullient coloration in the 1970s. In 1977, still owned by Mr. Tarnopol, it took a national first place and was awarded CCCA Senior Badge number 471. Subsequently, ownership would pass first to a collector in Maryland and then to Mr. Brinkerhoff.

As a board member of the CCCA, Mr. Goad was accustomed to attending "Hershey" each October. Among car enthusiasts "Hershey" is shorthand for the annual Eastern Division Fall meet of the Antique Automobile Club of America in Hershey, Pennsylvania. Hershey has for decades been something of a nationwide market fair for those who love and live pre–World War II cars. People show their cars, buy and sell them, and hunt for (and sell or swap) those pesky hard-to-find parts and accessories. In 2001, Criss went with Tom to Hershey because an auction of fine miniatures would be taking place a few miles away. While attending the AACA meet, the couple heard that a "no reserve" Imperial Palace/Blackhawk Collection auction was to be held on Friday in the Hershey Convention Center, and they went to investigate. Among the cars to be offered were a couple of Cadillac phaetons, a roadster, and the same V-16 sedan cabriolet Mr. Goad had so admired in Colorado five years earlier. The V-16 was in the auction because Mr. Brinkerhoff had traded fourteen Packards and Cadillacs to the Blackhawk Collection in exchange for a Duesenberg that he had once owned.

Although they hadn't come prepared with a letter from their bank saying they were good for enough money to buy a car, with some luck and help from a friend the Goads were able to buy a bidder's paddle and go inside. Criss had brought along the checkbook for her Merrill Lynch account in order to bid at the miniatures auction, and that helped, too. The bidding on the open Cadillacs ran up too fast and too high for the Goads, but near the end of the auction the green V-16 arrived on the stage. Criss had told her husband, "I want that car!" Tom made a bid, someone else bid, and Tom bid again. Sold! Criss wrote a check, which was held over the weekend until they could wire the money for the purchase price. Then Tom took Criss to her miniatures event, and went home to get the trailer (and fortunately, as it would turn out, a spare battery). Returning to the Convention Center, Tom had to ask how to start a V-16 Cadillac (the answer he received—turn the key and push the starter pedal). The car started right up and he drove it out and around the building. He stopped near the trailer and switched it off while he prepared for loading. But when he tried to restart the engine, the battery was completely dead. It seems that a lazy brake pedal return spring had allowed the brake lights to stay on, draining the battery. That was "Issue Number 1" (and the extra battery really came in handy!).

Driving the car, Tom had noted that the speedometer didn't work (Issue Number 2). And when he went for a refueling trip after bringing the car back home, he saw that filling the tank didn't prompt the gauge needle to move (Issue Number 3). The non-working spark control (Issue Number 4) was an easy fix with a piece of aluminum stock he drilled to replace the broken rocker arm bracket in the linkage.

Working with experienced V-16 hands at Classic & Exotic Service, Inc. and among fellow CCCA members, Tom Goad boldly set about finding and tackling the rest of the hidden issues. Fixing the speedometer involved shifting the rear axle in order to enter the back of the transmission to retrieve the driven gear for the cable (the gear had fallen into the transmission), and then installing a newly-cast end for the cable housing. The steering column had to be dissected in order to make the light switch and the manual throttle control easy to operate (Issues 5 and 6). A new thermostat to make the radiator shutters work (Issue 7) required removing and replacing the heavy hood and the radiator shell. Getting the vacuum tanks that supply fuel to the carburetors to work without leaking (Issue 8) required experimenting with various types of materials to find something capable of withstanding ethanol-laced gasoline. To get the quaint Visionall windshield wiper system working (Issue 9) he was able to use the rebuild kit that the Michigan Region of the CCCA sells as a club project, and to have the personal assistance of the man who designed the kit, Paul Ayres.

The Goads wanted this Cadillac to be able to hold its own in judged shows, and that was a big motivation for working to make all the gadgets, gauges and controls work properly. In particular, Tom had set a goal of entering the car in the upcoming Grand Classic (a judged national CCCA meet) and CCCA Museum Grand Experience (an annual themed gathering of Classics hosted by the CCCA Museum) on the grounds of the CCCA Museum at Hickory Corners, Michigan, both events to be held in early June of 2002. The big Cadillac was much improved by the time the deadline arrived.

At the Museum Grand Classic, Criss Goad's car took second place and scored 97.25 points out of a possible 100 (in spite of the not-yet functional fuel gauge). At the Michigan Grand Classic the following July, her Cadillac received the Senior Custom award with 98.0 points, and it was invited to the Meadow Brook Concours d'Elegance. Later in 2002, the Goads showed the car at the Cadillac-LaSalle Club's celebration of Cadillac's 100th anniversary in Dearborn, Michigan.

Over the next winter, Tom had the canvas roof covering replaced with a beige stayfast, a square-weave convertible top fabric. And then under the hood, he addressed some appearance and functional points. The visual aspect of an overhead valve Cadillac V-16 is very important, as it was designed to be seen, and Cadillac had used very specific finishes. Years before, Stan Tarnopol had left the intake manifolds and the carburetor air intake horns with a polished, bare aluminum surface, instead of the gloss black enamel that engine designer Owen Nacker had specified. Moreover, the exhaust manifold on the left side had lost a lot of the shiny black porcelain coating it was built with. There were also some fuel and coolant leaks to be remedied. With the help of Brian Joseph at Classic & Exotic Service, Tom was able to get the engine looking right, and keep it running right as well.

At the 2012 CCCA Grand Classic, Hickory Corners, Michigan. This view of the Goads' Cadillac (foreground) captures the dramatic curves and highlights of the 1930 V-16 styling. Parking lights echo the shape of the headlamps. Stainless steel wheel spokes were an attractive option. Accessory metal covers for the spare tires smoothly finish the car's external appearance (courtesy Nick Larisch).

At the 2003 Grand Experience, former owner Zach Brinkerhoff complimented Tom Goad on how well the Cadillac looked. Later he told the Goads that, knowing what they had paid for the car, if he had been at the Blackhawk Collection auction, he "would have bought it back in a heartbeat." Another triumph was a first-place award at the 2003 Michigan Grand Classic in the Premier Early class with 99 points.

When Tom finally tackled the non-functional fuel gauge (see Issue 3), it meant rebuilding the fuel gauge sending unit, since the wiring and the gauge checked out okay. Reaching the sending unit required some fancy extrication maneuvers, removing the rear seat, reaching through a small access hole in the body floor, and taking the unit out of the top of the gas tank from there. The cork float was missing, and the die-cast parts would barely move. The sending unit was sent out to be rebuilt and calibrated with the gauge, and once re-installed, it was at last possible to know when to stop for a fill-up.

After the Goads got Criss's V-16 sedan cabriolet sorted out, they showed and drove it extensively including on some long club tours, enjoying the big Classic in the manner in which it was meant to be enjoyed. Along the way, Tom did additional work on the car (like work on the cooling system in 2008), and that's part of the ownership experience. After Criss Goad's passing in 2007, Tom still referred to the car as "her car." When Tom passed away in 2018, a beautiful chapter closed on this stately Cadillac V-16. The next caretaker will have a well loved and cared for motor car.

26

Dayton Card's Diverted Convertible Coupe

In early April 1930, a Series 4335 V-16 convertible coupe left the Cadillac factory for the Don Lee dealership network in California. The engine number was 701777 and the body number was 91. It was subsequently diverted to New York City, and its paperwork was stamped at the loading dock May 29, 1931. Curiously, the same time stamp appears on the build sheet for another Series 4335 convertible coupe (engine number 701281) that was also shipped originally to Don Lee, Inc. in San Francisco, and later diverted to New York (see Chapter 17). Perhaps they were part of a package deal? It's very difficult to say with the information that remains.

The next we know of the car with engine number 701777, it was acquired from a seller in Canada by New Jersey collector and restorer Dayton Card. At the 1967 Annual Meeting of the Classic Car Club of America in Buckhill Falls, Pennsylvania, the car was awarded a score of 99.75 out of a possible 100, and received its senior badge. Sometime in the late 1960s, Mr. Card sold the Cadillac to Bob Kuhlman, who still owned it when he died near the turn of the last century.

Mr. Kuhlman's family kept the V-16 convertible coupe until 2013. His widow wrote to the next owner that it was "my husband's favorite toy ... we know we have given up a family member (I know it's only material) but the history and material attachment is so profound."[27] The purchaser told one acquaintance that this was the car he had always wanted. But life and time play tricks on us and sometimes force a change in priorities. In early 2015, that fellow consigned the convertible coupe to be sold at the RM Auctions Amelia Island event.

As built, this V-16 was painted Fargo Brown with Mountain Brown fenders, moldings, and chassis. The body pinstriping and the wheels were a gently contrasting Briarcliffe Beige. The interior was trimmed in dark brown leather. In sum, it would have been a tastefully understated ensemble. (The convertible coupe that was diverted to New York with this one was painted in three shades of gray, with light green pinstriping.)

Over the years, this motor car has been restored twice. Now the body is a light blue, with black moldings, deck lid, hood side panels and cove areas on the cowl. The fenders and chassis are black, and the wheels and body pinstriping are crimson. This eye-catching color scheme can be seen in a photograph of the car that graced the pages of *Automobile Quarterly* in 1984.[28]

---

27. Amelia Island Sale Catalogue, RM Auctions, March 14, 2015, page 175.
28. Borgeson, Griffith, "The Engine of Engines to Power the Car of Cars—The OHV Cadillac V-16 Engine," *Automobile Quarterly*, Fourth Quarter 1984, Kutztown, PA: Vol. 22, No. 4, pp. 340–365 at 344.

Striking color combination. **Pale blue graces the lower panels; black on the deck, moldings, fenders, hood sides; and red wheels with chrome spokes. Chrome hood vent doors and color-coordinated "lowboy" trunk complete the ensemble. When new, this elegant convertible coupe wore two shades of brown with beige wheels (courtesy Darin Schnabel and RM Sotheby's).**

The hood and cowl side vent doors have been chrome-plated (as was often ordered as an option on the 1930–31 V-16 cars), and the wheel spokes are either chrome plated or stainless steel (again, a commonly requested option). Pilot Ray driving lights augment the headlights, and a Cadillac-accessory "low-boy" trunk has been mounted on the luggage rack. Authentic accessory metal spare tire covers with attached rear view mirrors have also been installed.

There are some minor but noticeable discrepancies in the way the restorations have been carried out. The panel surrounding the gauges in the instrument cluster has been chrome plated. At times it has been difficult to find replacements in the original pattern of a black background with fine white cross-hatch lines overlaid. With the passage of time, exposure to the sun, and hands reaching for the ignition lock and the spark and choke controls, it's easy for the crisp white lines to fade and look worn. Before vendors found ways to reproduce the original effect, some owners stripped the panel to the bare brass and polished that, while others chromed it.

In the engine compartment, the intake manifolds have been chrome plated, instead of the original black enamel. And the carburetor intake air horns have been stripped of their black finish, with the underlying aluminum left exposed and polished.

The onset of increasingly chaotic economic times shortly after the Cadillac V-16 cars were introduced to the world meant that some of them were moved around quite a bit before they found a home. In the case of this car (and the one that was diverted with it) it took over a year from the time they were built until they went to customers. One can't

Creamy leather upholstery. The seats, door panels and dash pad are covered in ecru leather, complemented by light tan carpet and scalloped walnut trim boards on the doors. Split windshield with hinged panes is characteristic of cars built at Fleetwood's Pennsylvania factory before production was fully transferred to Detroit (courtesy Darin Schnabel and RM Sothebys).

help but wonder what the "back story" is—were they shipped to the Don Lee organization as demonstrators? Were they ordered for customers who suddenly couldn't afford a top-of-the-line motor car? And who caused them to be shipped across the country to New York? It may be that we'll never know.

On March 14, 2015, this car crossed the block at the Amelia Island sale conducted by RM Auctions, and it brought a price of $456,500.

***Opposite: Sparkling engine compartment of 1930 V-16 convertible coupe.* Intake manifold and carburetor air horn should be black enamel—otherwise, everything looks brand new. Designer Owen Milton Nacker meant for the engine to be seen and admired (courtesy Darin Schnabel and RM Sothebys).**

27

Richard Ancerewicz's Car

In March of 2009, an unrestored 1930 Cadillac V-16 Series 4380 all-weather phaeton emerged from many years of storage in a Michigan garage. From the photos posted on the message forum of the Antique Automobile Club of America it appeared that the car was largely complete and in solid, restorable condition. The top was tattered and the upholstery in shreds, and some of the trim parts (door handles, parking lights and the like) had been removed, apparently with an eye to beginning a restoration that never really got under way. The message included an asking price of $145,000, and claimed that the car had been sold new in Baltimore, that it was currently owned by the estate of the third owner who had bought it in the 1940s, and that the car had not been run in thirty years.

The all-weather phaeton that Richard Ancerewicz owned for many years had been previously owned by Floyd Harden (who lived in the same area in southern Michigan, known as Eastland). Floyd Harden worked as an hourly employee of Cadillac Motor Car Company, and he also owned a 1938 LaSalle 4-door convertible (painted mustard color, and equipped with one side-mount spare tire because there was no room in the trunk on that model). When Richard Ancerewicz had found out about the all-weather phaeton it had been sitting in a field for some time, and he tried to purchase it. Mr. Harden did not want to sell, despite Mr. Ancerewicz's importuning. At some point the car began to be the target of a sort of minor vandalism—such as rocks appearing on the seats—that made it seem like local kids were taking a destructive interest in the neglected old-fashioned

Driving in Detroit. **Richard Ancerewicz at the wheel of his 1930 Cadillac V-16 all-weather phaeton sometime during the 1960s. Keeping such cars running in those years, without ready sources of replacement (or remanufactured) parts was no mean feat (courtesy Guy Zaninovich).**

automobile. This development prompted Mr. Harden to change his mind about selling the car, and that worked out very nicely for Mr. Ancerewicz.

Mr. Ancerewicz was described by Doug Houston as an unusual fellow. He lived alone, and paid his bills by running a small electronic parts manufacturing operation. His brother was in charge of the engineering shop at Chrysler's missile-building plant, where Doug Houston worked. That was how Doug found out about the all-weather phaeton and its owner. Mr. Ancerewicz wanted to "keep the car original" but that may have been more about not wanting to spend any money on it. It was complete, solid and straight, notwithstanding the weather damage. Nevertheless, Mr. Ancerewicz got the car running and would drive it around.

Richard Ancerewicz's brother brought Doug Houston over to see the all-weather phaeton, and that was how Doug first saw a Cadillac V-16. Doug Houston knew a draftsman at Ford (a designer of progressive die equipment) named Wilbur Sanders, who owned another V-16 all-weather phaeton (one that was really in need of restoration), along with a lot of parts. Doug told Mr. Sanders about Richard Ancerewicz's car and about the parts that it needed, and Mr. Ancerewicz was able to purchase two carburetors and a clock for the car from Mr. Sanders. Richard Ancerewicz did some work on his car, but progress was very slow.

The engine currently in the car is number 702598, but the build sheet (as well as painted numbers stenciled onto the firewall at the factory) indicates that the original engine number was 702643. The build sheet also shows that the car was shipped August 25, 1930, to Cunliffe Cadillac in Baltimore, Maryland, but was diverted exactly three months later to Washington, D.C., on a special order. (Unfortunately, the Cadillac files

Uncovered in Mr. Ancerewicz's garage. **Following his death, arrangements were made to sell the V-16 Cadillac. Partial disassembly had been undertaken by Mr. Ancerewicz in hopes of restoring the car (courtesy Guy Zaninovich).**

Out into the light. **The headlamps have been reattached to Mr. Ancerewicz's all-weather phaeton, the frayed top has been raised and some of the dust wiped off of the original paint, as the car is posed for an online advertisement. Nails substitute for door hinge pins (courtesy Guy Zaninovich).**

that would have contained the documentation of that special order were discarded long ago.) A multi-tone color scheme is shown on the build sheet, with Rich Green for the body, and Vanderbilt Green for the body moldings, fenders and chassis. The wheels and the body pinstripe were Jade Green. Surviving Cadillac records indicate that the present engine (number 702598) originally powered a Series 4375 seven-passenger imperial sedan that was shipped new to Detroit. It is not clear when the original engine was replaced or by whom.

Mr. Ancerewicz owned the all-weather phaeton for the rest of his life, and after he passed away in June 2008, his estate got in touch with Mr. Guy Zaninovich, who posted a message and some photographs of the car on the AACA message forum. In due course, Mr. Ancerewicz's all-weather phaeton showed up on the Internet web site of Platinum Classic Motorcars of Macedon, New York, where myriad photographs were posted, documenting the "as acquired" state, and the progression from disassembly through restoration. Along the way, it was indicated on the web site that the car had been sold, but that the in-house restoration continued.

28

Monumental Mystery

APPROXIMATELY 10 YEARS AFTER IT was dedicated, the Lincoln Memorial in Washington, D.C., served as a dramatic backdrop for a photograph. Probably during the winter months (judging by the man's topcoat) a distinguished looking gentleman posed in front of the monument next to his new 1930 Cadillac V-16 sedan.

The trees planted by the National Park Service around the base of the memorial don't reach even to the level of the foundation stones (today those trees are grown and substantial). The camera sees the south face of the memorial, and one of the ceremonial

On a cool, clear morning. **An unidentified man poses next to a 1930 Cadillac V-16 sedan with the recently-erected Lincoln Memorial for a backdrop. The original image is in the Library of Congress, but there is no information identifying the gentleman or the occasion for the photograph (Library of Congress, Prints & Photographs Division LC-USZ62-99349).**

braziers that flank the front steps can be seen to the right of the structure. Off to the viewer's right, down the National Mall, lie the Washington Monument and the Capitol Building. Not a soul in sight but for the gentleman and his car.

The car is a Series 4375-S or 4375 seven-passenger sedan. It wears the plain radiator cap without an ornament, but the tires are whitewalls and the side-mount spare tires have the optional fabric covers. The license plate numbers can be discerned: J-8592. But which state issued it can't be made out. The style of the lettering and numbers is not inconsistent with 1930 District of Columbia plates—a letter followed by some numbers. But the resolution of the photo is not high enough to settle the matter.

Who was this well-to-do fellow who had someone snap his picture with his elegant transportation at such an evocative site? A business man visiting Washington to talk to his Congressman? A newly-elected Senator seeing the sights when no one is around? Maybe the car's owner took the photograph of a friend standing next to his car with the memorial as a backdrop. The seller of this photo said that there were no notations on the back of the original, and that he acquired it with a large number of unsorted old photos.

The same image can be found in the Library of Congress's Prints and Photographs Collection. Their information indicates that the photograph was taken in 1931 and that it was an Underwood & Underwood photo. Until it went out of business in the 1940s, Underwood & Underwood was a pioneer in the field of news-bureau photography (many older books contain photographs that credit Underwood & Underwood as the source). Unfortunately, the Library of Congress has no other information besides their title "Man standing with Cadillac near the Lincoln Memorial, Washington, D.C."

Perhaps the subject and occasion for this photograph will remain a mystery.

29

The Moir Family's Roadster

It's a rare thing when an automobile remains cared for in the same family for decades. Forgotten and neglected in a barn or shed? Perhaps. But to be kept in nearly new condition for over eighty years is truly remarkable. It happens that such a situation recently became public, and the car involved brought a record price at auction.

The 1930 Cadillac V-16 Series 4302 roadster, engine number 701761, was shipped to the Fitzhenry Cadillac Company of Worcester, Massachusetts. The surviving shipping order or "build sheet" for that car contains the instruction "TAG WHITTALL," the kind of instruction that generally points to the original owner (or a representative designated to pick up the new car). Apparently this roadster was destined for Matthew Whittall, a socially-prominent mill owner in the Worcester area.

This roadster was painted "Boone Brown" with "Thorn Maroon" for the moldings, the rear deck, and the wheels. A gold bronze pinstripe highlighted the fender edges and the body side moldings. "Rich Maroon" leather covered the seats and interior trim panels

Some of the earliest V-16 roadsters were equipped with a very fast-ratio rear axle (3.47:1) which was discontinued not far into the first year of production. But the later roadsters, like this one, were still pretty sprightly for their size, having a 4.07:1 ratio and significantly less weight to move around than their closed-car siblings. They were capable of 100 mile-per-hour speeds, and with mechanically actuated drum brakes, that sort of power and speed can be a handful. Mr. Whittall is reported to have been somewhat alarmed at the capabilities of his roadster, and around 1933 he traded the car for a Lincoln at Baker Ford Company in Brookline. Mr. John A. Moir, Sr., saw the car among the dealer's used vehicles, and bought it. Once the Great Depression really began to bite in the early 1930s, the market for large luxury cars lost most of its depth. At the same time, the new fashion for vehicles and any other industrial product was streamlining. The new cars were becoming so radically different in appearance that a two- or three-year-old car suddenly looked quite out of date. So when Mr. Moir bought this roadster, the price was a fraction of what it had sold for new. His son, John A. Moir, Jr., was about 6 years old.

This roadster was driven regularly until World War II when gas rationing persuaded the owner to store it. After the war, when his son returned to civilian life from the Army Air Corps, the elder Mr. Moir turned the Cadillac over to the young veteran. The younger Mr. Moir used the car during college and for a year after that, at which time his father convinced him to retire it from Boston driving. Over the subsequent years, the young man would acquire and care for cars for each letter of the alphabet (what became known as "The A-to-Z Collection").

The V-16 Cadillac remained with the Moir family, and in 1990 it was treated to a careful restoration by Curt Hardee of Hooksett, New Hampshire. The car was repainted,

Gently cared for in the family garage. **While still under the care of the Moir family, the roadster that John Moir, Sr., bought in 1933 looks as fresh as when it left the Cadillac factory in 1930. Family photographs are displayed on the license plate bracket and the front bumper (courtesy Joseph Scott).**

retaining the original colors. The seats were re-upholstered and the chromed items were replated. Correct 19-inch wheels and tires were installed, and the deteriorated radiator goddess and missing mirrors for the sidemount spare tires were replaced, along with the hood latches. Otherwise, the sleek Cadillac retained its originality. A friend of the author, who owns a 1930 V-16 roadster, visited the Moirs and took measurements of the interior of their car to help in the ongoing restoration of his own car.

In 2014, John Moir, Jr., decided to let go of a number of old cars, including the V-16 roadster. It was consigned to the Hershey Auction conducted by RM Auctions. Open Cadillac V-16 cars regularly command impressive purchase prices at these events, but this car surprised even the veterans. The pre-sale estimate had been around $650,000, which was somewhat high due to the unique history and correctness of the car. But when the hammer came down, the bidding had reached $1,000,000 (plus 10 percent buyer's premium). The new owner is a collector in Rhode Island.

30

Repurposed, Relinquished and Rescued

The "Madame X" cars were the upper tier of the early '30s V-16 Cadillacs. They represented a risk taken by Harley Earl's Art & Colour Section and by Fleetwood. The risk was, first, in styling—raked windshield, spare interior ornamentation—and trusting that affluent customers would appreciate the innovations. And second, there was an engineering risk—the slender "A" (windshield) and "B" pillars required new metallurgy and casting techniques in order to provide the same structural strength and integrity as the standard structures. And the Madame X models were priced about $1,000 more than their more conventional counterparts in the Fleetwood stable.

The Series 4155 imperial cabriolet was a five-passenger sedan without rear quarter windows. The roof was covered in leather or fabric, and the windowless rear quarter panels sported carriage landau irons, as though the rear part of the roof were collapsible. (In fact, if the series designation for the car were 4155-C, it would indeed have a collapsible rear roof section permitting passengers to take the air on a nice day.) A Series 4155 car would have fold-down "opera" seats in the rear compartment for two extra passengers, and a roll-up glass window between the front and rear seats. The car was a slightly smaller and very private limousine.

As a Madame X car, the Series 4155 had a raked windshield, thin chrome reveals with sharp corners outlining the side windows, painted interior window garnish pieces, and plain interior door trim (without the inlaid wood panels below the window sills as found on the standard cars). The effect was formal, but graceful.

The Series 4155 imperial cabriolet that bore engine number 703006, body number 13 was originally shipped on April 11, 1931, to the Don Lee dealership in Los Angeles and sold in southern California. According to the shipping invoice or "build sheet" for the car, it was all black except for the lower door panels, the lower rear body, the cowl and the hood, which were painted "Larchmont Blue," and the body pinstriping, which was done in "Gold Bronze." To add extra flash, the vent doors on the hood and the cowl were chrome plated, and the wheel spokes were stainless steel. A goddess-style radiator cap ornament was specified, and its serial number was given on the invoice. The interior of this car was trimmed throughout in a taupe pattern broadcloth supplied by New York textile supplier William Wiese & Company. The rear axle ratio was the slower of the options available, tending to indicate that the car was going to operate in hilly areas or spend most of its time in traffic.

Around 1940, after the newness, magnificence and shine of this car had worn off, a farmer on the Nevada-Idaho border cut off the rear portion of the body and converted

***As found, more or less.* The partial body of the vehicle on the right is the Madame X imperial cabriolet that Bob Hoffman found. The rear section had been removed long before. The red frame is from another project car of Mr. Hoffman's, and the partial frame stacked on top is of unknown provenance (courtesy Alan Merkel).**

the limousine into a boom truck for lifting and moving hay bales. The frame had been cut and dropped in the front and in the back, and a hoist mechanism had been installed. Eventually, the homemade truck's owner decided it was no longer useful, and it came to rest with some other discarded autos in a field behind a service station. The wire wheels with their stainless steel spokes were mounted on a farm wagon, but the rest of the contraption was left to sink slowly into the sod.

In the 1980s, Cadillac enthusiast and restorer Bob Hoffman travelled to Oregon to retrieve a 1933 V-12 Cadillac victoria that he had purchased. The seller told him about another Cadillac V-16 located on the border between Nevada and Idaho. Mr. Hoffman immediately discounted any chance of finding the car in question, since it was practically in Bill Harrah's back yard. In those days, Harrah's Automobile Collection in Reno (along with a high quality restoration shop and an extensive reference library) was world famous, and Bob was certain that any valuable cars anywhere near Reno would have been scarfed up already by Mr. Harrah and his staff.

Subsequently, Mr. Hoffman and a friend went to Idaho to pick up a 1934 LaSalle. They stopped at a gas station and took a look at some old cars sitting in the field behind the station. Mr. Hoffman called his friend's attention to one of the vehicles saying, "Look at that old Cadillac." The friend replied, "That's just a pickup truck." When they drew near, it became apparent that the truck had once been a glorious Madame X Cadillac. The frame had been cut and modified, and part of the body removed. When asked what had happened to the rest of the Fleetwood body, the gas station owner recalled that a lot of car bodies had been buried in a nearby landfill.

Reconstruction in progress. This is an indication of the work required to graft the rear portion of the sedan body from the car in Goochland County, Virginia, onto the remains of Mr. Hoffman's Series 4155 imperial cabriolet. The photograph was taken in Fred Weber's workshop in St. Louis (courtesy Jim Schild).

Reassembled and partially restored. The rear part of the body has been reconstructed, and the fenders and most trim items have been attached. The car subsequently showed up at the AACA's Hershey meet in October 1992 (courtesy Jim Schild).

Restored and respected. **The V-16 imperial cabriolet as it sits today at the Haynes International Motor Museum in the United Kingdom (courtesy Haynes International Motor Museum).**

Mr. Hoffman bought the truck, but gave up on finding the remainder of the body. But he did notice that the stainless-steel-spoked wire wheels had been mounted on an old farm wagon in the same field. He was able to buy the wheels off of the farm wagon, and he welded the frame back to its original conformation. Later, he bought the rear portion of a Madame X body that had been cut up years before in the woods in rural Goochland County, Virginia. Eventually, he sold the car and the parts he had assembled to Fred Weber in St. Louis, Missouri. Mr. Weber and his shop completed the restoration of the car and showed it at various venues, before consigning it to Christie's to be auctioned at their August 20, 2000, Exceptional Motor Cars sale at Pebble Beach. It was purchased for $149,000, and since then has resided at the Haynes International Motor Museum in Somerset, UK.

Today, the hood, the cowl and the lower panels of the doors and body are a deep blue, and the rest of the car is black. The roof is covered with black leather and padded. It looks like it left the factory yesterday, and most visitors to the museum have no idea how close this magnificent motor car came to annihilation.

31

Hopalong Cassidy's All-Weather Phaeton?

Bud Tinney, whose father was in the car dealership business before him, always liked old Cadillacs. Back in the 1980s, he purchased a 1930 Series 4380 V-16 all-weather phaeton. In early '30s parlance, "all-weather phaeton" referred to a four-door convertible with roll-up windows in the doors, and the consequent ability to seal out wind, rain, and other forms of precipitation. A true phaeton lacked roll-up windows, and the occupants depended upon fabric side-curtains with transparent inserts to keep out the elements when they turned unfriendly. Side curtains had to be retrieved, flattened, and installed in each of the doors when the rain or snow started, and they didn't always seal well around the edges and along the top. It was easy to become soaked before one had a chance to put the side curtains in place.

Cadillac's Series 4380 all-weather phaeton was a nicely proportioned car, visually, with a divider window like a limousine, between the driver's compartment and the passengers. When folded, the convertible top fit flush with the tops of the doors. The windshield was the split and nearly-upright design characteristic of the cars built at the Fleetwood plant in Fleetwood, Pennsylvania. The Series 4380 was a true five-passenger car, without even small opera seats for occasional extra passengers.

Bud Tinney acquired his Series 4380 (engine number 700503) through legendary V-16 Cadillac enthusiast, collector and restorer Jim Pearson. "Cadillac Jim," as he was known, had found out about the car when it was owned by Willie Christi, a garage owner in California, and had spoken with him about arranging a sale. Mr. Christi had said that the car had originally belonged to William Boyd, a movie actor who found fame portraying the fictional cowboy hero Hopalong Cassidy. But before a sale could be completed, the garage owner died, and another man came forward with a claim that the car had been promised to him. The garage owner's family denied this claim, and the matter was taken to court, where the judge forced a sale of the car and division of the proceeds of the sale between the contending parties. Bud Tinney was able to purchase the car after Jim Pearson flew out to California and was the high bidder at the court hearing. Bud then subjected the Cadillac to a conscientious restoration.

When it left the factory in March of 1930, this particular Series 4380 was painted black, except for the vent doors on the hood and cowl, and the wheels, all of which were painted "Mountain Ash Scarlet." The chrome-plated spokes on the wheels added extra flash, and with the optional 4.07 to 1 rear axle ratio, it was a quick car for one that weighed around three tons. The build sheet indicates that the car was shipped to Cadillac's Chicago Branch office with instructions to hold for payment. Typed at the top of the form is the word "TIFFANY." This has led some to speculate that the car was ordered for one of the members of the Tiffany jewelry family. However, at the time, a Mr. R.G. Tiffany was one of the principal figures at Cadillac's Chicago Branch. This writer considers it most likely that R.G. Tiffany was to be notified upon the car's arrival in Chicago, either as the actual purchaser, or as the person responsible for making sure the car was properly turned over to the customer who had ordered it.

Turning now to the garage owner's assertion that this was William Boyd's car, there are a couple of period photographs, copies of which turn up on the Internet from time to time, showing Mr. Boyd with a 1930 Series 4380 all-weather phaeton, but little or no documentation has been offered to prove that any surviving Series 4380 car was actually Boyd's. Even though the photos just mentioned are black-and-white images, it is clear that the car shown is painted in a different manner than that indicated on the build sheet for engine number 700503. In the photographs, the body is a dark color, and a lighter color covers the sides of the hood (including the vent doors) and the cove areas on the top of the hood and sides of the cowl (the area outlined by the so-called "LeBaron sweep" line).

By the time Bud Tinney acquired his car, the body (including the entire hood and cowl) had been painted maroon with a black belt molding (the fenders remained black) and with brown wheel hubs. The vent doors appear in a photograph from that time to have been stripped of paint for possible chroming. So, based on the limited evidence available, it's not possible to confirm or refute the garage owner's belief that this

***The car as acquired by Bud Tinney.* The Cadillac had been repainted with maroon body and black fenders and body molding. Mr. Tinney would undertake an extensive restoration (courtesy Bud Tinney).**

Rear Quarter. **As acquired, the left taillight had no lens, and the luggage rack and two of the vertical chrome bars protecting the rear of the body are missing (courtesy Bud Tinney).**

particular all-weather phaeton had been William Boyd's car, although the actor certainly drove one like it.

During the restoration conducted by Bud Tinney, the exterior finish was returned to its build sheet-specified color scheme, except that the body molding was also painted scarlet, like the wheels and the hood and cowl vent doors. The restoration efforts were rewarded with a score of 100 points at a Grand Classic event with the Classic Car Club of America.

In 2001, Mr. Tinney sold the Cadillac to collector Dave Lindsay in Manawa, Wisconsin. In April of 2016, the car was offered by Worldwide Auctioneers at their Houston Classic Auction, where it brought a sale price of $291,500. Afterwards, the car changed hands a couple of times in the Midwest before winding up once again in Wisconsin, in the care of Jeff and Rebecca Schreiner. Jeff had purchased a 1918 Roamer, and when that car was being delivered to his home, he saw on the transport truck a V-16 Cadillac. Intrigued, he asked the transport driver to give the new owner a note saying that if he ever wanted to sell the Cadillac, Mr. Schreiner would like to buy it. A week later he got a phone call, and after some negotiations, a price hadn't been reached. Mr. Schreiner called to see if the car was still for sale, and was told that it was on its way to Chicago for some paint work and possible sale to another prospect. Mr. Schreiner and the seller agreed on a price and Mr. Schreiner was invited to meet the truck in Janesville, Wisconsin. If he liked the Cadillac, he could have it. Otherwise it would continue on to Chicago. When the car backed out of the trailer and Mr. Schreiner saw it, there was no doubt. It went onto his trailer and home to Mondovi.

The "all-weather phaeton" as restored. **This body style, effectively a "convertible limousine," was a four-door convertible with weather-tight windows instead of loose, flexible side-curtains. A roll-up window could separate driver's and passengers' compartments like an enclosed-drive limousine, or the top and windows could be lowered for open-air touring. This car is very close to its original color scheme (save the scarlet body molding in place of a scarlet pinstripe) (courtesy Bud Tinney).**

The Schreiners purchased their car in June of 2016. Later, in October, the car suffered a front-end collision, and Jeff had to do extensive body work on the front fenders, have many of the chrome trim pieces re-plated, and re-paint the front end of the car. The horns had to be repaired and the goddess ornament reconstructed. Fellow Cadillac-LaSalle Club members sought out and located necessary parts, but Jeff Schreiner did all of the work, including the painting. Everything was completed just in time for the Amelia Island Concours d'Elegance in April 2017. At that event, the result of all the hard work was a First in Class award in the American Classics category for the Schreiners' V-16 all-weather phaeton.

In early 2019, the car was offered for sale on the web site of Hyman, Ltd. The old saying has it that we don't own the cars—we just take care of them for the next owner.

32

A Cadillac "Woodie" Convertible

Around 1985, Alan Merkel of White Stone, and Willie Meffert of Charlottesville, Virginia, travelled to Michigan and visited Melvin Patterson. Mel Patterson, now deceased, owned several Cadillac V-16s, and he would buy and sell and work on those cars. He acquired Ian Kiltie's rare Fisher-bodied V-16 convertible coupe when Ian died. (After Mel passed away that car went to Dennis Dow, also a Michigander.)

Alan bought from Mel Patterson V-16 engine number 702994 as a separate, stand-alone item. He didn't ask or find out anything about the prior history of engine number 702994 or where Mel Patterson got it. All that can be discerned from the build sheet is that the car that originally contained that engine travelled to Tulsa, Oklahoma, and to Kansas City, Missouri, before it finally found a purchaser in Chicago at the end of February 1932.

On the way home, Alan and Willie made a deal by which Willie would take number 702994, and Alan would receive from Willie another V-16 engine mounted on a chassis. (The engine and chassis Alan got would later go to Max Houston in Australia.) Willie already had (or was working on) a deal that would leave engine number 702994 with Ed Perkins in Guilford, Connecticut.

Mike Fairbairn of Ontario, Canada, had been interested in collector cars from his student days. He paid his way through college by finding and purchasing used Ford Mustangs that young kids had dressed up with funky wheels and tires and other personal touches that a mature purchaser would find off-putting. He wouldn't buy cars that needed bodywork or serious repair, just those that he could refurbish relatively easily. Once a car was returned to stock equipment and cleaned up with a detailed engine compartment, it would present as a nice, cared-for driver, and he would sell it for a tidy profit. After college there was some money left over, and Mike acquired a couple of cars he really liked, including a "K-Code" Mustang convertible with the special high-performance 289-cubic-inch engine, something like a Shelby Mustang with a drop top.

Mike was a regular attendee of the annual AACA Eastern Division Fall Meet at Hershey, Pennsylvania, and he would return home to Ontario by different routes. On one return trip, he and his wife saw a cardboard roadside sign that said "CAR SHOW NEXT EXIT," and they decided to have a look. When they arrived, there was a circle of six or eight Classics including a 1930 Cadillac V-16 roadster. Mike Fairbairn was taken with that car, looking at it and studying each detail from every angle. He spoke with the owner (who had no interest in selling), and left the show thinking about how to obtain a car like that.

By the 1980s, V-16 Cadillacs in good shape were bringing substantial prices, and Mike had little or no cash, so he figured that his best plan would be to buy a rough car and restore it himself. He went looking for a project car, and came to speak with Ed Perkins. Ed had a V-16 engine, chassis and other parts—basically everything but the body—and he wanted $21,000 or $22,000 for the lot. The two men worked out a deal whereby Mike would turn over a 1969 Shelby Mustang GT-350 and $7,000 cash. Mike just had to convince his wife to let him borrow the money. After a lot of persuading, she finally agreed, and Mike hitched an open trailer to his big late-70s Ford station wagon and went to pick up his project.

The chassis was in worse shape than expected, having sat in the weather, and the front axle was detached (the front end was supported by a jig with casters). Mike and Ed spent half a day hunting for and gathering V-16 parts for the car from Ed's garage. When they'd got everything together, they loaded the chassis on Mike's trailer and arranged the fenders and all the other parts on and around the chassis. Then Mike covered the load with a tarp and tied it all down like a haywagon with yards of nylon rope.

At the U.S.-Canada border, Mike declared a 1931 Cadillac V-16 to the customs agent, who wanted to take a look. So they went outside, and the agent asked, "Where is it?" Mike pointed and the agent said, "This on the trailer?" Mike nodded and the man let out a big belly laugh and said, "One thing's for sure, you ain't lyin'!" Mike paid the duty and drove the rest of the way home uneventfully, finally getting to bed in the wee hours of the morning.

About 7:00 a.m., Mike Fairbairn awoke to the sound of screaming. "Michael, get down here!" Having only had three hours of sleep, Mike got up and went downstairs to see his wife pointing at the still-covered mass of car parts on the trailer. "I mortgaged my house so you could buy THAT?!" Mike would spend some time "in the doghouse" for that, but he eventually got the chassis and the rest of the parts unloaded and stored.

Mike wanted to restore his car as a roadster, but found himself unable to locate and acquire a roadster body. But a man in Whitby, Ontario, had a Cadillac V-8 roadster stored in his backyard, covered with tarps. Every year, the man would lift the tarps and spray the car with oil to prevent rust. Mike bought the car, even though there were some differences between the V-8 and V-16 roadster bodies, and he sold off everything except the body. He had started the restoration work when he found out about a doctor who had begun collecting Classic cars.

Dr. David Klein of Staunton, Virginia, had an active medical practice when his own doctor told him that he needed to slow down and find a hobby, or he wouldn't be around for his next check-up. Dr. Klein picked Classic car collecting, and specifically, V-16 Cadillacs. There was a restoration shop near where he lived and he had begun acquiring cars and having them restored there. Dr. Klein offered to buy Mike Fairbairn's project and for the agreed upon price, Mike estimated he could throw in half again as much and be able to purchase a restored V-16.

For whatever reason, Dr. Klein and the restoration shop became unable to work together, a lawsuit ensued, and the judge ordered that the restoration project including engine number 702994 be sold. The purchaser was James W. Pascoe, who lived in Escanaba on the Upper Peninsula of Michigan.

Mr. Pascoe, a Korean War veteran, began and managed a construction company, and he loved old cars. He had a particular fondness for the slat-and-panel wood body surfaces used in older station wagons and "woodie" vehicles such as the Chrysler "Town and Country" models of the late 1940s. He made wooden body structures for mid-century Buicks, among other cars. When he purchased the unfinished V-16 Cadillac project, he

Unconventional coachwork. **In the early 1930s, "woodie" body construction was generally limited to station wagons, depot hacks, and other light commercial vehicles. Not until the early 1940s would that technique spread to passenger cars in significant numbers. This Cadillac portrays quite nicely what Fleetwood might have done with this type of bodywork (courtesy Mark Thomas).**

decided to design and build a woodie body for it. And that's what he did. He built a convertible coupe body with rumble seat and golf bag compartment and saw that the rest of the car was restored in a professional manner. He said that he put 2,000 hours into the project. Mr. Pascoe took the restored car to Cadillac-LaSalle Club events and met a hostile reception. Disheartened, he decided to sell the Cadillac.

Nine or ten years ago Mark Thomas saw an ad in *Old Cars Weekly* for a Cadillac V-16 with a wood body, located in Escanaba, Michigan. Mark lives in Birmingham, Michigan, a suburb of Detroit. He and his brother still own their family's home in Clintonville, Wisconsin, about 35 miles west of Green Bay. Clintonville is where four-wheel drive started in America—there's a museum in Clintonville that just acquired a 56,000 square-foot factory building to use.

Mark can get to the family home one of two ways. The southern route goes by way of Chicago and then north to Clintonville. The other route goes north into the upper peninsula of Michigan and down through Escanaba. But that route is longer and more likely to involve bad weather. So Mark didn't get around to following up on the ad and it dropped out of the magazine.

But about a year later, the ad re-appeared, and with a reduced price. Mark became interested again, and took the route through Escanaba to get to Clintonville. He had along with him Morgan, the son (of two) who is interested in cars, and they stopped and looked at the V-16. The car was a correct restoration, except that everything from the windshield pillars back and from the rear fenders and body sill up was constructed

***Profile view.* This unique hand-built body is reminiscent of the Series 4335 convertible coupe, with its upright passenger compartment. The woodwork evokes country estates and picnic outings (courtesy Mark Thomas).**

of exposed and finished wood, instead of metal panels over a wood framework. Mark was looking the car over and hesitating as he contemplated the price, when his son said that he would give him all the money he had if Mark would buy the car. He said that they would be joint owners. And so Mark agreed to purchase the car and his son became a 1⁄14 owner. They drove the car southwest to Clintonville.

In due course, Mark had the car shipped from Clintonville to his home in Birmingham and did what research he could regarding the car's history. He went to the GM Heritage Center and spoke with the people there, obtaining copies of the car's build sheets. He found that engine number 702994 originally belonged to a Series 4375 seven-passenger limousine that was shipped to Kansas City in April 1931, and then diverted to Chicago to be sold. Series 4375 cars were the second most numerous of the 1930 and 1931 V-16 cars built, totaling 438 hand-crafted motor cars. They worked hard—some were worked to death, some fell prey to the wartime scrap drives, and others were victims of neglect and the elements. This one's engine survived, made it onto another chassis, and acquired a new and unique body.

Mark reports that the car runs nicely, and that he has taken it to several Michigan Region Classic Car Club of America events. He told this author that he plans to submit paperwork to seek recognition of the car by CCCA as a re-bodied Classic. In the meantime, it's a beautiful, very enjoyable and eye-catching automobile.

In October 2019, the car was offered for sale by RM Sotheby's, without reserve, at the company's Hershey Auction in Hershey, Pennsylvania. A sale price of $82,500 (including buyer's premium) was realized.

33

The London Landaulette

After the First World War, a couple of Royal Navy veterans named Frederick Hartman (christened Friedrich Wilhelm Hartmann) and Ernest Samuel Lendrum formed an automobile distribution company in Albemarle Street, London, that became Lendrum & Hartman Limited. Lendrum & Hartman began distributing Buicks and became General Motors' sales agent in Great Britain, continuing to do business for the better part of the twentieth century.

When the Cadillac V-16 appeared on the scene in 1930, Lendrum & Hartman ordered two bare chassis that would be fitted with custom-designed bodywork by the distinguished Belgian firm of Van den Plas.

As a rule, Cadillac was extremely resistant to allowing outside coachbuilders to work their artistry on the V-16 chassis. Apart from the fact that General Motors already had extensive coach-building facilities of its own (Fisher Body and the recently-acquired custom body-maker Fleetwood) and would naturally prefer to keep the business "in-house," there was a strongly-felt need to maintain artistic control over the image of the V-16 line, and how the public perceived it. Harley Earl, head of GM's Art and Colour section, had spent years in California catering to the customization whims of a broad range of customers, and he knew how far those whims could go. GM management was aiming to create an aura of sophisticated elegance, and an eccentric customer commissioning a loopy or grotesque creation could "poison the well." Moreover, it was thought that the many different body styles offered to Cadillac V-16 customers, coupled with the eagerness of Cadillac to work with customers desiring alterations and personalized touches, would suffice to satisfy all (reasonable) tastes.

Nevertheless, several bare chassis were shipped by the factory, with full knowledge that these were going to be bodied by firms with no affiliation with, or control by, GM or Cadillac. The one we are concerned with here bore engine number 702297, was set up for right-hand drive, and was shipped from the Detroit factory on July 9, 1930. The bare chassis was shown at the London Motor Show at the Olympia in the autumn of 1930, and thereafter was turned over to Van den Plas. There seems to be some support for the idea that Queen Wilhelmina of the Netherlands commissioned or otherwise prompted the design and completion of this extraordinary automobile. A representative of the Queen is said to have confirmed that she would purchase the car, built according to Van den Plas's design. But as the extent of the financial difficulties triggered by the stock market crash became more and more evident, it is said that she decided owning and using such a grand conveyance might send the wrong message when so many ordinary people were suffering.

In any event, the car was completed as a "Saloon Landaulette Deluxe," a term that describes a limousine with a folding rear quarter. The finished motor car appeared in

Van den Plas custom landaulette body on a 1930 Cadillac V-16 chassis. **The cowl, hood, radiator shell, fenders, bumpers, gas tank cover and luggage rack are standard Cadillac. The body from the windshield back is Van den Plas. Taillights are from a 1929 or 1930 Cadillac V-8 car, and the headlights, though similar to stock in size and shape, are from another manufacturer. On a landaulette, the rear quarter of the roof from the rear door hinge pillar back could be collapsed and folded back, affording rear seat passengers the pleasures of open-air motoring. The anchors for the "S"-shaped landau irons double as support brackets for the folded roof section. The design was not a new one for this coachbuilder, as they had mounted similar bodies on 1929 and 1930 V-8 Cadillac chassis (courtesy Louman Automobile Museum, The Netherlands).**

the Olympia Auto Show in late October of 1931 before being delivered to its first owner, Arthur Ernest Guinness of the Guinness brewing family.

Ernest Guinness, as he was known, achieved a measure of fame for having arrested the Prince of Wales during World War I. Having encountered a young soldier on a bicycle with a chest full of medals, he could not imagine that one so young was entitled to so many decorations, and concluded that he must be a spy. Mr. Guinness had three daughters who figured largely in the contemporary London social whirl. They were known in society pages as "the Golden Guinness Girls" (or the Fabulous Guinness Girls). He bought Luttrellstown Castle in Ireland as a wedding present for daughter Aileen. We do not know how long he may have had his Cadillac V-16, or what adventures he and his family may have had in it. But a full page drawn and colored illustration of the Saloon Landaulette Deluxe in a 1931 Lendrum & Hartman brochure contains the legend "As supplied to the Hon. A.E. Guinness."

The car shown in the brochure is a stately four-door sedan for which the portion of the top from the rear door pillar back could be collapsed and folded, affording the rear-seat passengers an open-air riding experience without the full exposure to wind and sun that comes with a full convertible top. The body and hood panels are a blue-gray color, vivid without being flashy. The fenders and dust shields are black, as are the beltline molding, door pillars, roof, and upper rear panel. Blue-gray offsets frame the side windows, and the upholstery (as much as can be seen in the picture) is a dignified gray.

The bodywork is not a major departure from what Fleetwood was doing for Cadillac's offered V-16 body styles. The fenders and hood, along with the cowl as far back as the windshield frame, are stock Cadillac Fleetwood. Only the body from the windshield back is different. The windshield is bolt upright—Fleetwood and Fisher stayed at least 7 degrees from vertical, even on the more conservative jobs. The windshield glass is hinged at the top and framed in a bright metal channel. The lower edge swings out to allow

SALOON LANDAULETTE DE LUXE

Coachwork by Carrosserie Van den Plas, Brussels

(ON V-16 CADILLAC CHASSIS)

The body is painted in a charming shade of powder blue, wings, head leather and bonnet in black. Upholstery is in pale grey superfine box-cloth. Interior woodwork is in dull walnut.

This elegant body has wide doors and ample head room despite its low slung appearance. The interior is fitted with two armchair pullman seats and two extremely roomy occasional seats which face forward and are provided with side rests. Safety glass

As supplied to The Hon. A. E. Guinness

Lendrum & Hartman Image. **General Motors Corporation's London agent, Messrs. Lendrum & Hartman Limited, prepared a brochure for the London Auto Show, and one of the color plates featured the Van den Plas landaulette that was mounted on Cadillac V-16 chassis, engine number 702997. Original color scheme and interior trim were more subdued than the present symphony of red (courtesy Yann Saunders and the Z. Taylor Vinson Collection).**

ventilation, and brackets allow it to be locked in position. The door window frames have sharp corners and slender reveals or offsets, not unlike the Madame X Fleetwood models, although without chrome reveal moldings. Exposed barrel hinges and simple straight handles highlight the doors. The irons that lock the folding top in place are of a unique design that also serves to support the top frame and bows in the lowered position. The headlights are nearly as large as the stock Cadillac "Tilt-Ray" units (which were 13 inches in diameter), and the buckets are a slightly different shape, but to the untrained eye, they look like the usual 1930–31 V-16 lamps (but without the badge bar between them, or its distinctive cloisonné V-16 medallion). The taillights appear to be 1929 Cadillac units, rather than the 1930–31 V-16 style which mimicked the shape of the headlights. Seen as a whole, the outward aspect of the car has a personality of its own, but does not oppose or depart markedly from the Cadillac/Fleetwood esthetic.

Inside the car, the differences from Fleetwood trimming are more pronounced than the exterior distinctions. The wood inside the window openings is heavier, and the inlaid boards on the doors are part of a wood edging that runs the entire perimeter of each door trim panel. The top of the imperial division features an elaborate inlaid tray that runs from one side of the interior to the other. The cabinetry between the jump seats incorporates a rear-seat speedometer (not unlike what Fleetwood did with their sport phaetons, but without an accompanying chronometer). The jump seats themselves fold out to provide cushioned armrests. The rear seat is reminiscent of a pair of overstuffed easy chairs, separately adjustable and with elegant vanity units incorporating the chauffeur's microphone on the right side, and a fine clock on the left.

An ad in the British magazine *Motor* dated April 4, 1934, appears to refer to this car:

> Limousine Landaulet, 1930 Cad, double enclosed VandenPlas, leather forward, occasionals, £295, Alpe and Saunders, Providence Court, North Audley St [opposite Selfridges].

No one seems to know what happened to the car after that, until it showed up in a July 1959 ad in *The Self-Starter*, the monthly newsletter of the Cadillac-LaSalle Club, in which Jeffrey Watts of Levittown, Pennsylvania, was offering the car for sale. The ad read:

> 1930–31 Cadillac V16 with English built body; originally owned by Guinness of stout fame; designed by Van den Plas and built by Lendrum and Hartmann, Ltd. RHD, compartmented, folding landau back. English headlights (large), upholstery moth eaten but beautiful, paint rough, mechanically looks excellent [$300 … or maybe less].

According to Yann Saunders, the car showed up "in a deplorable state" at the May 1974 auction of cars that had been part of Movieland–Cars of the Stars in Buena Park, California, where it failed to find a buyer. In his list of surviving V-16 cars, Rick LeForge placed it at Lyon Classic Cars in Los Angeles. At some point, legendary V-16 expert "Cadillac Jim" Pearson acquired the car and still had it in 1976. He sold the unique vehicle to collector and auctioneer James Leake of Tulsa, Oklahoma, who undertook a substantial restoration. Yann Saunders saw the car in Tulsa in 1978, while the restoration was in progress.

Mr. Leake chose red for the car's body, with maroon fenders, body moldings, wheels and hood vent doors. The interior is trimmed in a dusty rose leather for the chauffeur's area and a similar shade of plush or velour fabric for the passenger compartment, with matching carpets. In the 1970s many high-end or aspirational automobiles were trimmed in napped fabrics. One recalls actor Ricardo Montalban crooning on TV commercials that a certain Chrysler model was offered in "genuine Corinthian leather or reeech crotched velour."

The Cadillac landaulette made its way to Europe again, and as late as 2011 it was photographed in the Louwman Automobile Museum in The Hague, Netherlands. On February 7, 2013, English auction house Bonhams offered the car at their Les Grandes Marques du Monde auction in Paris. It sold for €108,100 ($142,605) including buyer's premium. Then on May 31, 2014, Lucky Collector Car Auctions in Tacoma, Washington, offered the car at its Spring Classic Auction, but there was no sale. Meanwhile, Cosmopolitan Motors, LLC had the car for sale at a price of $350,000. Offered again by Lucky at their Fall Classic auction on August 31, 2014, the car failed to sell.

On January 15, 2020, Worldwide Auctioneers offered the landaulette at its Scottsdale Auction in Arizona. On that occasion the car brought a sale price of $152,500 (not including buyer's premium).

34

Simple Sedan

Bob Crane of Toms River, New Jersey, owns a nice collection of vintage cars, including several V-16 Cadillacs. He bought his first V-16 in April 1967 for $500 from a man in Beachwood, New Jersey, named Robert W. Ripley. Mr. Ripley drove a garbage truck, and he had survived a terrifying accident in which he'd fallen from a truck and his head landed in the path of the wheels. Soft sand saved his life, and he came away with nothing worse than tread marks on his face.

The car in question was a Series 4375-S seven-passenger sedan. Of the 3,248 V-16 cars that Cadillac built in the extended model year of 1930–1931, the 4375-S sedans were the most numerous, accounting for 501 units or something over 15 percent of the total production. These were roomy cars with full-width auxiliary seats ("jump seats") forming a middle row of seating. They were used as family sedans, corporate cars, and high-end livery vehicles, and most of them worked for their living. Nevertheless, with their fine interior appointments and careful construction, they were among the more elegant examples of the V-16 model line.

The V-16 sedan that Bob Crane acquired was loaded with challenges. The wood inside was in bad shape, including both the structural members that give the body its shape and strength, and the decorative inlaid trim in the passenger compartment. Mr. Ripley had owned the car since at least as early as March 18, 1949 (the date stamped on the registration certificate from the New Jersey Department of Motor Vehicles). For some time he had stored the stately vehicle in a building with a leaky roof, and before leaving it there, he had removed the hood and the engine valve covers. By the time Bob Crane came along, the engine was seized.

Bearing engine number 700208 and body number 112, Bob Crane's car had originally been painted several hues of green. The chassis, fenders, body moldings, and window reveals were what the Rinshed Mason Company called Highland Green, with the cowl, the lower panels of the doors, and the lower part of the rear body painted Rich Green. The wheels were Vanderbilt Green and an Apple Green body stripe highlighted the car's moldings and character lines. The interior was trimmed in green-gray wool broadcloth woven by William Wiese & Company, and sewn and installed by Fleetwood craftsmen. By the time Mr. Ripley put the car in storage, it had been repainted black with light brown wheels.

This V-16 sedan had been shipped new to Cadillac's Philadelphia branch on Shackamaxon Street in February of 1930, and optional equipment mentioned in the shipping order was limited to wire wheels and fender-mounted spare tires. No one today knows who first purchased this imposing motor car, but the buyer would have paid something over $6,000 for it at a time when ten fully-optioned Chevrolets could have been had for that sum.

Every hair in place. **These Series 4575-S sedans were the most frequently ordered of the 1930–31 V-16s. Deep red and plum color scheme on this car lends warmth to a very dignified vehicle. Stylized heron radiator ornament was an optional accessory that could be purchased from the dealer or ordered from the factory (courtesy Mark Hyman/Hyman, Ltd.).**

Of the surviving Cadillac V-16s, the 4375-S sedans are not as well represented as their original production numbers would indicate. Some of them were used until they wore out. Wartime scrap drives were more likely to capture more utilitarian vehicles than the sportier cars that owners might have hidden away or may simply have refused to part

A period photograph of the car. **The identities of the fashionably-dressed gentlemen posing with the car are unknown (courtesy Alan Merkel).**

***A rusty, dusty survivor.* As acquired by Bob Crane, the car shows the effects of long-term storage in a leaky building (courtesy Bob Crane).**

with. And the payoff for restoring a rusted and heavily weathered sedan is likely to be significantly less than for rehabilitating, say, a roadster (leading some to restore a sedan as an open car).

Bob Crane had his V-16 sedan for about a year, during which time he tried over and over again to free up the engine, with no success. Time and again he would rock it forward and backward, with the transmission in gear, in an effort to use the car's own inertia to break the pistons free. In 1969, he put the car up for sale and handed off the task of getting the engine to turn.

Alan Merkel had recently returned from military service in Vietnam and was a couple of months away from his discharge when he saw an ad in *Hemmings Motor News* for a 1930 Cadillac V-16 sedan, not running but complete, and in need of a total restoration. Without hesitating, Alan and his wife travelled to New Jersey from their home near Pittsburgh to see the car. Alan bought it, attached a hitch to the front bumper, and towed the car with a U-Haul pickup to a rented garage near his parents' home in Pennsylvania. There it would wait until Alan and his family moved to their new home in Virginia. At a rest stop on the Pennsylvania Turnpike, someone tried to buy the Cadillac, reassuring Alan that he'd made a good purchase.

During the next sixteen years, Alan worked on the car when his work and his family obligations permitted. He was transferred to California and took the car and crates full of parts with him. It was there, about five years after he bought the car, that he started it for the first time. Transferred back east to Pittsburgh, Alan kept working slowly but determinedly. Much of the wood (which forms the skeleton of early thirties car bodies such as this one) was weather-damaged and had to be replaced. He tried to do the work himself, but decided to have most of it done by a restoration shop, where the slats and some of the headers in the roof were replicated and replaced. By the mid–1980s Alan had the car back on the road, with nearly everything but the upholstery taken care of. In 1984, he was driving the big Cadillac significant distances, but the next year he learned that the car he had really dreamed of owning (a Series 4380 V-16 all-weather phaeton) was available. In order to acquire that car (which would require another 25 years to restore) he sold the seven-passenger sedan in October 1985 in the flea market at Hershey.[29] The buyer was John F. Folino of Northville, Michigan.

John Folino completed the restoration process. He finished the interior and installed a new fabric roof insert (in 1930 the auto industry had not yet learned how to stamp a one-piece steel roof for closed cars). He painted the car a combination of dark red on the body, and deep maroon on the fenders, chassis, moldings and outlined cove areas on the hood and the sides of the cowl. In February 2017, the Series 4375-S sedan showed up for sale on the Internet website of vintage auto dealer Hyman, Ltd. wearing two shades of maroon with gray broadcloth upholstery. In less than two weeks, the car was sold.

29. Among old car enthusiasts, "Hershey" is shorthand for the annual Fall Meet of the Eastern Division of the Antique Automobile Club of America. It draws vendors, restorers, collectors, spectators and others from all over the world.

35

Tragedy on the Test Track

SINCE THE BEGINNING OF THE automobile industry, manufacturers have engaged in testing of their products for a wide range of reasons. It's important to know that the car runs, and that it does so dependably. Otherwise, the manufacturer will not stay in business. It's also important to know whether, and under what conditions, it can be operated safely. Even before the days of Federal automotive safety regulations, the National Highway Transportation Safety Administration, and the Insurance Institute for Highway Safety, if a maker sold a dangerous vehicle, and people were harmed, the moral and material repercussions for all involved would be substantial. And finally, the capabilities and characteristics of the car are important marketing points that can distinguish it from competing products, and attract customers.

General Motors Corporation opened its Milford Proving Ground in 1924, and the facility was the automobile industry's first of its kind. It covered 1,125 acres (now expanded to about 4,000) in Milford, Michigan, which was then a small, relatively isolated village about a day's drive from Detroit. The rolling hills on the property allowed engineers to construct test tracks and road courses to simulate any imaginable road surface or maneuvering challenge. Suspension and structural designs could be subjected to any stress the real world could dish out, and the results could be studied and analyzed. High-speed and endurance testing could be done on a company-owned, closed course under controlled conditions. The next year, Ford and Packard opened their own proving grounds, and today it's standard practice.

The V-16 cars that Cadillac introduced in 1930 represented a major advance over previous models, in terms of elegance, comfort, and power. The new chassis and drivetrain had ample power and strength to carry the heavy, luxuriously-finished bodywork that well-to-do customers increasingly favored during the late 1920s. Determining just what that automotive "platform" was capable of was the goal of a testing program at the Milford Proving Ground. A team of "experimental drivers" headed by Willard ("Big Bill") Rader put prototypes and specially-prepared examples of production cars through their paces, in terms of endurance, speed and other performance criteria, with a view to continual improvement of the product.

When today we see video recordings of a contemporary car, say a Cadillac CTS-V, being tested or demonstrated under extreme circumstances (perhaps a "hot lap" at the Nürburgring), we are accustomed to seeing the driver outfitted with a fire-resistant racing suit, a five-point harness, and an engineered racing helmet. Often as not there's a full roll cage. Things were much different in 1930. Seat belts (let alone full harnesses) were still a novelty, even in aircraft. "Helmet" meant a soft aviator's head cover with detachable goggles that kept the wind out of one's hair and kept the scalp warm. Ordinary cloth overalls kept dirt and grease off of one's clothing, and everything was, quite literally, "seat of the pants."

It is amazing to imagine these brave souls coaxing early automobiles through high-speed runs with only rudimentary safety measures. The June 30, 1927, issue of "Clearing House: Co-Operative Bulletin of the Cadillac Organization" contains an extensive and exciting account of the nearly ten-hour endurance run in which a stripped-down LaSalle roadster maintained an average speed (including pit stops) of 95.2 miles per hour. Tires were run until they were threadbare (as shown in an accompanying photograph). The primary driver (Bill Rader, relieved by fellow GM driver Gus Bell) wore road grime and dust on the exposed parts of his face. The whole spectacle was witnessed by representatives of the press and of the Cadillac distribution network.

Three years later on July 15, 1930, a prototype 1930 Cadillac V-16 roadster was taken on a high-speed run at the Milford proving ground. The V-16 was a newly designed engine, larger and more powerful than any motor car engine GM had produced. The roadster likely had the 3.47 to 1 rear axle ratio that was installed on some of the early production V-16 cars.

At the wheel was Gus Bell. At 33 years old, he was an experienced dirt-track auto racer, and had been working as a professional experimental driver with GM for seven years. With him in the cockpit was 22-year-old newlywed Glenn McCallum, a third-year student at the General Motors Institute of Technology in Flint, Michigan. GMI students often participated in the testing and development work at the proving ground as part of their studies. The car was a prototype or specially built model with notable differences from production V-16 roadsters. The sides of the cowl had thin louvers instead of hinged vent doors like those in the hood side panels. The compartment doors on the valence panel below the body sill were plain, like the 1929 and 1930 V-8 cars. The running boards were covered with plain, fine-ribbed rubber mats. And the headlights were connected by a bar with the rectangular V-8 badge instead of the V-16 badge with red cloisonné background. The instrument panel was undecorated, with only a speedometer and one other smaller dial. To cut down on weight and wind resistance, the windshield, folded convertible top, and rear-mounted spare tire had been removed, but the fenders, bumpers, horns, and lights had been left in place. A surviving photograph shows Mr. Bell looking down the very long hood (which seems even longer without the windshield).

During the course of the run, something went wrong. The prevalent theory was that a tire had blown at or near 112 miles per hour, and Mr. Bell had lost control of the car. In any event, the big roadster left the track, flew through a fence, and ran down an embankment. Both occupants were thrown out, and Mr. Bell died instantly. Mr. McCallum died on the way to the hospital. GM engineers pored over the mangled wreckage, not satisfied that a tire blowout was the whole story. It is not known whether their investigation produced a more complete explanation.

One of the photographs of the car after it came to rest clearly shows that the treads of both front tires had been worn smooth except at the outside edges. That's the sort of wear pattern one would expect from over-inflation. And since the day's assignment was to take the car up to top speed, it would make sense that the air pressure in the tires would have been increased above the normal specifications. That the tread is worn smooth in the middle lends some support to the theory that a tire blew and that led to the crash. After the car came to rest, both front tires were deflated, and the right one had come halfway

On the job. **General Motors experimental driver Gus Bell poses with a prototype or "test mule" 1930 Cadillac V-16 roadster. Windshield and top have been removed for reduced wind resistance. Older V8 badge on bar between headlights belies the V-16 power beneath the hood. Mr. Bell and engineering student Glenn McCallum were killed when this car left the test track at 112 m.p.h. (courtesy Yann Saunders/The [New] Cadillac Database).**

off the rim. It would have been hard to prove that one or the other had failed before the car left the track.

Newspaper accounts of the accident included photos of the deceased, including one of Gus Bell at the wheel of the LaSalle roadster that Bill Rader had piloted for the 1927 endurance feat. One paper printed a tribute acknowledging that tragedy is sometimes the price of knowledge.

36

Reload, Re-Use, Recycle

THE 1930 CADILLAC V-16 ENGINE number 702987 was installed at the factory in a Series 4260 sport phaeton. This jaunty, open body style was indeed sporty with the top down. With the top raised, it looked, even when new, a bit dated and old-fashioned. The forward edge of the top header extended beyond the top of the windshield, and there were no side windows to keep out rain or wind. With the side curtains in place, the anachronistic effect was intensified. Sport phaetons (and touring cars) were on their way out. Of the 3,250 1930 and 1931 V-16s produced, only 82 were sport phaetons. By way of contrast, 250 of the Series 4380 "all weather phaetons" (with roll-up windows and a fitted, weather-tight top) were shipped in the same two-year period.

By the early 1940s, fate had consigned this particular sport phaeton to a less dignified existence. It was purchased inexpensively by a young southern California man named Charles Dimmitt. Mr. Dimmitt took the Cadillac on a trip to Las Vegas, Nevada, and back, and not long afterwards he discarded the sport phaeton bodywork and set about making the chassis and drivetrain part of a racing "special." Thus, this once-luxurious V-16 joined the various cars that contributed their engines, frames or other parts to the hot rod craze. Many GIs returning from service in World War II (and other young car nuts) had taken up the sport of cobbling together a fast car out of found or cheaply-bought parts, and running their creations on dry lake beds or other improvised tracks to see who could go fastest. Racers formed clubs, and the clubs formed associations that organized the time trials and races, and determined who had bragging rights.

Charles Dimmitt was a member of the Autocrats, a club under the auspices of the Southern California Timing Association. He dreamed big. He became president of the club, and he built a big car. He started with the chassis and engine from the sport phaeton, and reorganized them. He lengthened the frame and positioned the engine well behind the front wheels. The lower half of a 1939 Lincoln Zephyr coupe formed the main portion of the bodywork. Added sheet metal covered the frame rails as they passed by the engine on the way to the spring shackles in front of the radiator. The radiator shell came from a 1937 Ford pickup truck. Painted green and orange, the car seemed to go on for days. Some considered it to have been the biggest car that ran on the dry lakes in the 1940s.

Behind the V-16 engine was its stock clutch and transmission. A second transmission, placed backwards behind the first, was intended to increase the final drive ratio. In 1948, Mr. Dimmitt raced his creation at El Mirage Dry Lake in Class D, but at 107.52 mph, his best time was almost 20 mph behind the fastest speed that day. Rather than re-engineer his behemoth to try for more speed, Mr. Dimmitt elected to transform it from a serious racer into a street rod in which to cruise and be seen.

Dry lakes racer. **Charles Dimmitt took a salvage yard Cadillac V-16, lengthened the chassis, adapted Lincoln Zephyr bodywork, and took his beast to El Mirage Dry Lake in 1948 to try for a speed record. The car was ferocious, but not fast enough to beat the competition (courtesy Dick Shappy).**

Returning the frame to something like its original dimensions, Mr. Dimmitt removed the second transmission and attached (or continued to use) an independent front suspension setup that used coil springs and telescoping shock absorbers (rather than the solid axle, semi-elliptic sprung front suspension that stock 1930 and '31 Cadillac V-16 cars were built with). The body used 1930 Cadillac V-16 fenders, but the hood, cowl, passenger compartment and rear body were designed and executed by Mr. Dimmitt. A number of 1932 Cadillac parts were used (such as the front fender parking lights). The radiator grille was a modification of the 1933 Cadillac grille, and the bumpers were fabricated to look like 1933 Cadillac V-8 or V-12 bumpers. The wheels sported large, purpose-built, knock-off spinners with V-16 emblems decorating them.

In its shape and contours, the body evoked many of the sleek, streamlined sport coupes of the day, even if the car would dwarf most of them. The workmanship on the shaped panels and fabricated doors and openings was impressively professional, and Mr. Dimmitt must have turned some heads. He appears to have made and enjoyed a street-legal car of unusual and unique character, although some bits seem never to have been constructed—hood side panels, a completed instrument panel. One of the top panels of the hood either had not been made, or had been lost along the years. And fabricated items like the bumpers and the hub spinners waited in vain for plating. In his later years, Charles Dimmitt restored old Indian motorcycles. Paul Schinnerer, who knew him as Charlie, said that he was a very accomplished metalworker and a member of the pile driver's union. He recalls that the roadster wasn't quite finished when Mr. Dimmitt died in 1975. But there were about 50 motorcycles at Charlie Dimmitt's funeral.

***From racer to street rod.* Mr. Dimmitt switched gears and repurposed his dry lakes racer as a street roadster. A talented metalsmith, he fabricated much of the bodywork himself and adapted Cadillac parts for the rest. The project was still unfinished when he passed away (courtesy Dick Shappy).**

The Dimmitt roadster passed to a fellow named Art, who kept it but didn't start or run the car. Art passed away and the project remained incomplete.

Not long ago, a California friend of restorer and collector Dick Shappy called him on the phone and told him about a very interesting V-16 Cadillac located outside Los Angeles. Intrigued, Mr. Shappy persuaded his friend to go take photographs of the car, from which he discerned that the engine was from a 1930 or 1931 Cadillac. Once he had the engine number, he could determine that it originally powered a Series 4260 sport phaeton. The photos showed a time-worn but solid artifact from an important era in automotive history.

Informed by the seller that only cash was acceptable, Mr. Shappy flew from his home in Rhode Island, laden with currency. Having successfully salved the curiosity of the TSA personnel, he still had to convince the seller to honor their bargain over competing offers from two other interested folks. In fact, when Mr. Shappy met with him the seller said that he had decided he wanted more money, and Mr. Shappy said he'd have to think about it. Talking the matter over with some knowledgeable friends he became convinced the car was worth it, and he persuaded the seller to take the cash he'd brought, let him have the car, and let him have time to come up with the rest of the seller's new price.

***Opposite: Veteran engine.* Charles Dimmitt replaced the Cadillac updraft carburetors with Stromberg downdraft units. Air intake scoop atop carburetor was installed by Dick Shappy. Steering shaft passes parallel to the engine manifolds to reach the steering box in front of the engine (courtesy Dick Shappy).**

Business-like cockpit. Dick Shappy finished the interior of the car in a straightforward manner consistent with similar cars of the period. Instrument panel is from a 1932 Cadillac. Gear lever and hand brake are original to the V-16 chassis (courtesy Dick Shappy).

Once he had successfully acquired Mr. Dimmitt's beast, Dick Shappy had it shipped to his facility in Warwick. After examination, he decided to limit his restoration efforts to making the car drivable and (relatively) safe. He believed that, in the form he found the car, it represented a significant historical treasure, linked as it was to the era of dry lakes racing and the age of customizing and personalizing cars.

In 2012 this unique V-16 car was featured in two consecutive issues of the Cadillac-LaSalle Club's monthly publication *The Self-Starter*, with photographs and information about its history and highlights.[30] As the custom roadster sits today, a '32 Cadillac instrument panel has been installed and the missing interior has been cut, sewn and fitted. But the rough primer finish on the body panels and the oxidation patina on the trim parts remain. Mr. Shappy had a hood top panel fabricated to match the surviving one, but he left the engine compartment open on the sides.

Dick Shappy would take the Dimmitt roadster out for a drive from time to time, and he describes it as a fast running car, with an engine that runs really well. He is inclined to believe what was told to him, that Charles Dimmitt installed a high performance camshaft.

Put up for sale on Mr. Shappy's website "as is" in March 2011, the car ultimately caught the attention of a new caretaker, and in 2017 a deal was done and it was off to a new home. So far, this Cadillac has been a flashy supercar, a cheap used car, a purpose-built racer, a custom project, and an historic artifact. That's quite a series of past lives. Now, let's see what the future holds.

30. Milici, Chris, "The Dimmittmobile," *The Self-Starter,* Cadillac-LaSalle Club, Inc., Detroit, MI, Vol. 55, No. 2, February 2012; pp. 18–22.

Milici, Chris, "'Hot Rodding' Cadillac Style—Cadillac action on the dry lakes," *The Self-Starter,* Cadillac-LaSalle Club, Inc., Detroit, MI, Vol. 55, No. 3, March 2012; pp. 11–15.

37

Old Yeller

Some people like to give their cars names. For some a car is like a riding (or racing) horse—it must be fed, sheltered and cared for, and it will serve its owner if the owner meets those obligations. Rick LeForge of Menlo Park, California, has owned five Cadillac V-16s over the years and some other Cadillacs as well. The V-16s had names, and one of them was named after the title character in a Walt Disney movie about a stray dog that a boy adopts and loves.

That car was a Series 4355 imperial sedan cabriolet (body number 4), a five-passenger limousine with leather-covered roof, solid upper rear quarters and decorative landau irons. It was one of 52 built, and the new car price would have been about $6,400. Old Yeller got its name from the bright yellow paint job it wore when Rick bought the car. When new, it had a more subdued color scheme, with milk-chocolate brown fenders, chassis, hood sides and upper surfaces (including the wide beltline molding). The door panels, the lower portion of the body in back, the reveals or offsets around the door windows, and the "widow's peak" down the top of the hood were a lighter *café au lait* color. But the car had been restored in 1948 (including replating the chrome trim, repainting the car, and re-covering the top in light-colored canvas).

We don't know the name of the original purchaser, only that the car was shipped from the factory February 13, 1930, to Los Angeles. The second owner, a man named Haswell Parker, told Rick LeForge what was probably a fanciful story that the car had been one of six that were prepared for the New York Auto Show and that subsequently toured the country. This car, he said, was "liberated" (purchased) before the tour was finished.

Rick first saw Old Yeller during the 1950s, on the street, in a community in the south bay area around San Francisco. He recalls that a friend may have seen it first and told him where to look. He said that the owner wanted an outlandish price for the car (a relative term indeed, as at the time, $1,000 for a pristine Cadillac V-16 would have seemed outlandish). Not content to give up, Rick and his friend revisited the owner repeatedly, each time showing up in a different Cadillac V-16. Eventually, the owner agreed to part with the car for what Rick describes as a "reasonable price."

By the time Rick wrote about Old Yeller in 1963 for the Cadillac-LaSalle Club's newsletter,[31] the odometer showed 50,000 miles. The chrome plating job that had been done in 1948 was deteriorating, but the paint and the top looked fine. The original upholstery was almost like new. Rick used the car for a "go to meet" car participating in club and other enthusiast activities with it.

---

31. LeForge, Rick, "Happiness Is a Sixteen Cylinder Cadillac," *The Self-Starter*, Cadillac-LaSalle Club, Inc., Detroit, MI, Vol. V, No. 6, April 1963: pg. 11.

***A formal five-passenger limousine.* Fully restored in the Nethercutt Collection, the sedan cabriolet that Rick LeForge used to call "Old Yeller" shows a well-proportioned and dignified presence. Windowless rear quarters provide ample privacy. "Cadillac Herald" radiator ornament harks back to the early days of the marque's history (courtesy The Nethercutt Collection).**

In the mid–1960s, mere mortals could afford the big Classic cars of the 'thirties, and Rick LeForge was fond of the multi-cylinder Cadillacs. In early 1965, he came to terms with "Cadillac Jim" Pearson regarding Rick's acquisition of a 1933 Cadillac V-16 convertible coupe. In exchange, Rick would give Jim Old Yeller and a 1931 Cadillac V-12 sport phaeton (then a restored chassis with a stripped-out body). But Jim lived in Kansas City, Kansas, and Rick was living in the Los Angeles area. So Rick decided to enlist a friend's help and use Old Yeller as a tow vehicle to haul the sport phaeton. On May 20, 1965, the two intrepid adventurers rigged a trailer brake and running lights for the sport phaeton, and set out on a 1500-mile road trip.

Rick kept a log of the trip and regaled Cadillac-LaSalle Club members with a condensed version of it in the club's newsletter *The Self-Starter*.[32] Apart from one flat tire, overheating that was caused by a disconnected water pump shaft (discovered only after they'd removed and boiled out the radiator), and a periodically run-down battery (from all the extra lights), the trip was tiring but successful. Without having warned or prepared Jim Pearson for their arrival, they pulled up to his house at 10:30 p.m. with lights blazing, and enjoyed the expressions on the faces of Jim and his family.

Subsequently, Jim Pearson sold Old Yeller to the Nethercutt collection, where it has been treated to a thorough restoration. The original interior remains exactly the way the Fleetwood craftsmen trimmed it. The big limousine now wears its original color combination and in every way presents the appearance it had when new.

32. LeForge, Rick, "Turn Left at Tucumcari," *The Self-Starter*, Cadillac-LaSalle Club, Inc., Detroit, MI, Vol. VII, No. 11, September 1965: pp. 4–10.

38

Blue Boy

ONE ORIGINAL PURCHASER OF A 1931 Cadillac whose identity we know was United States Representative Ira Clifton Copley. The car that he ordered was a Series 4375 seven-passenger imperial sedan with engine number 703108 and body number 411. He specified "Yale Blue" (which was the color of his alma mater) for the lower body panels and the offsets for the windows. The rest of the car—fenders, chassis, roof and body molding—was black. The front compartment was trimmed in black leather, as was customary for cars intended to be chauffeur-driven. The passenger compartment was upholstered in fine cloth, and privacy was afforded by silk window curtains and a roll-up

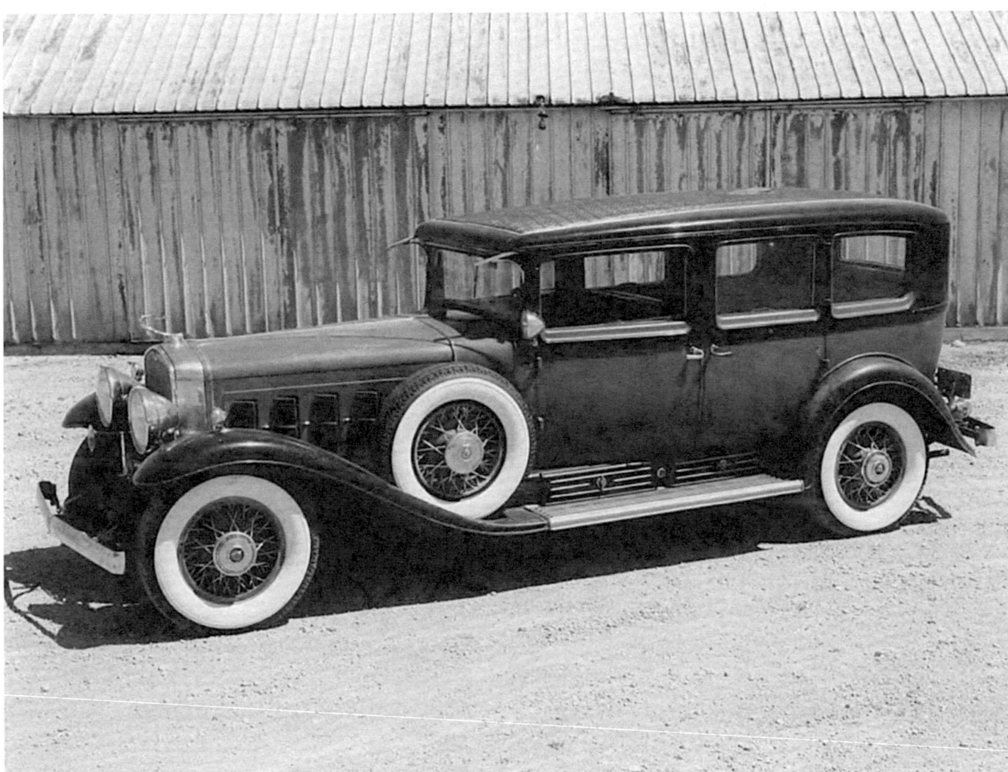

Blue Boy. **Origin of the car's nickname is apparent from the blue paint on the lower part of the body and the window offsets. Original finish shows some wear, but overall the car is very presentable (courtesy John Groendyke).**

window between front and rear compartments. Mr. Copley saw to it that a little bronze medallion, cast with his initials, was affixed to the outside of each of the car's rear doors, just below the window.

Per Mr. Copley's specification, the car came equipped with a Lorraine spotlight on the driver's side, Kelch hot-air heater system with registers in both compartments, front and rear, wire wheels with stainless steel spokes, and dual fender-mounted spare wheels and tires. Another optional accessory on the car, first offered in 1930, was a Cadillac radio. The new V-16 limousine was shipped to Mr. Copley's home town of Aurora, Illinois, on June 18, 1931.

In addition to calling for a radio and Kelch heater, the Cadillac shipping order or "build sheet" for Mr. Copley's car has an interesting instruction that was stricken through before the car was delivered: "INSTALL YALE LOCKS ON EACH SIDE OF HOOD." At this distance from the early 1930s, we can only speculate as to why it might have been thought necessary to secure the engine compartment in that manner.

After graduating college, Ira Copley took over a struggling gas and electric company from his father and built it into a successful conglomerate before selling his interest in it in 1926. In the same timeframe, he began acquiring newspapers in Illinois and later in California. From 1911 to 1922 he represented Illinois's 11th Congressional District as a Republican (except for two years when he threw in with Theodore Roosevelt's Bull Moose Party). By the 1930s, he was a successful man in the newspaper business with the means to purchase and keep a new V-16 Cadillac motor car.

According to one of the subsequent owners of this limousine, Mr. Copley kept the car for the rest of his life, and it remained in his estate for some years after he passed away in 1947. Around 1960, a deliveryman purchased the car from the estate and later sold it to early Cadillac V-16 enthusiast Elmer Franzen. Mr. Franzen, in turn, sold the car to "Cadillac Jim" Pearson.

Gaylord Ray Pearson, Jr., was better known as Cadillac Jim for having amassed a prodigious stock of parts (and an equally prodigious knowledge) of mostly early 1930s Cadillacs. In the 1950s, he had travelled around the Midwest from Cadillac dealer to Cadillac dealer buying up their obsolete parts. He also bought and sold a large number of the Classic Cadillacs, including V-16s, that had survived the scrap metal drives of World War II and the other perils that faced these cars, once they were no longer new. For years, he was the "go-to guy" for anyone trying to restore or maintain a Cadillac from the late '20s and early '30s. He knew all about the cars, and he could provide the necessary parts. Cadillac Jim called our subject V-16 limousine "Blue Boy" and enjoyed its well-cared-for condition and eye-catching color scheme.

Cadillac dealer and long-time enthusiast Bud Tinney recalls seeing the car during the 1960s when he visited Jim Pearson at the latter's home in Kansas City, Kansas. It was then (and remains today) a remarkably well-cared for and pristine automobile. At one point, Mr. Tinney was sitting in the driver's seat while Cadillac Jim in the back seat crooned over the car's intercom, "Buy me! Buy me!" Mr. Tinney recalls that although he was tempted by the delightfully original car, he didn't buy it. Almost, but not quite.

Rick LeForge, another long-time Cadillac V-16 collector and restorer (and friend of Cadillac Jim's), has an explanation for the gentle use this car received during its youth (when most such cars would have been driven a lot and subjected to substantial wear). When the accessory radios were installed, a capacitor was connected at the generator to minimize noise from the engine's ignition system. Jim Pearson had noticed that

A gathering of friends. **From left to right: Evangelist T.L. Osborne, Mrs. Osbourne, Louise and Jim Pearson, Rich LeForge, and Ray Pearson. For decades Jim "Cadillac Jim" Pearson was the "go to" man for V-16 Cadillac parts and know-how. The car on the right is "Blue Boy," a 1931 Cadillac V-16 Series 4375 limousine. Rick LeForge had just driven the car on the left (a 1930 V-16 4355 sedan cabriolet) from California to the Pearsons' home in Kansas City, KS (courtesy Jeff Pearson).**

the capacitor on his car was loose, and that when he went to secure the connection, he observed a small spark. There was apparently a slight but steady current drain as a result of the way the capacitor (or perhaps the entire radio system—control head, circuit box, batteries and speaker) had been installed. Unless the car was driven daily, it would probably have been murder on batteries. If the owner had to recharge (or replace) the battery each time he wanted to use the car, it would not likely get a lot of use.

Subsequent to Jim Pearson's ownership, the big Cadillac became the property of a Massachusetts collector, who sold it in 1992 to Don Armacost, CEO of Peterson Manufacturing Company and owner of the Armacost Museum near Kansas City, Missouri. Thereafter, Ira Copley's well-cared-for limousine, the one Cadillac Jim nick-named "Blue Boy," was owned by John Groendyke of Enid, Oklahoma. In January 2016, Mr. Groendyke

Well-preserved interior. **Showing some wear in spots, the interior of this car is remarkably close to new for a car well over eighty years old. Leather for the front seat and door panels is typical of chauffeur-driven cars of the time. Rear seat foot rests have been pivoted back against the seat cushion. Silk window shades are rolled up above the rear compartment windows. Cargo net remains in place on ceiling of rear compartment for gloves or other light-weight items (courtesy John Groendyke).**

showed the car at the Concours d'Elegance of America at the Inn at St. Johns, Plymouth, Michigan. There it was given the award "Most Original—The Way It Was."

In late 2019, Mr. Groendyke decided to thin out his collection of Classic cars, and Blue Boy was offered for sale. The venue would be the RM Sotheby's Arizona Auction, held in Phoenix, January 16–17, 2020. The winning bidder at that venue got a definite bargain, paying $65,000 (plus buyer's premium) for the car.

39

Papa Tino's Coche

Celestino Camilo Vega, Sr., was born in 1870 in Gijon, on the north coast of the western part of Spain in the province of Asturias. He came to the United States at the age of fourteen and became a citizen in 1896. He went into the cigar making business, and in 1908 he moved from Chicago to Tampa, Florida, and formed the Celestino Vega Cigar Manufacturing Company. For twenty years he did very well selling La Venga cigars, but he closed the factory in 1928 when labor union demands became too onerous, and he retired. For the rest of his years "Papa Tino," as he was known by younger family members, led an active life, enjoying golf (at which he was very good—he held hole-in-one records at two Tampa-area golf courses) and engaging in numerous civic projects.

Cadillac's V-16 cars were announced in late 1929 (not long after the stock market crash) and they were first displayed to the public in early January 1930. Shipments to dealers, however, did not begin in earnest until February. On the nineteenth of that month, thirty-one cars were shipped to dealers across the United States and in Canada. Of that number, two were four-door convertibles, officially designated "all-weather phaetons."

Until the late 1920s, most cars sold in America were what we would call convertibles—roadsters, phaetons, or touring cars—with folding fabric tops. Closed coupes and sedans were a relatively recent development, and they generally cost more. By 1930 closed cars were really catching on, because the occupants were protected from inclement weather. The open cars of the day generally had no windows. Your only protection from a sudden rain storm was to stop the car, raise the top, retrieve and deploy flexible side-curtains, and hope that the wind didn't drive too much water through the gaps around the edges of the side-curtains. In 1929, Cadillac introduced a four-door open V-8 car with roll-up windows that formed a weather-proof seal with the top and the windshield. No more fumbling for side curtains and fussing to get them in place before everyone got wet. The marketing folks called these cars "all-weather phaetons."

The first 1930 V-16 convertibles shipped from the factory were body style 4380 all-weather phaetons. The first one of these built was kept at the factory, destined for former General Motors Corporation finance committee chairman John J. Raskob (famous for causing the Empire State Building to be built). The second and third were delivered to the Claude Nolan Cadillac dealership in Jacksonville, Florida, as part of that February 19 shipment mentioned earlier. The first one of those, the car with engine number 700189, and the first V-16 all-weather phaeton sold to the public, became the pride and joy of Papa Tino Vega. According to Vega family lore, however, the car was originally intended for one of the Fisher brothers at their Miami winter residence. A death in the

Returned to regal glory. Prior owner Steven Nannini of Tucson, Arizona, lovingly brought this 1930 Madame X landaulette back to the magnificence of its early days. Although he elected not to paint it black, the light tan cloth top covering is consistent with what the first customer requested when the car was sold. The interior fabrics and trimming have been painstakingly reproduced (courtesy Joseph Scott).

1930 Madame X Landaulette. The collapsible rear quarter of this body style converts a formal limousine into an open-air carriage for touring. Later Madame X styles, like this one, traded the upright, split windshield for a fashionably raked one-piece design. Shipped new to Antwerp, this car later served with a fire department in Switzerland, before returning to the United States (courtesy Yann Saunders).

1930 Roadster. The Series 4302 roadster was the least expensive of the V-16 styles offered by Cadillac. Ironically, it is the one that seems to be most sought after by modern collectors. This one had devolved into a bunch of parts strewn across a field in Virginia. Completely restored, the former basket case now resides in sparkling splendor at the San Diego Automotive Museum (courtesy Robert McGinnis).

Opposite: A rare non–Fleetwood 1930 V-16. This boat-tailed speedster was designed and built by the recently-formed Italian coachbuilder Pininfarina for an Indian Maharajah. Cadillac allowed only a few bare chassis to be sold, hoping to ensure that the image of the V-16 in the mind of the public was not sullied by poor designs or sloppy workmanship. This car, retored to its original color scheme and seen at the 2005 Pebble Beach Concours d'Elegance, is a unique gem (courtesy Ronald Verschoor).

1930 Series 4235 convertible coupe. Roll-up windows for open cars were a relatively recent development in 1930. This let the buyer have the sportiness of a roadster without the bother of trying to deploy side curtains in a sudden rainstorm. This car was sold new to a businessman in Buffalo, New York. Since 1966, it has been in the collection of Josiah Lilly III, now part of the Heritage Museums and Gardens that he founded in Sandwich, Massachusetts (courtesy Heritage Museums and Gardens, Sandwich, Massachusetts).

1930 town sedan. The Series 4361-S town sedan came was a five-passenger, "close coupled" car with a permanently-mounted trunk. With a folding rack on which an additional trunk could be mounted, this style was a perfect car for long trips or for everyday family use (courtesy Wellington Morton).

Inviting driver's seat of a 1930 town sedan. A comfortable, adjustable front seat faces a full set of instruments and conveniently placed controls. Fine inlaid wood adorns the door and continues above the instrument panel. Lush wool broadcloth and fine carpet surround the occupants. A small crank over the windshield raises the windshield glass for ventilation on warm days (courtesy Wellington Morton).

Creamy leather upholstery of a 1930 closed coupe. The driver's seat of this Series 4376 coupe shows the split windshield of the "Pennsylvania Fleetwoods," the cars built in the old Fleetwood Metal Body Company plant before all operations were moved to Detroit. The seats, door panels and dash pad are covered in ecru leather, complemented by light tan carpet and scalloped walnut trim boards on the doors. The hinged windshield panes can be unlatched and the lower edge pushed outward to let air enter the cabin on warm days (courtesy Darin Schnabel and RM Sotheby's).

A 1930 Series 4380 all-weather phaeton before restoration. This four-door convertible sedan (a style then known as an "all-weather phaeton") would require an extensive restoration to bring it back to its original state. Veteran Cadillac dealership owner Bud Tinne, who oversaw the restoration, confided that he thought the all-weather phaeton design was the hardest to restore because of the work required to line up the door openings and body pillars (courtesy Bud Tinney).

A 1930 V-16 rebodied as a wood-bodied convertible coupe. In the early 1930s, "woodie" body construction was generally limited to station wagons, depot hacks, and other light commercial vehicles. Not until the early 1940s would that technique spread to passenger cars in significant numbers. The engine and chassis under this car had long since lost their original body when a Korean War veteran in Escanaba, Michigan (who made and installed replacement woodie bodies for cars originally built with them) decided to build and install a convertible coupe body (courtesy Mark Thomas).

Crafted by custom coachbuilder Van den Plas. One of the few bare V-16 chassis that left Detroit to be bodied by one of the great coachbuilders of the day, this sedan by the Belgian firm Van den Plas appeared at the London Motor Show. It was purchased by Nawab of Bahawalpur, a local ruler in what is now Pakistan. In this photo, the restoration of the car is nearing completion in Pakistan. The design and fittings are entirely consistent with Cadillac (and Fleetwood) standards of art and craftsmanship. Stephen Grebel headlamps replaced the original Cadillac Tilt-Ray units. The raked windshield is similar to Fleetwood's Madame X design, but incorporates a top swivel hinge for ventilation. The sun visor was installed by Barker & Co. of London. Items yet to be completed include the missing crank hole cover and the bright-metal windsplits for the hood vent doors (courtesy Amer Ahmad).

A 1932 sedan. 1932 brought rounded edges and fewer straight lines as the concept of streamlining took hold in the transportation industry. This sedan was originally painted in a "Tunis Blue Pearl" color with "Avon Blue Opalescent" for the wheel rims. Owner Quentin Robbins has reproduced that finish on his car. Metallic or iridescent paints were a new thing in 1932, and Cadillac would not resume offering them until 1937. Paint companies experimented with fish scales, ground glass, mica, and metal shavings in an effort to find a coating that would hold up and retain its luster (courtesy Quentin Robbins).

1933 V-16 driver's compartment. By 1933, art deco touches are beginning to show up. The driver of a 1933 V-16 was surrounded by high-class appointments. The use of inlaid exotic wood and high-quality cloth is expanded and refined. The instrument cluster is balanced by the similarly-shaped (and carefully decorated) glove box door with control knobs in between. The lenses covering the gauges are convex to minimize glare, and art deco influences are clear in the numbers and graphics of the gauge faces. An owner could have his name engraved on a small brass plaque (courtesy Mike Fairbairn/RM Sotheby's).

1934 V-16 front ensemble. The 1934-1937 Cadillac V-16 cars enthusiastically embody art deco design themes and aeronautically-inspired streamlining. Elegant biplane bumpers (strengthened here by aftermarket vertical guards) were a one-year-only feature. They proved fragile in practice, even though the mounting brackets were spring-loaded. The flying goddess hood ornament could be ordered (courtesy Steve Plunkett).

1934 V-16 roadster, a latter-day realization. Among the designs that Fleetwood offered, but that were not ordered new by customers was this stunning two passenger roadster. By the mid–1930s the roadster body style was largely obsolete, having been overtaken by convertible coupes with roll-up windows. This car shows just how sporty and flashy a twenty-foot-long automobile could be. Massive proportions of the 1934–1937 V-16 chassis are highlighted by the two-seat passenger compartment. Separate fenders and absence of running boards evoke contemporary race car design. Opening in the raised hood panel accommodates the cowl vent (courtesy Ronald Verschoor).

1936 town sedan. Although the wheelbase is the longest of any production American car (154 inches), and the overall length is a hair shy of twenty feet, the proportions of the town sedan body lend a visual appeal and litheness uncommon to such a large car. This car was bought in the mid–1990s as a parts car for another restoration, but the purchaser decided to restore it instead (courtesy Chad Chambers).

1937 V-16 sedan. The accessory trunk adds to an already impressively long automobile. The effects of the mid–1930s streamlining craze on automotive design are readily apparent in the sculpted lines of this sleek sedan. Cigar-shaped door handles, teardrop head- and taillights, "speed streak" louvers, pontoon fenders and curves everywhere else make the car look fast standing still. This car arrived in Great Britain early in its life and remained there for years (courtesy Steve Plunkett).

Opulent passenger area of a 1937 V-16 limousine. This inviting enclave is as comfortable as it looks. Hidden roll-down silk shades for the rear and quarter windows can provide extra privacy, and the window behind the driver's seat keeps conversations confidential. The seat back cushion and lower cushion adjust separately, fore and aft, and the side armrests sport smoking kits and storage pockets. Cadillac offered a wide selection of fabrics and stitching patterns to suit the tastes of discerning customers (courtesy Steve Plunkett).

1937 formal limousine. First owned by Hollywood mogul Edgar J. "Eddie" Mannix, this car is rumored to have been loaned to Vivien Leigh and Clark Gable during filming of *Gone with the Wind*. Leather roof covering and closed rear quarters lend an air of formality to an already dignified motor car. Current owner Skip Tetz showed this car and achieved a First in Class award at the 2016 Pebble Beach Concours d'Elegance (courtesy Skip Tetz).

Engine compartment of a side-valve "flathead" V-16. Where the 1930 through 1937 engines were designed to be seen and visually appreciated, the 1938 through 1940 engines were much more subdued in appearance. This one is barely visible, deep in its bay, under the air cleaners, carburetors, and manifolds. These business-like power plants produced the same horsepower with half the number of moving parts, significantly less weight, and a low profile that accommodated more modern styling trends (courtesy Tom Hamilton).

1939 formal limousine. The 1938 through 1940 V-16 cars shared their body shells with the top series of the V-8 Cadillacs (Series 75). This Series 9033F body style featured solid upper rear quarters (no quarter windows) and leather roof covering. With a large, dignified car to start with, these additional attributes accentuated privacy and elegance (courtesy Tim Stentiford, Motorland Classic Cars).

Interior of a 1939 V-16 imperial sedan. Seen through the leather-trimmed opening of the imperial division window, the wool broadcloth and inlaid wood trim show the understated elegance of a late-series V-16 passenger compartment. The cloth material selected by the man who restored this car for the rear compartment turned out to be a Rolls-Royce fabric selection. Chauffeur compartments were typically upholstered in leather, then considered a more utilitarian material (courtesy *The Self-Starter*).

A rare custom-bodied late-series V-16. The Derham Custom Body Company of Rosemont, Pennsylvania, was one of the few that survived the Great Depression and the Second World War. This variation on a Series 9057 coupe was ordered by DuPont executive Harry G. Haskell, and the Derham records for the project have survived. The smooth, swooping curve from the roof backward, the leather roof covering, and the formal backlight are some of the modifications made to create a unique V-16 coupe (courtesy The Nethercutt Collection).

1930 V-16 engine. Designer Owen Milton Nacker crafted Cadillac's overhead-valve V-16 engine to be seen and appreciated as a work of art. This beautifully rehabilitated engine once again displays the painstaking attention to detail that characterized the spectacular 1930 V-16 Cadillac powerplant. Wiring and tubing is mostly concealed, and porcelain, enamel and brushed aluminum surfaces gleam. Essentially two straight-eight engines sharing a crankshaft and camshaft, it featured separate fuel, ignition and manifolding for each side (courtesy Jaroslav Koniček).

Fisher family occasioned a change in plans, and the new V-16 was offered to Mr. Vega instead.

Mr. Vega got a great deal of enjoyment and use out of his Cadillac. He played golf every day except Sunday at the Rocky Point Golf Club and in later years at the Palma Ceia Golf and Country Club. He would also take his grandchildren to school in the car or to go swimming at the Sulphur Springs spa. In the early 1950s, Papa Tino hired a house painter to paint the car (with a brush). The chrome parts of the car were painted silver, and the rest of the exterior was painted red. In the mid–1950s, nearing 85 years of age, he realized that he could no longer drive the car, and shortly thereafter it went into storage.

In 1958 and 1959, some high school friends of Papa Tino's granddaughter were given permission to get his car running again. It took some tinkering, but they were able to enjoy local excursions in the car, as other drivers honked and waved. Papa Tino Vega died in 1963, and his Cadillac passed to his son Celestino Camilo Vega, Jr. Sadly, the son died a year later. Papa Tino's only grandson, nicknamed Milo, then inherited the car, which he stored at the cigar factory where he worked, Corral, Wodiska y Ca., Inc., manufacturers of the premium Bering Cigars.[33]

In the early 1980s, Milo Vega agreed to sell his grandfather's Cadillac to collector and restorer Charles LeMaitre of Hardwick, Massachusetts. Mr. LeMaitre didn't have the car

***Protective but not pretty.* The coat of red paint applied by a housepainter was solely to prevent rust. This is the way Alan Merkel received the car in the 1980s. He would begin a meticulous restoration (courtesy Alan Merkel).**

33. The Corral, Wodiska y Ca., Inc., factory was built by Milo Vega's maternal grandfather Manuel Corral, also from Asturias, Spain. The building, at 1302 N 19th St. in Tampa, is now office space.

for long before Gifford Oborne of Warren, New Jersey, bought it from him. Mr. Oborne had built a respectable collection of V-16 Cadillacs, but up to that point he didn't have an all-weather phaeton.

Beginning in the late 1960s, Alan Merkel (then living near Pittsburgh) had been gathering information about the surviving V-16 Cadillac cars. He owned a 1930 V-16 seven-passenger sedan on which he'd almost completed a 16-year restoration. On a cold, snowy day in January 1985, he visited Gifford Oborne, who had graciously permitted Alan to view his collection and to obtain the engine and body numbers from his cars. Mr. Oborne gave Alan free rein to inspect not only his stable of restored cars, but also future projects stored in semi trailers on the property. In one of those trailers, Alan came upon the red V-16 all-weather phaeton from the Vega family, and immediately knew he wanted to own and restore it.

Alan had first seen a picture of a 1930 Cadillac V-16 all-weather phaeton in the September 1962 issue of *The Self-Starter,* given to him by a college friend. Alan joined the Cadillac-LaSalle Club and determined that someday he would own a car like the one in the photo. Seeing the Vega family car in the trailer rekindled that desire. Later, when he spoke to Gifford Oborne, his excitement was amplified when Mr. Oborne said he probably would not be able to complete all the projects he had acquired, and that he would be willing to sell the all-weather phaeton. Alan could not afford to buy the car at that time, but Mr. Oborne kindly agreed to hold the offer open for a year, to permit Alan to come up with the purchase price.

After the restoration. **Alan Merkel poses proudly with his Cameo Ivory V-16 all-weather phaeton. Powerful engine and fast rear axle ratio combine to make this a quick car for such a big Classic (courtesy Alan Merkel).**

Three months early, the following October, Alan Merkel sold his V-16 sedan at the flea market associated with the AACA Eastern Division Meet in Hershey, Pennsylvania,[34] and was able to buy the V-16 all-weather phaeton. The restoration of this car would require 25 years. Although the brushed-on paint job applied by Mr. Vega's house painter had prevented any rust from harming the sheet metal, the underlying wood structure had been heavily damaged by insects. Mr. Oborne had taken apart the two rear doors to begin the work of replacing the wood framework, but he had gone no further.

Alan Merkel worked steadily and meticulously, and finished the restoration in 2010. One V-16 restorer told the author that the all-weather phaeton is the hardest body style to restore, owing to the precise alignment needed for the center-hinged doors with the rest of the body, and the way the windows meet the center posts, the windshield, and the convertible top. Everything has to line up correctly.

Today, the car is painted Cameo Ivory (a Cadillac color from the 1970s) with black for the chassis and the undersides of the fenders. The rear axle gearing is 3.47 to 1, a ratio that Cadillac offered on some of the very early V-16 open cars. That allows the car to maintain highway speeds without "over-revving" the engine, making it a pleasure to drive on modern roads. And Alan does believe in driving and enjoying the car, having logged about 4,000 miles since returning it to the road. He participates in six to eight local shows during the course of a year.

Alan Merkel has communicated with members of the original owner's family, and they were delighted to know that Celestino Camilo Vega, Sr.'s "coche," as he called it, has been so lovingly cared for. No doubt Papa Tino would be pleased, too.

34. The Antique Automobile Club of America's Eastern Division annual meet in Hershey (known simply as "Hershey" to old car people) draws vendors, exhibitors, browsers and buyers from all over the world.

40

An Ex-Pat Returns

A Series 4381 V-16 coupe was one that could not be mistaken for a chauffeur-driven vehicle. It was very clearly a family car, with room for five and with an enclosed luggage compartment in the gracefully curved rear deck behind the cabin. There was also the customary folding rack over the gas tank cover to carry an accessory trunk, should more space be needed. Of the two individual front seats, the one on the right could fold completely out of the way to permit rear seat passengers to enter and leave with ease. The windows were large and gave an airy feel to the passenger compartment, as well as ample opportunity to view the passing world. On the outside, the windows were framed with bright-metal reveal moldings.

Pleasing proportions. **The Series 4381 coupe is a well-balanced design with plenty of window area and graceful body lines. Bright metal reveals for the window are a distinctive touch, similar to the "Madame X" cars. The front passenger seat folds forward to allow entry to a very comfortable rear seat.**

***Plenty of luggage space.* The handle on the rear deck opens a spacious luggage compartment. The fold-down rack accommodates an external trunk.**

This particular car (engine number 703026 and body number 116) was shipped new to Cadillac of Canada in Toronto. It was delivered as a "CKD" or "complete knockdown" vehicle, meaning that it was only partially assembled, and would have to be put together before the purchaser drove it away. Historically, CKD has been a way to avoid paying high importation taxes or tariffs. Curiously, engine number 703026 corresponds to a blank record sheet among the factory shipping documents known as "build sheets." The same is true for the next four engine numbers, and the reason for that is no longer known.

The name of the original purchaser of this Cadillac coupe is not known, but whoever owned it in 1938 brought it with them to Britain for a vacation. As they sometimes do, events intervened, and with the onset of World War II, the owner returned hastily to the States. His car was left to languish, abandoned at a hotel in London's West End. Then in 1956, it showed up on a used car lot on the Great Western Road leading out of London. The dealer was not able to get the car running, and so Mr. John Rolfe of Sussex was able to purchase it, engine partly dismantled, for £50.

Mr. Rolfe did considerable work on the car. Getting the engine going involved such measures as replacing the distributor cap, freeing the pistons, and installing new rings. An extensive repaint of the body and installation of new upholstery were undertaken as well, and the nearly-completed restoration was featured in an article in the November 1962 issue of the British magazine *Motor Sport*.

At about the time that the *Motor Sport* article appeared, Mr. Rolfe moved to San

***Elegant control center.* The driver has plenty of room, and a full complement of instruments (from left to right, fuel gauge, oil pressure, clock, speedometer, coolant temperature, and ammeter). Levers on the steering wheel hub are the light switch and the hand throttle.**

Francisco, and subsequently to Oregon. In those days, an immigrant to the United States could only bring a limited amount of cash with him. On the other hand, he was allowed to bring an automobile, and Mr. Rolfe brought the V-16 coupe with the intention to sell it and use the proceeds for living and other expenses. Sell it he did, to Jon Lundberg of Berkeley, California, who owned it when V-16 enthusiast Craig Watrous saw it about 1963. Mr. Lundberg traded the Cadillac to Joe Mikula for a Series 4376 V-16 2-passenger coupe. About a year later Mr. Watrous acquired the Series 4381 car.

Mr. Watrous kept and enjoyed the five-passenger car, and it was still in his care when he passed away in May 2009. Subsequently, Mr. Stephen Babinsky of Lebanon, New Jersey, purchased the car and he has maintained it as a delightful driver. After fifty-plus years, the repaint that Mr. Rolfe had done shows some checking and a few instances of peeling. But the car is very presentable overall, quite drivable, and a source of pleasure to owner and viewers alike.

41

Roadster Number 73

On June 11, 1930, the Cadillac factory shipped a Series 4302 V-16 roadster to Newark, New Jersey. A two-passenger car with rumble seat accommodations for two more to ride *al fresco*, it had a folding fabric top but no roll-up windows to seal out the elements. The build sheet depicts a black car with "silver leaf" pinstriping and chrome-plating for the hood and cowl vent doors and for the wheel spokes. The only optional equipment specified was a pair of fender-mounted spare tires.

Paradoxically, although the roadster was the least expensive of the (expensive) Cadillac V-16 model line-up, that body style consistently brings the highest sale prices today. No one knows who the original purchaser was, but years later, this particular roadster (body number 73 of the 105 1930–'31 V-16 roadsters) found its way to the collection of pioneering old car enthusiast Albro Case of Windsor Locks, Connecticut (heir to the Case farm equipment manufacturing family). In the 1960s, Mr. Case sold it to restorer Richard Terhune of Charlottesville, Virginia, who undertook a restoration of the roadster. When the work was finished, the car wore maroon paint on the fenders, chassis, wheels, body moldings and deck lid, with a light tan on the hood, cowl, doors and side panels. The passenger compartment and rumble seat were trimmed in maroon leather, and a beige canvas top finished the ensemble. In the course of the restoration process, the original engine (number 701954) was removed, reportedly because of a cracked block, and was replaced with engine number 701070. Engine number 701070 had been rescued from a destroyed Series 4361-S town sedan that had been originally delivered to New York City.[35] (All we know about that town sedan is that it was black with an ivory pinstripe and had a tan broadcloth interior.)

Until the late 1970s, most buyers and owners of V-16 Cadillac cars were unconcerned whether the engine in a particular car was the one that came with it, so long as the existing engine was correct for the year the car was built. Once the big Classics began commanding higher prices, however, and the availability of factory "build sheets" permitted simple verification of the correct numbers for a given Cadillac car, people began to pay more attention to engine swaps.

Mr. Terhune sold the restored V-16 roadster to rare book dealer and antiquities

---

35. Style number 4361-S denoted a five-passenger sedan that was "close-coupled" or configured without the extra footroom (or room for folding auxiliary seats) found in the larger sedan and limousine bodies. In exchange for the interior space, these cars had a built-in luggage trunk behind the body, in addition to the customary folding luggage rack over the gas tank cover (onto which an additional removable trunk could be mounted). Thus, the driver and passengers could bring along more clothing and personal items for extensive travel than might be possible with other body styles.

As restored the first time. **Richard Terhune added wind wings, twin spot lights and Pilot Ray driving lights. The original black paint was replaced with a more colorful scheme. Restorers of open V-16 cars frequently add accessories that were available but not necessarily ordered for that particular car (courtesy Alan Merkel).**

collector Laurence C. Witten II of Easton, Connecticut. In 1972, Mr. Witten sold the car to businessman and philanthropist William Gannett of Hopedale, Massachusetts, who used it for local outings and drove it sparingly. Not entirely happy with the maroon and tan color combination, Mr. Gannett decided to have the car restored again, with a new look. During 1989–1992, Mr. Al Rogers of Charlton, Massachusetts, undertook a complete restoration of the Cadillac, investing over 3,000 hours. Mr. Gannett asked for and received a no-expense-spared treatment for the car, and Al Rogers described him as the perfect client, advancing money when he was going to be away so that the project kept going. On one occasion, Mr. Gannett said that he was "going south" and when Mr. Rogers asked, "To Florida?" Mr. Gannett replied, "No, I don't like the hot weather. I'm going to the South Pole." He took an excursion that circumnavigated Antarctica and used helicopters to bring passengers to points of interest.

Mr. Rogers returned the finished roadster to Mr. Gannett with a dark green body and black fenders, moldings and deck lid. Chrome-plated spokes highlighted the wheels, and the interior was done in tan leather. Once again, beige canvas was fitted for the convertible top (and used to cover the spare tires).

On April 30, 2005, the car was offered at the auction held by Bonhams & Butterfield at the Larz Anderson Auto Museum in Brookline, Massachusetts. The selling price (including premium) was $280,000, just reaching the low end of the auction company's pre-sale estimate. The buyer was Lew Webb, a major collector in Southern California. Twelve years later the roadster showed up at the 2017 Santa Monica auction conducted by

Restored again. At the behest of William Gannett, the 1930 roadster received black paint on chassis and fenders, and dark green on the body. Canvas covers and rear view mirrors grace the spare tires. Once again, chrome-plated spokes highlight the wheels (as called for in the build sheet) (courtesy RM Sotheby's).

The other Number 73. This roadster is part of the collection of the AutoMuseum Volkswagen (Autostadt Zeithaus) in Wolfsburg, Germany. The engine, number 701954, was removed from the car that now has engine number 701070. The body of this car is a modern reproduction of an original Fleetwood roadster body (courtesy Fred Bausch).

RM Sotheby's. At that sale, it brought $797,500, reflecting the current high-price market for V-16 roadsters.

The original engine from the car (number 701954 that Richard Terhune replaced when he conducted the car's first restoration) was sold to William Meffert, another enthusiastic restorer, also from Charlottesville, who worked for Mr. Terhune. In turn, Mr. Meffert sold the engine to fellow restorer Alan Merkel, who later sold it to Oklahoma collector and restorer Walt Dietzel. Mr. Dietzel installed the engine in a V-16 chassis and mounted a reproduction roadster body on it. Somewhere along the line the cracked block or other ailment that occasioned removal of engine number 701954 from its original engine bay was remedied. At this writing, the car Mr. Dietzel assembled rests in the collection of the AutoMuseum Volkswagen in Wolfsburg, Germany, and it has a body tag that indicates that it (like the roadster introduced at the beginning of this chapter) is also number 73. Hmm.

42

A Custom Coach Fit for a Prince

When Cadillac introduced its super-luxury V-16 cars in 1930, there was no intention to limit the marketing effort to the United States. Half a dozen of these cars in an assortment of body styles were shipped by General Motors to Europe for a grand tour of the continent to allow potential prospects to see the cars in person and to appreciate their spectacular design and craftsmanship. General Motors' London sales agent, the firm of Lendrum & Hartman, Ltd., was eager to participate in promoting the new cars, and requested that two bare, right-hand-drive chassis be sent to them, on which would be fixed bodies made in Europe to appeal to the tastes of European customers. In response to the request, chassis bearing engine numbers 702297 and 702298 were shipped from the factory July 9, 1930. Both were then fitted with bodies exquisitely crafted by the Belgian coachbuilding firm of Van den Plas. Engine number 702297 received a very proper and formal landaulette body, made for Queen Wilhelmina of the Netherlands. She did not take delivery (reportedly because she was advised that it could be seen as an unwise extravagance in a time of growing economic difficulty). That car became the property of Arthur Guinness of the famous brewing family (see Chapter 33).

The second bare chassis received a very stylish and sporty close-coupled sedan body with raked windshield, center-hinged doors, and free-standing step plates in place of running boards.[36] From the cowl forward, the car retained Fleetwood design, except that Belgian-made Willocq et Bottin Supralux headlights were substituted for the standard units and the badge bar between the headlights was eliminated (with the V-16 emblem being fastened instead directly to the radiator stone guard). From the windshield back, however, the styling was quite distinctive, though not far removed from what Cadillac offered. The sill line of the body made a dramatic downward dip, contrasting with the level belt line. That's not dissimilar to the "carriage sill" seen on the 4200 series Fleetwood models. The drip molding over the doors descended in a loose "S" curve to become the lower border of the rear roof quarters and back panel. That and the raked windshield are not unlike what can be seen on the Madame X (4100 series) Fleetwood designs. The step plates (and rounded ends of the fenders where the running boards would have met them) are more of a European touch. Although the body has an integral luggage trunk

---

36. This author is heavily indebted to Mr. Amer Ahmad of Lahore, Pakistan, for providing extensive, detailed information about the right-hand drive V-16 Cadillac, engine number 702298, and its ownership history. Without Mr. Ahmad's help, this chapter would not have been possible.

Parked on the street early in its life. **This is the 1930 V-16, engine number 702298, newly bodied as a custom town sedan by Van den Plas and being taken on a tour of Europe by Captain Frederick Hartman (principal of the firm of Lendrum & Hartman, Ltd, GM sales agent in London). Visible distinctive features include step plates instead of running boards, large chrome-plated door hinges on the center-hinged doors, raked windshield, and non-standard headlamps.**

with fitted cases, the body is longer, with a more fluid silhouette, and with more passenger compartment room than Cadillac's town sedan models.[37]

A sunroof could be opened over the front compartment, and the interior featured generous application of inlaid tiger maple, including a substantial beverage service in the rear compartment. The instrument panel and controls are standard Cadillac V-16 components, although the gasoline gauge is calibrated in Imperial gallons. The exterior of the car was painted a light gray and French gray, with the darker shade on the fenders, exposed chassis parts and body belt line. The four exposed hinges on each door were chrome plated and the distinctive door handles were sourced from Italy (the same door handle design may be seen on the Pininfarina-bodied Cadillac V-16 ordered by the Maharajah of Orccha).

An interesting side-note about this and other right-hand-drive V-16 chassis is that the water pump, which is on the right-hand side of the engine, becomes difficult to service without first removing the steering gear box and shaft (which sit right next to the water pump on these cars).

Captain Frederick W. Hartman (one of the "names" in the company) had intended

37. In the Van den Plas design, the integral trunk extends rearward almost to the end of the gasoline tank cover, and there is no room for a luggage rack (and additional trunk) as there is on Cadillac's 4361-S and 4161-S town sedan models.

to use 702298 as a sort of rolling advertisement, driving it around Europe, displaying it at local concours d'elegance and generally demonstrating, to people with the means, that the Cadillac V-16 was equally at home filling the role of a chauffeured limousine, or serving as an owner-driven grand tourer. And once Captain Hartman and the car had made their circuit of the continent, they wound up back in Britain for the London Motor Show. There the car was noticed and appreciated, but it failed to find a buyer. In the March 1931 issue of *The Motor*, Lendrum & Hartman advertised the car for sale at a price of £2,350.

His Highness Sadiq Muhammad Khan Abbasi V (1904–1966) was the Nawab of Bahawalpur, a princely state in what is now Pakistan. In the Mughal Empire of south Asia "Nawab" was an honorific title given by the emperors (who were Muslims of Turkish-Mongol origin) to subservient Muslim rulers of semi-autonomous states within the empire. The title "Maharajah" was granted to non–Muslim (usually Hindu) subservient rulers within the empire.

In 1931, the Nawab was in his late twenties. He was very fond of fine motor cars and in his position he could afford any that he liked. He would summer in England with his British wife at a large estate he owned in Surrey. When he saw the advertisement for the Van den Plas-bodied Cadillac V-16, he already owned sixty-odd personal cars, including four Rolls-Royce Silver Ghosts, three new Phantoms, a Mercedes SSK, and three 1929 Packards, all of which were back home in Bahawalpur, where he was encouraged not to drive himself. In the U.K., however, he could freely exercise his enjoyment of motoring, with his chauffeur and retinue following in other cars to his permanent suite and parking place at London's Savoy Hotel. This Cadillac was just the thing.

The Nawab personalized his new acquisition with an indigo blue Lalique art glass radiator ornament in the shape of a peacock's head (Tete de Paon) that glowed with a concealed electric light. A man who abstained from alcoholic beverages, he had the furnishings removed from the liquor cabinet in the rear compartment. And he had his monogram painted on the rear doors. In 1933 the coachbuilding firm of Barker & Co., Ltd. performed some modifications to the car—the fenders were painted black, a black leather roof covering was applied, spotlights were installed (the one by the driver had been made by Stephen Grebel of Paris), and a sunvisor was installed across the top of the windshield. Afterwards, the car, with approximately 6,000 miles on the odometer, was shipped to Bahawalpur to join the Nawab's other cars at the Sadiq Garh palace.

The rulers of the princely states in British India used their cars to impress their peers and the public, and quantity was important. The British colonial authorities frowned on ostentatious displays by these very wealthy men, but re-bodying and repainting one's existing cars could give rivals the illusion that one owned more vehicles than one did.

In 1934, in anticipation of the visit to Bahawalpur state by the Commander-in-Chief British Army India (and later Viceroy), the V-16 and three Rolls-Royce cars with open coachwork were sent to Barker & Co., the Nawab's favorite coachbuilder. Barker & Co. made some more substantial changes to the Nawab's V-16, giving it a more formal presence. The body was repainted in a dark green. The interior was re-trimmed in maroon leather and matching carpet. The chrome-plated hinges and the garnish moldings around the windows were painted the same color as the body. Mounting hardware for state and personal flags were attached to both fenders, the radiator stone guard, and the top of the windshield. A rear-view mirror was fitted to the right-hand "A" pillar (a good idea with

***Still presentable prior to restoration.* In the mid–1930s, the body was re-painted dark green and the fenders black. A sun visor was added above the windshield. This photograph, taken about 2012, shows some flaking of the paint on the hood, scuffing on the front bumper and a missing right front fender lamp, but overall the car has held up well after decades of storage (courtesy Amer Ahmad).**

these cars!) and the Grebel spotlight was removed, leaving only the bumper-mounted Lucas lamp. The Lalique ornament was replaced with a plain radiator cap, now that flags would be flying in front of it.

From 1935 through the Second World War, the Nawab's V-16 Cadillac was used in Bahawalpur for official transport of visiting princes and other dignitaries, clocking an additional 1,500 miles mainly travelling among the seven palaces at different locations within the state. After the War, British India was divided into India and Pakistan. In August 1947, British forces were withdrawn from the subcontinent and later that year, the Nawab acceded his State to Pakistan. Though only 43 years old, he was suffering from the effects of diabetes, and spent more time in the United Kingdom than in Bahawalpur. From this time until 1969, the V-16 Cadillac and the Nawab's other fine motor cars were locked up in the Palace's private garages.

Nawab Sadiq Muhammad Khan Abbasi V passed away in 1966, and the Pakistani government administered his estate, apportioning his assets among ten sons, ten daughters and three surviving wives (Begums). The Cadillac V-16 went to Princess Shafiqa Abbasi, who was a favorite among his daughters, born to a wife of American origin.[38] She considered it to be just an old car, and her nephew Prince Salahuddin Abbasi acquired it from her. The Prince's father (Abbas Khan Abbasi) had succeeded to the title of Nawab (although without any administrative or political power). When Nawab Abbas Khan Abbasi died, Prince Salahuddin Abbasi was recognized by the family as the Nawab and successor to the once-ruling Abbasi family.

38. Her full sister, Princess Sadiqa Abbasi, was able to get a right-hand-drive 1929 Packard 740.

Returning to its original state. Shown here recently with upholstery well under way, a two-tone grey color scheme has been adopted, as was originally applied. Roof covering is still being installed, and a number of the trim parts have yet to be fastened (courtesy Amer Ahmad).

Sporting details. **Willocq et Bottin Supralux headlamps of Belgian manufacture replace the original Cadillac Tilt-Ray units. The raked windshield is similar to Fleetwood's Madame X design, but incorporates a top swivel hinge for ventilation. The sun visor was installed by Barker & Co. of London. Items yet to be completed include the missing crank hole cover and the bright-metal windsplits for the hood vent doors. Stephan Grebel driving light formerly served as a spotlight (courtesy Amer Ahmad).**

In 2012, after eighty-one years and three generations, the Cadillac V-16 Van den Plas sport sedan left the Abbasi family and came into the care of Mr. Amer Ahmad (whose brother-in-law Rizwan Butt had become the owner of the car). Because of the dry climate in Bahawalpur, the car had little or no rust. The paint showed areas of flaking and other evidence of age and wear, and the leather upholstery, though not torn, had become delicate. The original headlights were missing, replaced by a large Grebel spotlight and an old British headlight. Very few other parts were missing—notably the piston for the engine-mounted vacuum pump, and the vent pipe for the fuel tank. Brass floats had replaced the cork originals in the carburetors.

This car has now been sympathetically restored in Pakistan by Mr. Ahmad, a hands-on enthusiast, and it is fully functional. The missing headlamps have been reinstalled and new tires mounted. The original two-tone paint scheme has been duplicated, based on matching original paint remaining in areas covered by badges or other parts

Opposite: Nearly finished. **The fabric top covering is still in progress and the hubcaps are unfinished. But the distinctive features of the Van den Plas coachwork are clearly visible. The sinuous curve of the drip molding leads back to the built-in trunk and extended gas tank cover. Individual step plates replace the running boards and the fender edges have been rounded off where they once adjoined the running boards. The center-hinged doors sport uniquely-styled handles and chrome-plated barrel hinges. The indigo Lalique peacock's head radiator ornament originally installed by the Nawab of Bahawalpur will be lighted from below at night (courtesy Amer Ahmad).**

that were not removed when the car was repainted in the 1930s. Recently, Mr. Ahmad's son, Oosman Bashir of Lahore, bought the car from Mr. Butt.

The restoration of this unique car has occasioned several YouTube videos featuring the engine being started and run, the mesmerizing close-order drill of thirty-two exposed rocker arms working their valves, and the stuck clutch being freed by tipping the rear axle off jack stands while the wheels are spinning. It will not be long before this magnificent example of American technological achievement clothed in elegant European coachwork can be seen as it was when the Nawab first took the wheel.

43

The Fire Wagon

ROYAL LITTLE WAS AN AMERICAN businessman who started out in the textile business with a desire to make a name for himself and a business empire. He founded Specialty Yarns Corporation in 1923 on borrowed money, and by the late 1940s, his company (then called Textron) was reporting sales of $125 million. In the 1950s he began acquiring businesses in other industries. Today, Textron is a conglomerate with assets in the billions of dollars, and its component companies include Bell Helicopter, Cessna Aircraft Company, Jacobsen lawn tractors, and various aerospace and defense businesses. Mr. Little retired in 1960 when Textron had become one of the top 100 companies in the country, and in 1979 he wrote *How to Lose $100,000,000 and Other Valuable Advice*. He died at his home in the Bahamas in 1989.

In 1932, Mr. Little married another New Englander, Augusta Willoughby Ellis. In 1931, prior to their wedding, Mr. Little had graced her with a gift. At a dealership in Philadelphia, an order was placed in her name for a new Cadillac V-16 Series 4620 five-passenger sport phaeton. Though not a true dual-cowl phaeton (with hinged panel behind the front seat back that would be lifted to allow the rear seat passengers to enter) the Series 4260 cars had a roll-up windshield for the back seat. There was also a duplicate speedometer and a Jaeger chronometer for the entertainment of the rear passengers.

This particular sport phaeton was entirely red, inside and out, except for the wire wheels, and not just any shade of red, mind you. The paint color specified on the build sheet was "Satan Red," an actual Duco designation. (The color ordered for the wheels was "Puritan Cream.") The build sheet called for upholstery leather "to match Satan Red," and indicated that the car, with engine number 703166, was sent to Philadelphia in September of 1931. And amid the shipping information is the instruction "Tag Miss Ellis" and a notation that the car was "sold."

Not surprisingly, Miss Ellis named the scarlet car her "fire wagon." She became and remained fond of her Cadillac, and it would be part of her life for more than four decades, through her marriage to Mr. Little and beyond. She paid the car the following tribute:

> As much satisfaction as I have had in owning my beautiful fire wagon (because the car is bright red), the single strongest sense of enjoyment has been a personal one, that it was possible to have a car that for forty years I drove enjoyably. It always measured up to my expectations and gave me always the quietest imaginable joy. No one could have been more pleased with the car from the beginning of ownership.[39]

---

39. "Fire Wagon Returns to Cadillac," *The Self-Starter*, 1974 annual edition, The Cadillac-LaSalle Club, Inc., pp. 9–10.

***The Fire Wagon*. The car that Royal Little gave to his then-fiancée Augusta Willoughby Little was painted (and upholstered) in the color Satan Red, with Puritan Cream wheels. The new owner referred to the car as her "Fire Wagon."**

Mrs. Little also owned and flew a private airplane, a Buhl Airsedan, that was painted the same color as her Cadillac.

In 1974, Mrs. Little decided that it was time to relinquish ownership of the Fire Wagon. But she wanted to ensure that her car found a permanent home, and was not subjected to the indignities of the marketplace. Her attorney realized that a former classmate of his by the name of Robert Lund was then the General Manager of the Cadillac Motor Car Division. A letter was prepared and sent, and in due course, Mrs. Little's car returned to the company that had manufactured it. During her ownership, the odometer had recorded a mere 44,000 miles.

Cadillac performed a factory restoration of the car that included removal of a modern power steering unit that had been installed during Mrs. Little's ownership. Mrs. Little was not a large woman, but her car certainly was large, and one could certainly understand why she would have had a power assist installed for managing the nearly-three-ton beast. When the restoration was complete, GM invited Mrs. Little back to see the results.

In the ensuing years the red sport phaeton has been a jewel in the crown of the General Motors Heritage Center. GM has supplemented the original restoration by adding some period-correct enhancements. A set of Pilot Ray driving lights (an early version of cornering lights and a Cadillac accessory) were installed. And in 2005 (ostensibly to keep the car comfortable among the flashy concept cars and other special vehicles in the collection) GM decided to paint the fenders, dust shields, body moldings, and spare tire

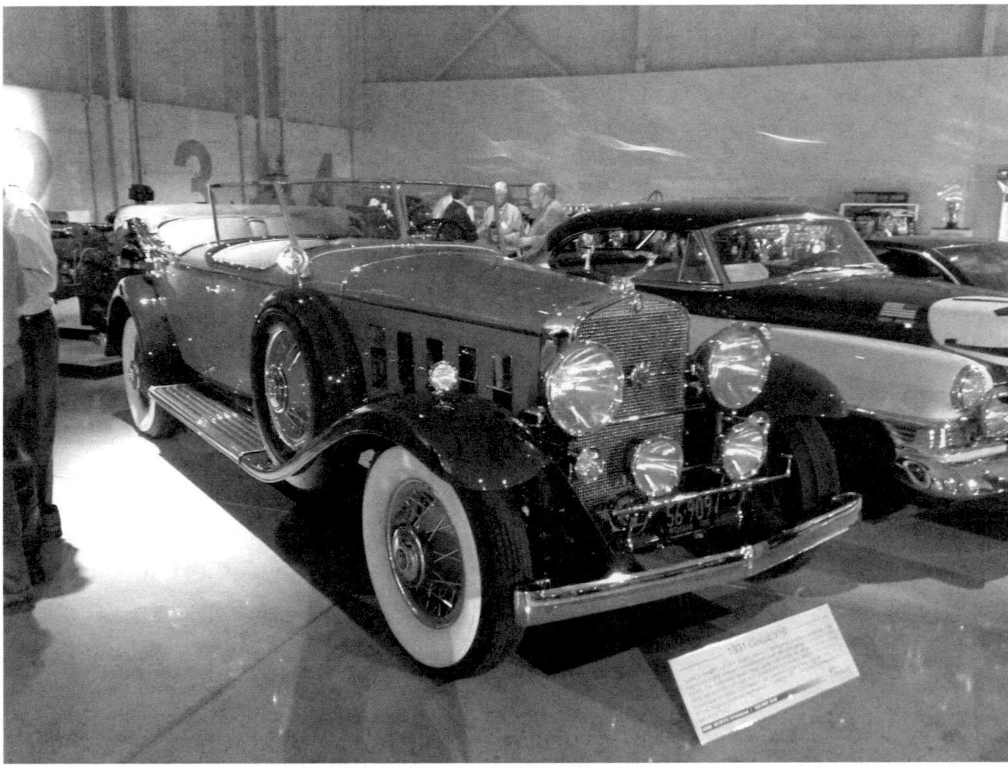

Revised color scheme. **General Motors officials decided to update the sport phaeton's color scheme from over-all Satan Red to one including contrasting maroon for the fenders, chassis and moldings, and to replace the red leather upholstery with light tan. Today Mrs. Little's car is part of GM's Heritage Center Collection in Detroit, Michigan.**

covers a deep maroon, and to chrome plate the hood vent doors and wheel spokes. The red leather upholstery was redone in a light tan color. But the body remains arrayed in Satan Red and the moniker "Fire Wagon" still fits, if not nearly as emphatically as when Mrs. Little drove around in it.

44

A Lucky 1932 Survivor

In terms of sales, the 1932 model year was a low point for the entire U.S. automobile industry. The Great Depression had settled in, and the hope that the economic difficulties triggered by the 1929 stock market crash might be swiftly rectified had largely evaporated. Especially hard hit were the manufacturers of high-end luxury motorcars. Success in that market segment is as much dependent on customer optimism as it is on the existence of people with the means to afford a special conveyance.

Cadillac built 299 1932 V-16 cars (and one more chassis that may have been used for a 1933 car). Those cars represented the first major styling change and technological update for the V-16 line since its introduction at the beginning of 1930. Streamline curves began to replace straight lines, corners were rounded, fenders flowed into the running boards, external sunvisors over windshields disappeared, and head and taillights took on teardrop contours. A mechanical fuel pump replaced the old vacuum tanks, shock absorbers could be adjusted from the driver's seat, helical gears silenced the transmission, and the popular "freewheeling" feature was introduced.

One particular 1932 V-16 car was a seven-passenger sedan (variously designated Series 5175-S or Job No. 32-16-212—Cadillac used two classification systems that year). One of forty-seven such cars produced, this car is reported to have been sold new to the owner of a brewery in Denver, Colorado, who drove it sparingly. In the 1940s or early 1950s, the car came into the possession of a group of Army enlisted men, and when it broke down while they were returning to their base, the hapless GIs opted to trade it in at a used car lot for something that would get them back in time. A doctor purchased the car from the used car lot and reportedly towed it to his family's farm, using an Austin-Healey as the tow vehicle (one can only imagine how well that went). The Cadillac was still being stored at the farm when the doctor passed away. Subsequently, a somewhat rambunctious little girl began using the Cadillac as a playhouse, and to prevent further damage to the interior, the doctor's widow had it towed to a house in Great Bend, Kansas, where it could be garaged.

In 1985 or 1986, Cadillac-LaSalle Club member Greg Gottschalk and several college friends travelled to Great Bend to attend a car show. There wasn't much to see at the car show, so the friends decided to drive around town. On the first street onto which they turned, a lady had her garage door open and there inside sat an unrestored 1932 Cadillac V-16 sedan. She told the boys that it had belonged to her late husband (a doctor), and she told them about the GIs trading the car in to the lot where her husband later purchased it. She said that she would trade it for a new Cadillac. Neither Greg nor the other young man interested in the car had that kind of money available, so they took down her phone number and left. Some years later the other fellow tried to contact the widow, but she

Garage bound. **This 1932 V-16 sedan was spotted in a Great Bend, Kansas garage by Greg Gottschalk and some college friends in the mid–1980s. Still-shiny paint, straight bodywork, and good interior woodwork grace a car that was then a half-century old (courtesy Greg Gottschalk).**

had moved and the phone number was no longer in service. Greg had written down that the data plate on the car's cowl indicated job number 32-16-212 and body number 14. He recalls that the odometer indicated relatively low mileage.

According to one story, about 1989 the local Lincoln-Mercury dealer (from whom the doctor's widow customarily bought her regular driving-around cars) persuaded her to part with the 1932 Cadillac in exchange for a new Mercury. The next purchaser traded an airplane to the Lincoln-Mercury dealer for the V-16, and transported the car to southwestern Canada. Greg Gottschalk attempted to verify that story and contacted the Lincoln-Mercury dealer in Great Bend. The owner (who had begun working there for his father in the mid–1980s) could not recall a 1932 Cadillac sedan making an appearance at the store, and no one he asked had any such recollection.

In the October 2011 issue of *Hemmings Motor News* an ad appeared offering a 1932 Cadillac V-16 seven passenger sedan: "original survivor, stored for decades, 37,000 original miles, $150,000 obo." The location was given as "BC, Canada" and a contact phone number and e-mail address were included.

The man who placed the ad said that the doctor's widow had sold the Cadillac around 1989, and that he had bought it in 2001. He described it as in very good condition mechanically, with original black paint and a usable interior (but one that needed attention—mentioning a rip in the driver's seat). He provided some indoor photographs that showed a very nicely preserved original car, but he would not give the engine number. He said that the car was running and drivable, and that he was selling due to

A peek under the hood. Thin layer of dusty oil on the valve covers and no-longer-porcelained exhaust manifolds show that the car was driven and used. 1932 V-16 modifications included air cleaners (far left) and a simpler distributor cap with plug wires attaching on top (right) (courtesy Greg Gottschalk).

his age. At about the same time the Cadillac was also advertised in a publication in Norway.

In March 2016, the same seller placed another ad in *Hemmings*, with a photograph of the '32 V-16 sedan, posed outdoors with an elderly gentleman, and an asking price of $149,000. After appearing in several subsequent issues of the magazine the ad was dropped, perhaps because the car was sold. A magnificent survivor, it's likely that this car will endure (whether in its present form, as a meticulous restoration, or as a re-fashioned open car is an open question). It will be interesting to see where it turns up next.

***Opposite: Through the back door window.* The upholstery in this 1932 sedan is in pretty good shape. The rear edge of the door trim panel has been tacked after apparently having come loose, and the clock is missing from the quarter window vanity unit (courtesy Greg Gottschalk).**

45

Hubert Dalton's Limousine Brougham

HUBERT K. DALTON WAS BORN in England in 1866 and immigrated to the United States at the age of 16. Starting as a toolmaker and machinery salesman, he became a very successful businessman. His enterprises included manufacturing metal lathes, a nursery business (he enjoyed breeding orchid hybrids), and making and marketing an automobile bearing his name (the Dalton was produced during 1911 and 1912). About 1930, Mr. Dalton sold his tool and die company to General Motors, and in 1931 he built a magnificent colonial revival home in Rumson, New Jersey (Willowbrook, designed by New York architect Alfred Brusselle, has been expanded over the years, but still stands proudly on Rumson Road).

In January of 1932, Mr. Dalton ordered a new Cadillac V-16 limousine brougham. The term "limousine brougham" described an elegant open-front town car for seven passengers. A detachable cover formed the roof over the leather-upholstered driver's compartment. The sumptuous rear compartment enveloped the passengers in fine broadcloth with elegantly inlaid wood trim pieces. Folding jump seats provided additional seating in front of the sofa-like rear seat.

Seven V-16s were built in this body style that year, and Mr. Dalton's was body number 3 (with engine number 1400185). Although the 149-inch wheelbase was only one inch longer than that of the 1930–31 V-16 cars, the 1932 V-16s looked longer because of the gentler curves of the body lines, and lengthened hood. Legendary General Motors head of styling Harley Earl is reported to have considered the 1932 Cadillac the most beautiful of all the designs he had a hand in. New for 1932 were a mechanical fuel pump for the engine, driver-controlled variable shock absorbers, and "freewheeling" capability.

According to Cadillac records, this car had originally been shipped from the factory to the Howland B. Jones Cadillac Company at Red Bank, New Jersey, but was diverted to Cadillac's Newark Branch for sale to Mr. Dalton. The paint colors called for were Thessalon Green for the body, black for the fenders and chassis, and Robin Hood Green for the wire wheels. The pinstriping was to be Robin Hood Green, except that the window reveal beads would be body color. Whitewall tires were specified.[40]

---

40. The shipping order or "build sheet" for the car had a second page that apparently contained the upholstery and interior trim specifications. That second page has unfortunately not survived.

Poised and ready to tour. **1932 V-16 limousine brougham (open-front town car) body contours are more rounded than the corresponding 1930 or '31 design. Accessory trunk would most likely include fitted suitcases and a hat box. Sumptuous wood interior appointments are visible through the windows (courtesy Robert Blakeman).**

Mr. Dalton likely employed a driver, as this style of motor car was nearly always a chauffeur-driven conveyance. Leather, in those days, was considered utilitarian and plebian, and owner-driven cars would be ordered with cloth upholstery up front. This particular car clearly was well cared for over the years, notwithstanding that a restoration was undertaken at some point.

From the time the car left the hands of Hubert Dalton (who moved to Hawaii in 1941) until the 1970s, not much is known of its ownership history. But then, enthusiast and vendor Leo Gephart acquired it, and some time later, Warwick, Rhode Island, restorer and collector Dick Shappy succeeded to ownership. It was during this period that the car was given a restoration.

The Barrett-Jackson company offered the car for sale at its Scottsdale, Arizona, auction, held in early January 2003. At that time it still bore Rhode Island license plates. The successful bidder was a collector in Andover, Massachusetts. In 2005, attorney, philanthropist and avid car collector Robert Blakeman of Valley Stream, New York, bought the car from a showroom in Arizona, and began work to get it running well. Until his death in April 2018, Mr. Blakeman showed the Cadillac proudly at various car shows on Long Island.

In October 2018, Mr. Blakeman's limousine Brougham was offered at the Hershey Auction conducted by RM Sotheby's. Today it has a dark blue body with black fenders

Seven hood doors ventilate the engine. **The longer hood for 1932 accommodated two more vent doors. Radiator has a built-in die-cast grille, instead of the detachable wire mesh screen used for the previous two years (courtesy Robert Blakeman).**

and pale blue pinstriping. "Pilot Ray" driving lights that point in the direction of the front wheels, and that echo the shapes of the car's headlights, are mounted behind and above the front bumper. And a correct accessory trunk occupies the luggage rack at the rear of the car. The hammer fell, and for $143,000, including buyer's fee, a new owner took over the care of the 1932 Cadillac V-16 Hubert Dalton ordered so long ago.

46

A Sleek 1932 Convertible Coupe

In 1932, Cadillac produced 299 V-16 motor cars, less than ten percent of the number of V-16 cars it had built during 1930 and 1931. The 1932 model year was an especially difficult one for luxury automobile makers, as what would come to be known as the Great Depression really sank its teeth into the American population. Suddenly many who had money no longer had any. And those who did were wary of being seen as flaunting it or as lacking empathy for others. A total of 14 V-16 convertible coupes (style number 32-16-168) were built, and very few of those survive.

The convertible coupe was a more civilized version of the roadster. Unlike a roadster,

Rear-mounted spare tire. **Standard equipment for the early 1930s V-16s was a single spare mounted in the back (with a two-piece bumper to make room for the tire). Most of the cars that were sold and that have survived sport the dual fender-mounted spare tires. Roads of the time were often rough, and flat tires were common (courtesy Fran Roxas).**

No crossbar. **The new front end for 1932 eliminated the crossbar between the fenders, on which the headlights had previously been mounted. Now each headlight and horn had its own stanchion anchored to the fender at two points. The "badge bar" between the headlights also disappeared, and the V-16 badge was mounted directly to the new die-cast grille (courtesy Fran Roxas).**

it had roll-up windows that sealed out the weather (no need for cumbersome and inevitably inadequate side curtains, in the event of rain or wind). But with the top down, the same sort of open-air motoring could be experienced by two people (and perhaps two hardy rumble seaters). And although a single rear-mounted spare tire was standard equipment, most convertible coupes like their roadster counterparts, were ordered with twin fender-mounted spares.

One convertible coupe that was not ordered with fender-mounted spare tires bore engine number 1400163 and body number 4. By 1959 it had made its way to northern Minnesota, where it lived in a shed that housed a sawmill. After a year of chasing rumors, Cadillac-LaSalle Club member Elmer Franzen of Minneapolis discovered its resting place and began a five-year campaign to persuade the owner to part with the car.

In 1964, the Cadillac's owner pulled it out of the shed, cleaned the dust and debris off, and parked the car in his yard next to a busy state highway. Mr. Franzen worried that someone else would beat him to the prize, but no one else had any better luck talking the owner into a deal. Finally, in the winter of 1965, Mr. Franzen's umpteenth visit was rewarded by the owner's abrupt offer to let Mr. Franzen purchase his old car. Mr. Franzen jumped at the chance and had the car towed away as quickly as possible after the deal was struck.

Elmer Franzen found himself with a very complete and solid car that today might have been simply put back together and shown as an unrestored original. But in the 1960s the special attractiveness of original cars was not as widely appreciated as it is today. Mr.

***Before restoration.* This 1932 V-16 convertible coupe arrived at Fran Roxas's restoration in solid original condition. Rectangular item behind the front wheel is the battery box. For 1932, fenders flowed into the running boards and the lights were teardrop-shaped. The number of hood vent doors increased from five to seven, and the hood stretched closer to the windshield (courtesy Fran Roxas).**

Franzen described his efforts to acquire the car, as well as his intentions to undertake a restoration, in a February 1966 article in the Cadillac-LaSalle Club's monthly newsletter *The Self-Starter*.[41] The black and white photographs accompanying the article indeed showed a solid automobile, and the text indicated that the parts not shown in the photos were boxed up and in good condition.

Mr. Franzen never got to see the convertible coupe restored, but it did remain complete. Subsequent owners included V-16 expert, restorer and collector Wayne Merriman and New Jersey collector and restorer Gifford F. Oborne. When Mr. Oborne's cars were sold at auction after his death in 1986, Massachusetts collector and dealer James King acquired the 1932 V-16 convertible coupe. Mr. King sold the car to Mr. Ronald Benach of Chicago fifteen or twenty years ago. According to Mr. Benach, the body was on the frame, but a lot of parts were thrown into the passenger compartment. He brought the Cadillac to renowned restorer Fran Roxas for a complete renewal. Today the car wears a handsome dark green color with a light tan cloth top and matching spare tire cover. The original-equipment stainless steel spokes and trim rings on the wire wheels provide additional visual interest without overpowering. The absence of spare tires in fender wells lets

41. Franzen, Elmer, "If at First You Don't Succeed, Try, Try Again," *The Self-Starter*, Cadillac-LaSalle Club, Inc., Bloomfield Hills, MI, Vol. VIII, No. 4, February 1966: pp. 12–13.

Long graceful lines. **The absence of side-mounted spare tires allows the eye to follow the long sweep from front to rear. The "streamline" ideal began to take hold in 1932, relaxing corners and straight lines all over the automobile industry. In successive years Cadillacs would embrace aerodynamics ever more enthusiastically. The restrained use of it here is pure classic beauty (courtesy Ronald Benach).**

the eye follow the graceful curve of the front fender into the running board, accentuating the car's length. The balance and proportion of the lines and details are truly impressive. Harley Earl, head of General Motors' Art and Colour Section, is known to have had a special fondness for the 1932 Cadillac designs, blending as they did traditional coachbuilder's features with influences from the incipient streamlining movement.

This rare and impressive 1932 Cadillac has competed successfully at the Pebble Beach Concours d'Elegance, winning its class. Even resting in its owner's garage, it continues to bear witness to the engineering and artistic excellence of another age.

47

Model for a Die-Cast Model

BEGINNING IN THE 1960S, SEVERAL companies have designed and marketed scale models of Cadillac V-16 cars, executed in polystyrene plastic, resin, or die-cast metal. Sizing has ranged from 1/48 up to a hefty 1/12 scale. Generally, the designer approaches a V-16 owner and asks to measure and photograph the actual car, and that information is translated into a miniature replica. In some cases, we know which car was used to pattern the model.

V-16 engine number 1400095 was installed by the Cadillac factory in a 1932 Series 5130-S five-passenger Fleetwood-bodied sedan. The car was painted entirely in a shade called "Tunis Blue Pearl" except for the rims of the wire wheels, which were done in

Iridescent paint. **This 1932 Cadillac was originally painted in a "Tunis Blue Pearl" color with "Avon Blue Opalescent" for the wheel rims. Owner Quentin Robbins has reproduced that finish on his car. Metallic or iridescent paints were a new thing in 1932, and Cadillac would not resume offering them until 1937. Paint companies experimented with fish scales, ground glass, mica, and metal shavings in an effort to find a coating that would hold up and retain its luster (courtesy Quentin Robbins).**

"Avon Blue Opalescent." A "Silver Leaf" pinstripe highlighted the car, and the wheel spokes were gleaming stainless steel. An eye-catching car, it would have been a family vehicle, with ample foot room in back and no divider window behind the driver.

Cadillac records indicate that when it left the factory on January 20, 1932, this V-16 sedan was driven to a dealer in Columbus, Ohio, on speculation. It didn't find a home there, and on October 17 it was returned to the factory for credit. On October 28, 1932, it was sent by boat across Lake Erie to Buffalo, New York. This time, the heron radiator ornament was replaced with a goddess, and additional accessories included a screen to keep bugs out of the cowl vent, decorative license plate frames, and a "Handy Kit" (which included polishes and cleaners, a dust mitt, a light bulb kit and a tire gauge).

The new Cadillac was to be charged to Klepfer Brothers, which was a major Buick dealer. When the owner of the Buffalo Cadillac dealership died in 1931, just as the severity of the Great Depression was becoming clear, no one stepped up to take over the franchise. So Klepfer Brothers and General Motors arranged for the Buick dealer to sell Cadillacs through part of its extensive downtown showroom, and that continued until 1936.

There's no way to tell who the original purchaser was, but this V-16 sedan was pretty well cared for over the years, as it suffered few or none of the ills that befell many of its brethren. Fast forward to 1991, when Portland, Oregon, resident John Phillips bought the car from a widow in Rochester, New York. It had taken him a while to find a V-16 Cadillac

Front ensemble. **For 1932, the sides of the tombstone radiator shell were rounded and a diecast grille replaced the attached stone guard used the two previous years. Headlights and fender lamps are smaller and bullet-shaped. Trippe driving lights mounted on the bumper bracket are extra-cost accessories. Crank hole cover is decorative, as 1932 is the first year that no provision was made to hand-crank the V-16 engine to set timing (courtesy Quentin Robbins).**

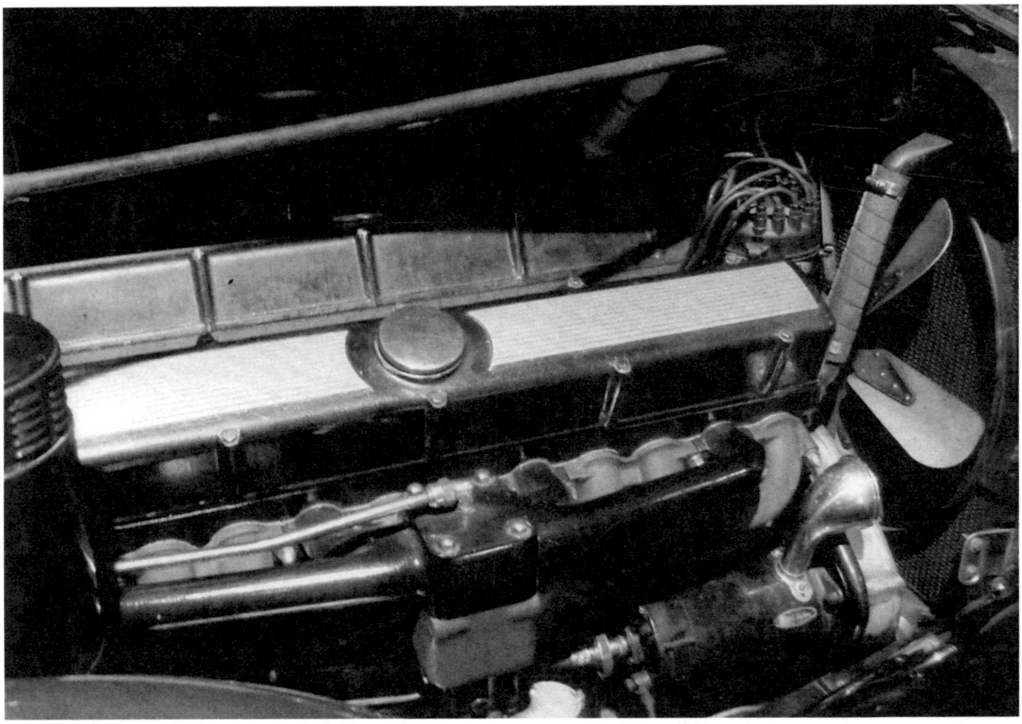

1932 V-16 engine. **Improvements over the 1930–1931 engine include: one-piece distributor cap that simplifies tune-ups and maintenance; air cleaner/silencer (lower left) to keep out dust and reduce intake roar; air scoop atop generator to prevent overheating and to enable increased capacity; and fan shroud ring to increase engine cooling efficiency. New Detroit Lubricator carburetor is barely visible, lower center of photograph (courtesy Quentin Robbins).**

of his own, and this one was a nice original car. His recollection was that the widow's late husband had owned the car from the 1970s or '80s. It had sat idle for some time, but it wasn't hard for Mr. Philips to get it running. He recalls it was a smooth-running car, and he taught his wife to drive it.

Four years later, John Phillips placed an advertisement for the V-16 sedan in the February 1995 issue of *The Self-Starter,* the monthly newsletter of the Cadillac-LaSalle Club. The ad text claimed 56,000 actual miles on this "exceptional unrestored gem." It went on to describe the car as "100% complete, no rust or rot, runs and drives great, nothing broken, dented or damaged." The price was $75,000, although the owner said he'd consider a trade for a 1932–1941 Cadillac for up to $30,000 of that amount.

Quentin Robbins, an art teacher and old car enthusiast who lived near Woodland, Washington (about 20 miles from Portland), and who had never before seen a V-16, saw the ad and went to take a look. When Mr. Robbins said he'd only come to see the car, Mr. Phillips said, "Make me an offer." Taken a bit by surprise, Mr. Robbins responded with an amount that was substantially less than the asking price, and when Mr. Phillips asked, "Cash?" he replied, "Yes." The response was "Sold!" and a deal was done. As Quentin Robbins drove back home, he wondered to himself what he'd just done.

By the time John Phillips had acquired the Cadillac, it had been repainted a dark maroon color, and when Quentin Robbins took possession, he noted that some blistering and peeling were visible in places. Mr. Robbins was able to find examples of the

Tufted wool broadcloth and fine woodwork. The sumptuous rear compartment features silk window shades, wind-up clock, assist handles and lull straps. Adjustable seat features fold-down center armrest, and lady's and man's smoking sets are built into the quarter window sills (courtesy Quentin Robbins).

original blue paint color on the underside of the cowl vent, and of the wheel rim color on the back side of the wheels. Armed with that information, he had the car returned to its factory-specified colors. He notes that the color combination in the build sheet was not among the combinations offered in the 1932 Cadillac Sales Data Book. But it is known that Cadillac was happy to provide any paint color or combination that a V-16 purchaser requested, only discouraging the use of colors that would fade quickly or otherwise not work out. At the same time as the repainting, Mr. Robbins had a new fabric insert installed in the roof,[42] and he had some of the chrome trim repainted.

In the early 2000s, representatives of the Danbury Mint contacted Mr. Robbins about measuring and photographing his car in order to produce and market a scale model 1932 Cadillac V-16 sedan. The finished model, issued in November 2003, was executed in black with silver pinstriping. Later in September 2008, a limited edition of the model was issued, with black fenders and with the body painted a blue similar to the color of Mr. Robbins's car. According to the company both editions of the model car have been sold out (although examples do turn up on auction websites and other re-sale venues).

Mr. Robbins doesn't drive his car long distances, but will trailer it or drive to local shows. At a Classic Car Club of America event the car received an award for its original upholstery. He says that he has never been sorry for his (at the time) extravagant purchase of this venerable motor car.

42. Prior to 1936 or 1937, automobile manufacturers were unable to stamp one-piece metal roof panels for closed coupes and sedans. A weather-resistant fabric was stretched over wood slats and ribs instead. The arrival of the all-steel top was a great advance in the ability to keep a closed car on the road.

48

A Special Sedan for an Opera Singer

ONLY 125 V-16S WERE BUILT BY Cadillac for the 1933 model year. The catalog stated that there would be no more than 400, but that turned out to be an optimistic upper limit. What we now know as the Great Depression was only a couple of years old when that catalog was laid out, and it's understandable that people were still expecting that a recovery was imminent. There has been much second-guessing as to why the economy ailed for so long, but whatever the causes, the Cadillac V-16 program never returned to the frenzied sales pace of the spring of 1930. That's not to say that Cadillac didn't continue to innovate and improve the cars, or maintain the highest standards of precision and excellence of design.

Streamlining takes hold. **Cadillac design for 1933 incorporates a significant amount of streamlining, with skirted fenders, rounded corners, bullet-shaped lamps, and slender door handles. Airfoil-shaped hood side vents, echoed in fender decorations, help to depict speed, whether the car is moving or still (courtesy Mike Fairbairn/RM Sotheby's).**

The 1933 model year was the second year of the streamlining process at Cadillac by which the stylistic conventions of the "carriage paradigm" were supplanted by the principles of aerodynamic design born of the burgeoning aircraft industry. The 1932 model year had seen rounding of body and window outlines,teardrop shapes for external lights, and blending of the joints between separate body parts. Now for 1933, the sides of the fenders extended down to "skirt" or cover the open spaces behind the wheels. On the V-16 cars, instead of the previous year's vertical doors, each side of the hood was vented by three long, horizontal louvers shaped like airfoils (with two small vertical doors at the front of the panel). The radiator shell became completely rounded, and the die-cast grill had a vertical crease down the center, as though parting the onrushing air. "'No-Draft' ventilation" of the interior of the car was accomplished for the first time by the use of hinged vent panes in the door window openings.

Mechanically, the 1933 V-16s continued the important developments introduced in 1932—a mechanical fuel pump, Detroit Lubricator carburetors, adjustable shock absorbers ("ride regulation"). New for 1933 was a higher compression ratio (5.7 to 1). The controlled free-wheeling feature introduced in 1932 was discontinued for 1933 and thereafter.

The build sheet for the 1933 Cadillac V-16 Series 5575-S seven-passenger sedan with engine number 5000024 and body number 5 (of 21 such sedans built that year) tells an interesting tale. The document directs that the car be shipped to the G.W. Shroyer & Company Cadillac dealership in Dayton, Ohio. In addition, it contains an instruction

***Jewel-like instruments and fine inlaid wood.* The driver of a 1933 V-16 was surrounded by high-class appointments. The instrument cluster is balanced by the similarly-shaped (and carefully decorated) glove box door. The lenses covering the gauges are convex to minimize glare, and art deco influences are clear in the numbers and graphics of the gauge faces (courtesy Mike Fairbairn/RM Sotheby's).**

Comfortable room for seven. **Expansive rear seat is augmented by folding auxiliary ("jump") seats that are themselves quite pleasant to ride in. Fine wool broadcloth begs to be stroked (courtesy Mike Fairbairn/RM Sotheby's).**

to "TAG—GEORGE WASHINGTON SHROYER."[43] Moreover, the notation "VERBAL 12/9 G.W. SHROYER" would appear to indicate that the order was placed by Mr. Shroyer himself.

George W. Shroyer, founder of the dealership with his name, had served as Mayor of Dayton (1914–1917), and was an accomplished businessman. Born in 1865, he left school at age 15, and worked as a travelling salesman. In 1894 he opened G.W. Shroyer & Co. and sold bicycles and associated parts and accessories. At least as early as 1909, and well into the 1930s, G.W. Shroyer & Co. would be a dealer for Cadillac motor cars. He would have been 68 years old in 1933.

Unlike most build sheets for V-16s sold in the early 1930s, this one contains extensive specifications for personalized touches (and the instructions continue onto the back of the sheet). Instead of a painted pinstripe on the body moldings and fender edges, this car would have an inlaid, 9⁄32-inch bright-metal strip. Two different cloths were to be used, and a tufted and pleated style for the interior trim was specified. A lamb's wool carpet provided warmth and comfort in the rear seating area, and a hat rack was included. A Kelch hot air heater was installed with registers in both front and rear compartments.[44] Black paint from the Jones-Dabney Company (instead of

43. Numerous Cadillac build sheets from the period indicate that a car was to be shipped to the G.W. Shroyer dealership, but this build sheet also indicates that the subject car is to be tagged for Mr. Shroyer himself.

44. The build sheet cautions: "Do not cut sheepskin mat for register in rear compartment."

the usual material from Rinshed-Mason) was to be used on the entire exterior of the car, its wheels, and the portions of the wheel discs that were not left with a chrome finish.

An intriguing special feature of this car, as called for in the build sheet, is an accessory called "Cadillac Electric Curtain Control." Offered only in 1933, curtain control permitted the driver to raise or lower the silk curtain for the rear window by moving a toggle switch mounted below the car's instrument panel. According to Cadillac literature describing available accessories for dealers, this device would quickly eliminate glare from following headlights, particularly during rainy weather or when the windshield was dirty. Cost to the customer was $13.50 (in 1933 dollars, of course!).

Clearly, the car that was the subject of this build sheet was ordered for someone with particular preferences. Unfortunately, there is no record of the identity of the original purchaser. But as we will see, there is an intriguing clue. In 1963, the car had made its way to Dean's Used Cars in Lynwood, California, a city between Los Angeles and Long Beach. There were several other 1930s Classics on the lot—Cadillacs, Cords, a Pierce-Arrow. The proprietor liked V-12 and V-16 cars. On June 14, Arthur H. Kusuhara of Canoga Park, California, bought this 1933 V-16 Cadillac off of the lot. Mr. Kusuhara recalls that the dealer told him the car had been sold new to a famous (woman) opera singer. There had been a little metal plaque on the dashboard engraved with the name of that opera singer (sadly, that plaque was no longer with the car). When the author spoke with him, Mr. Kusuhara was unable to recall the name of the opera singer, but he thought it might have been Lily Pons, the French-American coloratura soprano and actress, whose stellar career reached from the 1920s into the 1970s.

Arthur Kusuhara kept his V-16 sedan until the early 2000s, and the next owner was restorer and collector Dick Shappy of Providence, Rhode Island. In 2006, Mr. Shappy sold the car to Mike Fairbairn, one of the three founding partners of RM Auctions of Blenheim, Ontario, Canada.[45] Mr. Fairbairn undertook an extensive restoration of the car, partly at RM Auto Restoration, and partly with his own crew. His wife, a furniture maker, restored and refinished the delicately inlaid and formed woodwork in the passenger compartment.

Among the challenges encountered in the restoration process was renewing the exterior bright metal trim. Instead of a painted pinstripe along the body moldings and the edges of the fenders, this car was decorated with a fine band of polished stainless steel, bonded to the steel body parts before they were painted. Over the years, the fenders had been bumped, and the edges with their stainless steel trim damaged. Mr. Fairbairn and his team determined to construct new outer lips for the fenders all around. New stainless steel strips were milled and metal-formed to conform to the fenders and body. These were soldered in place and then masked when the car was painted. When the painting was done, the painted surfaces were masked so that the stainless steel could be polished.

Before the restoration was completed, Mike Fairbairn showed the bare, running chassis at the 2008 Pebble Beach Concours d'Elegance (including driving the bare-bones car in the associated Tour d'Elegance, while clad in old-fashioned driving duster and leather aviator's helmet). His wife had designed and constructed a finished

45. In February 2015, RM Auctions formed a strategic partnership with Sotheby's to become RM Sotheby's.

Accessory Facts — Numbers 11 and 12 — Page 3

THE NEWEST ACCESSORY THE CADILLAC ELECTRIC CURTAIN CONTROL

CADILLAC'S newest auxiliary equipment at its pre-showings at the various meetings recently held at the Factory received the most enthusiastic reception of any accessory ever introduced by Cadillac and since has been adopted as standard equipment on the V-16. It was welcomed not only as a *new* accessory with a new and *additional* market, but as a definite help to the new car sale.

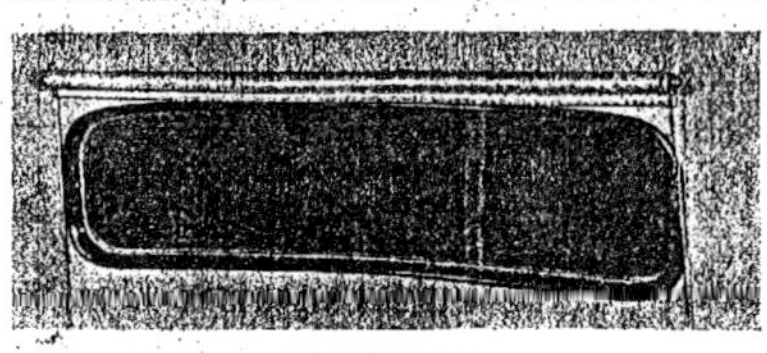

THE CURTAIN UP

This Electric Curtain Control has an important safety factor. How many times when driving at night would you have pulled down the rear curtain in your car to keep the glare of the headlights of the car behind out of your rear view mirror, off your windshield, and therefore out of your eyes? How many times have you been driving in bad weather—particularly rain—or with a dirty windshield—

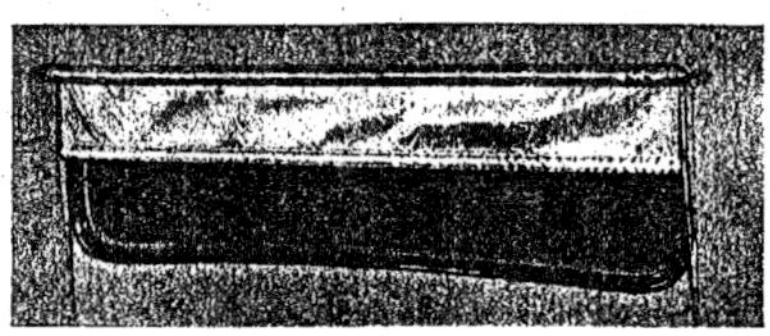

THE CURTAIN PART WAY DOWN

when the glare of the lights behind have reflected against your windshield and made that covering of raindrops or film of dirt like an impenetrable screen through which you could not see? With the new Electric Curtain Control a flick of the unobtrusive switch on the dash and your rear

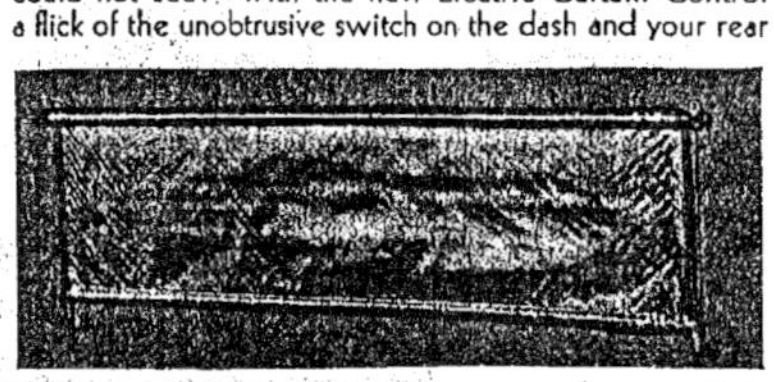

ALL THE WAY DOWN

curtain is instantly down—giving you maximum visibility. Another upward pressure when the danger is past and your curtain is briskly snapped up.

There is no visible evidence of anything other than a standard roller installation, save for the tiny switch below the instrument panel, within easy reach of your hand. A facsimile of this switch is reproduced here. The mechanism of the Electric Curtain Control is all contained within the roller, and that roller is no larger than standard curtain rollers as used in Cadillac-LaSalle cars. The mechanism is very simple. Within the roller are two coils—with connections for directing the flow of current from either end of the coils. When energized by electric current—supplied by the car battery—the coils are magnetized propelling or repelling—by change of current direction—a field core sliding within the coils. To this sliding field core is attached a brass shaft twisted like a corkscrew. This shaft slides through a fixed slot attached to the outer roller shell. When the driver presses down on the switch, the shaft is propelled, the roller unwinds and the curtain is instantaneously lowered. When the switch is pressed upward and the current flow is reversed, the shaft is repelled, the roller winds in the opposite direction and the curtain is snapped upwards as though by magic.

THE SWITCH ON THE INSTRUMENT PANEL

Wherever the switch is released—half down—three-quarters down—there the curtain is held firmly in position by an automatic brake incorporated within the roller mechanism. The roller proper revolves on ball bearings within the roller brackets to insure quiet and frictionless operation. The construction of the entire mechanism is so rugged, its design and action so simple, that once installed and operating properly there is nothing to get out of order.

The roller and brackets and switch are the major component parts of the Cadillac Electric Curtain Control. The standard curtain installed in the car body is removed from its regular roller and attached to the Electric Curtain Control roller when making installation. Factory installation is recommended on C Series Cars by specifying the control on the sales order with group equipment accessories. Field installation can be accomplished on past models without any complicated work. The only major operation—besides transferring the silk from the standard to the electric roller—is leading the armored cable provided from a point below the back of the rear seat down to the frame channel, along the channel, and up the pillar post to the instrument panel. One and three-quarter hours time is allowed for field installation, which brings the installed price of the Cadillac Electric Curtain Control to $13.50. The control proper lists at $10.00 uninstalled.

Without question this newest Exclusive Cadillac Accessory is going to be an important sales and profit item during 1933. Get a few in your Showroom on Show cars and on Demonstrators, and watch them sell themselves.

***"Electric curtain control" accessory.* For 1933, a V-16 closed-car buyer could order a remote-operated power sunshade for the rear window. This page from the "Accessory Facts" periodical that Cadillac provided to its dealers illustrates and describes the features and installation of this optional feature.**

and functional, leather-upholstered temporary driver's seat for the occasion, as well as a temporary mounting for the driver's instruments. Substantial attention had to be paid by the restoration team to giving normally concealed parts (like the backs of instruments, internal wiring, and structural braces) a presentable finish. The unusual configuration garnered an enormous amount of attention from other contestants as well as the general public. Subsequently, at the 2011 Pebble Beach Concours, the '33 sedan took second place in the American Classic Closed category.

In 2015, Mr. Fairbairn offered the Cadillac for sale through RM Auctions' Amelia Island event on March 14 of that year. The selling price of $550,000 far exceeded the pre-sale estimate, and was more in line with prices for open Classics of the era.

49

Executive Privilege

From May 27 through November 1, 1933, the city of Chicago was host to a World's Fair that was billed as "A Century of Progress," and that commemorated the founding of the Town of Chicago in 1833. At that exposition, several American automakers exhibited factory concept cars that displayed aerodynamic styling in a way never seen before. From Buffalo, Pierce-Arrow brought its sinuously streamlined "Silver Arrow." "Suddenly," said the accompanying advertising copy, "it's 1940!" Packard showed a one-off special sport sedan (actually a limousine) designed by Raymond Dietrich (which car won the designation "The Car of the Dome" referring to its place of honor under the giant 12-story dome of the exposition's Travel and Transportation Building).

Ford displayed the teardrop-styled, rear-engined "Briggs Dream Car" that would inspire the 1936 Lincoln Zephyr. Duesenberg brought an opulent, Rollston-bodied Model SJ Arlington Torpedo sedan that acquired the nickname "Twenty Grand" for its astonishing price tag. And Cadillac submitted a fastback, two-door, five-passenger V-16 "Aerodynamic Coupe."

Cadillac's gleaming black aerodynamic coupe was a concept car from the cowl back. The forward part of the car—hood, front fenders, headlights, grille, bumper—was very identifiable with the production 1933 V-16 cars (although the fenders were a bit more teardrop-shaped). But the passenger compartment and back end of the car were not like anything else. A one-piece metal roof arced gracefully from the top of the windshield over the seating area and smoothly down the back of the car, ending at a narrow valence that connected the tips of the comma-shaped rear fenders. It was a continuous, undisturbed curve that promised to slip through the air without effort. No spare tires sat in the fenders to trouble the onrushing air (the spare was stowed in the trunk). Sparkling narrow chrome reveals outlined the windows. Instead of perching atop the right-hand taillight, the license plate was tucked into a recessed area in the trunk lid, where it could not hinder the wind's flow.

The next year, Cadillac included in its radically restyled production V-16 offerings a body style that was essentially the same as the car that had represented the company at the Century of Progress. The 1934 Series 5799 had the same all-metal roof and fastback profile as the World's Fair Cadillac, but it was constructed on the new 154-inch wheelbase of the '34 V-16 chassis with an overall length of exactly twenty feet. With a windshield slanted backward 35 degrees, the Series 5799 wore the new 1934 V-16 "face" with a raked and narrowed radiator shell, and it carried the eye-catching "biplane" bumpers that adorned all of the '34 Cadillacs. In all, eight such rakish V-16 cars were built during the 1934 through 1937 model years (and twelve on the V-8 and V-12 chassis). Several of these survive today.

World's Fair concept car. **Cadillac exhibited at the 1933 "Century of Progress" Chicago world's fair a sleek, streamlined concept car embodying art deco details (note the bumpers and the horns especially). The next year, a production version of the revolutionary concept retained most of the features of the concept (with, *e.g.*, the 1934 biplane bumpers, radiator shell and headlamps). Chrome window reveals were dropped.**

The first production V-16 Aerodynamic Coupe was also the sixth 1934 V-16 car, and it bore engine number 5100006. It is generally believed to have been built for William Knudsen, who, at the time, was Executive Vice President of General Motors. In 1963, Cadillac-LaSalle Club member Robert Mellin, who extensively researched the history of the 1934–1937 V-16 Cadillacs, reported that Mr. Knudsen's family chauffeur, Mr. Blain Evenson, had watched as the car was built at the Fisher Custom Shop in Detroit. He provided Mr. Mellin with a description and photographs, saying that in addition to aluminum used in the body shell, the car sported quartz embellishments for the steering wheel hub and for the knobs and escutcheon plates for the window cranks. There was a regular carpet for the rear seat area, and a winter carpet that was made out of goatskin. Mr. Evenson said that he drove the car about 50,000 miles (the license plate read "V-1600"). He believed that it had been sold in the New York City area.

Mr. Evenson related an incident in which he took the Knudsen family to the station in Hot Springs, Virginia, to board a train home. He then drove the V-16 (at speeds of 65 to 75 miles per hour on mid–1930s roads) and easily beat the train to meet the family at the Michigan Central Station in Detroit and drive them to their home on Grosse Ile. Cross country driving in the 1930s was not without its surprises. Mr. Evenson told of another trip during which he crested a hill in the 1934 Cadillac only to encounter a herd of sheep, one of which he hit, sending him and the car off the road.

Although he had no solid confirmation, Mr. Mellin believed that the Knudsen V-16 aerodynamic coupe had most likely survived, as a 1934 aerodynamic coupe had been advertised for sale by Giant Motors of Little Ferry, New Jersey, in 1956. Because only three 1934 V-16 aerodynamic coupes were built in 1934, and he could account for the other two, he concluded that the 1956 advertisement referred to Mr. Knudsen's car.

At this date, it's not clear whether (or where) the first production 1934 V-16 aerodynamic coupe still exists.

50

An Oil Man's Family Car

BASCOM H. ROGERS WAS AN ACTIVE participant in the "oil boom" in Texas and Oklahoma during the early twentieth century, as vice-president of an oil company, and owner of various oil and gas leases, mineral rights, company shares, and so forth. In 1934, he was a married man with a son and a daughter (another daughter would follow two years later). He must have been doing very well to have ordered a new V-16 Cadillac Series 5875-S seven-passenger sedan. Shipped to the Greenlease Moore Cadillac dealership in Oklahoma City, the twenty-foot-long car was painted Mountain Brown Extra Light, including the wheels. The interior was trimmed in a special-order cloth (front and rear, since there was no divider window or chauffeur's compartment).

The shipping order or "build sheet" for the car (engine number 5100012) is one of the relatively rare ones that actually identifies the car's original purchaser (Bascom H. Rogers). It specifies a number of special features—a silver-plated goddess hood ornament, a "Master" radio, painted metal covers for the fender-mounted spare tires, and a monogrammed lap robe made out of the same material used for the seats, with piping and a plush backing. Further details, set forth in Fleetwood special body order number 126, are lost to us, due to destruction of the special body order files. All told, the price for this car would have been close to, if not in excess of, $8,000. By comparison, a new Ford would set the buyer back only about $600.

The car went back to the factory in 1937 for some significant updates. Hydraulic brakes (newly offered on Cadillacs that year) were retro-fitted, some suspension modifications were made, and an upgraded frame cross-member was installed. There is a handwritten notation on the build sheet that a special suspension part (pitman arm) was shipped to Oklahoma City on May 14, 1937, for installation on this car. Clearly, it was intended that the car would continue to be regularly used.

On May 1, 1939, Mr. Rogers sold the car to Mark Barnhart of Holdenville, Oklahoma, who kept the car registered for a number of years and then appears to have laid it up for storage in a Quonset hut in eastern Oklahoma. In March of 1941, Bascom Rogers and his wife were divorced, and the following September, he died of pneumonia at the age of 40. The 1934 V-16 sedan would not see the light of day again until October 12, 1964, when William Pine bought it (along with an Auburn). He owned the car almost four years and on August 1, 1968, famed casino owner and mega-collector William (Bill) Harrah signed a purchase authorization to add the car to his auto collection in Reno, Nevada.

On March 10, 1973, the Harrah collection sold the car as part of an adjustment of their inventory, and Bascom Rogers's V-16 sedan wound up at Batey Chevrolet in Elk Grove, California. In 1977, early V-16 enthusiast Ron Renaldi bought the car, and about a year later he sold it to Gunnar Henrioulle. Mr. Henrioulle told this author that by that

Still proud, if a bit worn. **Emerging after years of storage, this 1934 V-16 seven-passenger sedan is complete and generally straight. The fragility of the elegant 1934 "biplane" bumpers is evident, notwithstanding the spacers that have been added at both ends. At twenty feet of overall length, these cars required careful maneuvering when parking (courtesy Jim Tait).**

time the car was "a very beat up sedan," but one that was "straight, not too rusty." The doors were intact, although the hinges were loose.

Left unprotected, these automobiles don't weather well. So-called composite bodies were still the rule in the mid–1930s, although all-steel bodies were becoming more common. In a composite body, the main structural members are shaped hardwood pieces glued and screwed together. The metal panels are fastened to the hardwood framework and the welded joints between adjacent panels are lead-filled and filed smooth. Most of the roof is a fabric covering stretched over wood slats and backed with wire mesh. Left to the elements, water begins to infiltrate and the wood rots and separates. Soon the doors sag, the upholstery disintegrates, and the metal panels, posts, and openings rust away. Restoration of such a victim becomes an economically intimidating prospect, with expenditures likely exceeding the market value of the finished product.

Mr. Henrioulle devised a plan for this car, to bring to life a body style that was offered for the 1934 V-16 line, but was never ordered by a customer—a Series 5857 seven-passenger touring car, a four-door convertible without roll-up windows. (Touring

Opposite: 1934 V-16 seven-passenger sedan as reacquired by Monty Holmes. **Monty (back to the camera) would get the doors properly rehung and working before selling the car to Jim Tait (courtesy Monty Holmes).**

Enormity of the project is apparent. **Sprung or dislodged door hinges, missing roof structure, shredded cloth, delaminated glass and missing parts betray the time and expense entailed in bringing a car like this back. On the positive side, the major body surfaces are straight, and there's no obvious rust through (courtesy Monty Holmes).**

cars, with their lack of weather protection, were generally considered old-fashioned by the mid–1930s, but Cadillac included a design for one in the 1934 Fleetwood catalog, in case a buyer should harbor a strong preference for a bygone style.) The goal, according to Mr. Henrioulle, "was to actualize a beautiful car," and not to realize a profit. Finances, however, did not work out for him, so the ambitious project was abandoned.

In 1998 or 1999, the sad sedan was purchased from Mr. Henrioulle by restorer Monty Holmes of Seattle, Washington. Mr. Holmes had been restoring a 1934 V-16 convertible sedan that had been messed with quite a bit (the engine had been removed and used to build a race car, while a Mercury V-8 had been installed in the emptied engine bay). Another unrestored V-16 would be an extremely helpful reference for reassembling his project car.

After some years, Monty Holmes sold the sedan to a man in California, who intended to restore it. Unfortunately, that fellow only got as far as rebuilding the engine before bankruptcy overtook him. Monty bought the car back, completed the engine work, and rehung the doors. Then he sold the car to fellow Washington State resident Jim Tait.

Mr. Tait has been undertaking the complete restoration for which this noble veteran motor car has been so long due. He has replaced the wood slats that support the roof and has installed a new fabric covering. He removed the body from the chassis so that the frame and suspension could be cleaned and made right. And he has steamed and shaped

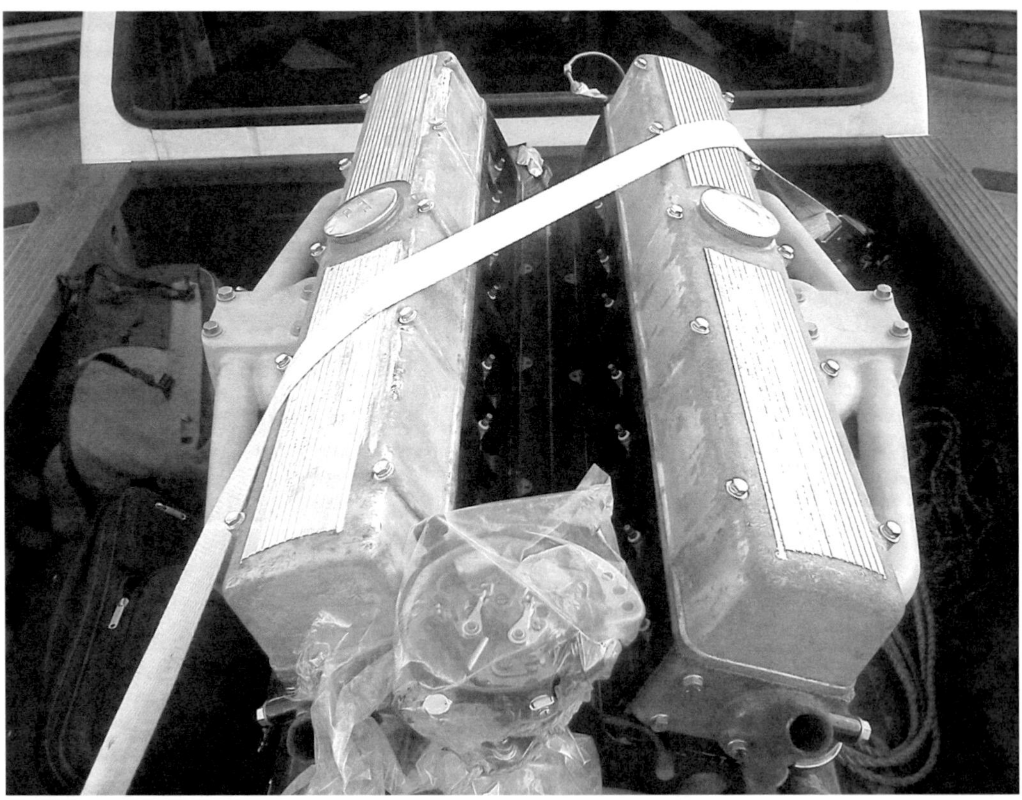

***Rebuilt engine.* Mechanical concerns have been seen to. Carburetors remain to be attached, along with distributor cap and plug wires (courtesy Monty Holmes).**

Nearing completion. **Paint and chrome are just about done at this point. Window and interior remain to be done, but this car is a far cry from its previous state (courtesy Jim Tait).**

black walnut for the interior window garnish moldings. As of 2018, he was hoping to have the upholstery redone that fall.

The project has required Mr. Tait to learn skills he hadn't had, and to make a lot of parts for the car (that were either missing or unusable). Stan Squires, a pioneering expert on the 1934–1937 V-16s, had a detailed drawing of the battery box, and that enabled Mr. Tait to reproduce one for his car. (On these cars, the battery and battery box are installed in the car, as an assembly, from underneath the right front fender. The shop manual recommends that two men be assigned to the job of removing or replacing the battery.)

Once the process is complete, this 1934 V-16 will join the relative handful of restored survivors of the 208 V-16 cars that were built during the 1934–1937 model years. The dramatic size, art deco styling, and advanced (for the time) engineering make these cars really impressive, and the V-16 engine makes them truly spectacular.

51

A Playboy's Convertible Victoria

Hugh McLeod Fenwick (1905–1991) was a tall man, over six feet, and barrel chested. Outgoing and charming, he was raised largely apart from his well-to-do parents, and his academic career was overshadowed by extracurricular activities (such as lettering in football and polo at Harvard). He trained in flying at Pensacola Naval Air Station, and aviation became a long-term passion. He would wed three times and in 1934 he was married to Millicent Vernon Hammond, who would later be elected to represent New Jersey in the United States Senate. He was president of Aviation Utilities of New Jersey and president of Fenwick & Co. an insurance brokerage in Newark. He held memberships in the Harvard Club of New York, the Racquet Club of Washington, and the Aviation Club of Hicksville, Long Island, along with being a leading polo player in New Jersey.[46] One woman described him as of a type who "made a specialty of marrying ladies with money … he's coarse, he's funny. He has a lot of charm, ghastly as he is. Oh, he's full of charm. He can charm the birds off the trees."[47]

Mr. Fenwick ordered a new 1934 Cadillac V-16 convertible victoria, style number 5885, engine number 5100044. Fewer than 60 Cadillac V-16s were built in 1934. This one would be the only 1934 V-16 ordered as a convertible victoria, and the shipping order or "build sheet" records Body No. 1. One of the most impressive and exciting body styles employed with the 1934–1937 V-16 chassis, the convertible victoria was a five-passenger open car for which the convertible top incorporated blind rear quarters. With the top raised, the car was a formal conveyance with deep privacy for the rear seat passengers. Lower the top, and open-air motoring could be enjoyed with almost the spacious comfort of a phaeton. Interestingly, the Cadillac Motor Car Company sent a letter out to all distributors and dealers on May 2, 1934, saying this body style would be built only on special order (at a list cost, FOB Detroit, of $4495 for the V-8 version, $5195 for the V-12 and a whopping $8150 for the V-16).[48]

Hugh Fenwick's car was finished in black lacquer, with green leather trimming the passenger compartment. A short list of optional equipment—silver goddess hood ornament, "Master" radio, flexible "banjo" steering wheel, chromed license plate frames, and chrome plated hubcaps—appears on the shipping order or "build sheet," and reference is

46. Shapiro, Amy, *Millicent Fenwick: Her Way*, New Brunswick: Rutgers University Press, 2003 at pg. 68.
47. *Id.* at pg. 65.
48. The (New) Cadillac Database, 1934–1937 production. By contrast, a 1934 Chevrolet Master two-door cabriolet had a retail price of $695.

***Only one that year.* This is the only 1934 Cadillac V-16 built as a convertible victoria, style number 5885, as it was when it was owned by Robert Friggens in the early 1970s. In this design, the commodious rear seat area gave the passengers near-complete privacy when the top was raised, and open-air exhilaration when it was lowered (courtesy Robert Friggens).**

made to Special Fleetwood Body Order No. 154 for detailed specifications. Unfortunately, the Fleetwood special body orders are lost to us. The horn button on the steering wheel hub was engraved with Mr. Fenwick's initials (H. McL. F.) and the car number (No. 22).[49] Hugh Fenwick owned and drove his car for almost four decades, and he took it with him on overseas trips during the 1930s.

Bob Friggens of Albuquerque, New Mexico, has loved fine cars since high school, when he took a shine to a neglected 1941 Cadillac Fleetwood 60 Special sedan. He restored that car and went on to a successful career in engineering, acquiring along the way a number of pedigreed motor cars (including film star Al Jolson's 1932 Dietrich Packard convertible sedan). In January 1970, he acquired the only 1934 Cadillac V-16 convertible victoria, style number 5885.

Mr. Friggens had heard about the car from a man in the Midwest, and had negotiated with another gentleman in North Carolina to purchase it. He set off first to Chicago, to pay a finder's fee to the man who gave him the lead on the car. Then he flew to Washington, D.C., and hitchhiked to Hickory, North Carolina, where he found his way to Gateway Auto Sales. Gateway was an 8-foot-by-8-foot wooden "office on skids with a row of worn out old gray government cars for sale." Mr. Friggens's contact for the sale of

49. For the 1933 through 1937 model years, Cadillac would personalize a V-16 car with the owner's name (or initials) and the car number. In 1933, this was done on a brass plaque on the instrument panel. For 1934 through 1937, the engraving was done on the horn button.

Imposing but graceful. **The front ensemble of the 1934–1937 Cadillac V-16 cars embodies art deco design themes and aeronautically-inspired streamlining. Elegant biplane bumpers (strengthened here by aftermarket vertical guards) were a one-year-only feature, as they proved fragile in practice (courtesy Steve Plunkett).**

the 1934 Cadillac was Gateway's proprietor, a Mr. Joe Smart, who immediately asked if he had the money with him. Mr. Friggens handed over a cashier's check and Mr. Smart made a phone call and then wrote out a receipt for a "16 sil cat." He told Mr. Friggens he would drive him to the car's location.

After a long drive, all on back roads, the two men arrived at the estate of Hugh McLeod Fenwick in Aiken, South Carolina. Mr. Fenwick met them at a large stone garage, and the men socialized for about an hour. Bob Friggens said that he intended to restore the car, and Mr. Fenwick was pleased to hear that. Stashed in the trunk of the car were a set of cylinder head gaskets that were thicker than the stock gaskets. When Mr. Fenwick had taken the V-16 convertible touring overseas, the thicker head gaskets reduced the engine's compression ratio, and decreased the potential for damage from knocking with the poorer quality and lower octane gasoline then found in Asia and Europe. Mr. Fenwick had another V-16 car, on which he had had the wells for the fender-mounted spare tires modified so that his hunting dogs could drink water from them. Among his hunting companions were Dwight Eisenhower and pharmaceutical executive Robert Wood Johnson II.

Bob Friggens serviced his new acquisition and drove it home from Aiken to Albuquerque, a long and complicated journey. A few examples of the challenges he encountered give an idea of what he and the V-16 convertible endured. On a long hill east of Asheville, North Carolina, the car's floorboards caught fire. On Interstate 40, east of

Flashy fender skirts. **The fender skirts, with discs that mirror the car's hubcaps, are seen on Fleetwood design drawings for the 1934 Cadillac V-16 cars, but were not offered on production cars. The luggage trunk seen mounted on the rear of the car is of a different design than what Cadillac offered as an accessory (courtesy Steve Plunkett).**

Jackson, Tennessee, at two in the morning, a section of the radiator blew out. Later, while travelling through Arkansas at about 1:30 a.m., the car's electrical system failed, and Mr. Friggens found himself backing carefully down an I-40 entrance ramp, using his flashlight. Eventually, car and new owner made it home, safe and sound.

During 1970 and 1971, the car was Bob Friggens's major restoration project. He had all of the chrome trim replated, with the exception of the windshield frame. He repainted the car (black as it was originally done), and replaced the exhaust system. He fabricated new running board covers and side trim, cut a wood pattern on a lathe to spin new wheel covers (some were missing), and made a new rear compartment ash tray and a new valley cover for the engine. He replaced the interior trim, including new door moldings, he rebuilt the folding top system, including hinges, bows and pads, and he repaired or replaced the instruments. Work was done on the engine, clutch, brakes, steering, and suspension. With these and myriad other tasks, he finished with a good-driving, reliable automobile.

In the July 1972 issue of *The Self-Starter*, the Cadillac-LaSalle Club's monthly publication, Mr. Friggens placed an ad for the 1934 V-16 convertible victoria. This author was able to peek under the tarp the evening before the Cadillac was shipped from Bob's home to its new owner in Texas, and it was truly a magnificent car, gleaming gloriously.

George J. Patterson of Houston, Texas, succeeded to the ownership of the convertible victoria. He subsequently offered it for sale. Beginning in 1979, the next owner, Illinois resident Jon Freeman, undertook a new complete restoration, effected by renowned expert Fran Roxas. The car acquired a deep maroon exterior finish and black convertible

Evolution of an icon. **The beautifully designed OHV V-16 engine that debuted in 1930 is still there for 1934, but changes have been made. The improved air filter, intake silencer, and cold-air intake system largely block view of the black enamel and brushed aluminum valve covers. The more conventional distributor cap isn't as neat as the flat-top 1930 model, but it's easier to service. Clean firewall is permitted by adoption of a discreet mechanical fuel pump and hidden oil filter canister (courtesy Steve Plunkett).**

top, along with fender skirts of the type shown in contemporary Fleetwood design drawings, and bumper guards (doubtless a handy addition, given the fragility of the 1934-only "biplane" bumper design). The process was completed in May 1981 and the car appeared in a Kruse auction in August 1996.

Noted collector Steve Plunkett of Ontario, Canada acquired the car and showed it at the 2008 Meadow Brook Concours d'Elegance. Thereafter, the big Cadillac entered the collection of Oklahoma collector John Groendyke where it remains today.

52

He Drove a Cadillac V-16

A MEMORABLE AUTOMOTIVE ADVERTISING CAMPAIGN from the 1930s featured nothing more than a full-page image of a poised, stylish, and obviously well-off man or woman situated in a setting evocative of upper-class life (onboard a yacht, engaged in the hunt, relaxing in a private club) with no words but the statement in fancy typeface: "He [or she] drives a Duesenberg." There was no hint of a car in the image—just the commanding presence of the type of person the viewer should want to emulate by purchasing a Duesenberg. It was a splendid illustration of the maxim "less is more," and it was quite effective. During the economically turbulent 1930s, some of the fortunate people who sailed above the storms were hesitant to indulge in the extravagance of a bespoke luxury motor car. These ads told them it was okay.

In 1933, Cadillac issued an advertisement that consisted of a blank page with a fine line around the border. Centered was a small Cadillac crest above the following words:

> "The Nineteen Thirty-three production of the
> CADILLAC V-SIXTEEN
> will be limited to Four Hundred Cars
> custom built to order
> creating an entirely new plane of fine car
> ownership."

Cadillac sought to indicate exclusivity, and at the same time, to evoke "The Four Hundred," the designation popularly used to describe the top tier of New York society (Mrs. William Astor's ballroom supposedly accommodated 400). It would be hard to stereotype the people who purchased Cadillac V-16 cars, but there were a number of fascinating characters among the customer base.

Charles Allen Ward was a larger-than-life figure. Born in Seattle, Washington, in 1886, he left home at 17 and worked at transitory employment in various western states (and on the Pacific Ocean). Before World War I, he became involved with the insurgency being led by Mexican rebel Pancho Villa. By 1916, Mr. Ward's activities south of the border enabled him to return to the U.S. financially secure, but a few years later, he managed to get himself arrested and convicted of possession of cocaine and morphine. He began serving his prison term at the end of 1920 in the Leavenworth Federal Penitentiary. While in prison, he met, became friends with, and assisted Herbert Bigelow, a St. Paul, Minnesota, businessman serving time for income tax violations. In 1925, after both men had been paroled, Charles Ward approached Mr. Bigelow for a job at his company, Brown & Bigelow in St. Paul. Then as now, Brown & Bigelow, Inc., is a manufacturer and distributor of printed promotional materials and novelties such as calendars, playing cards and

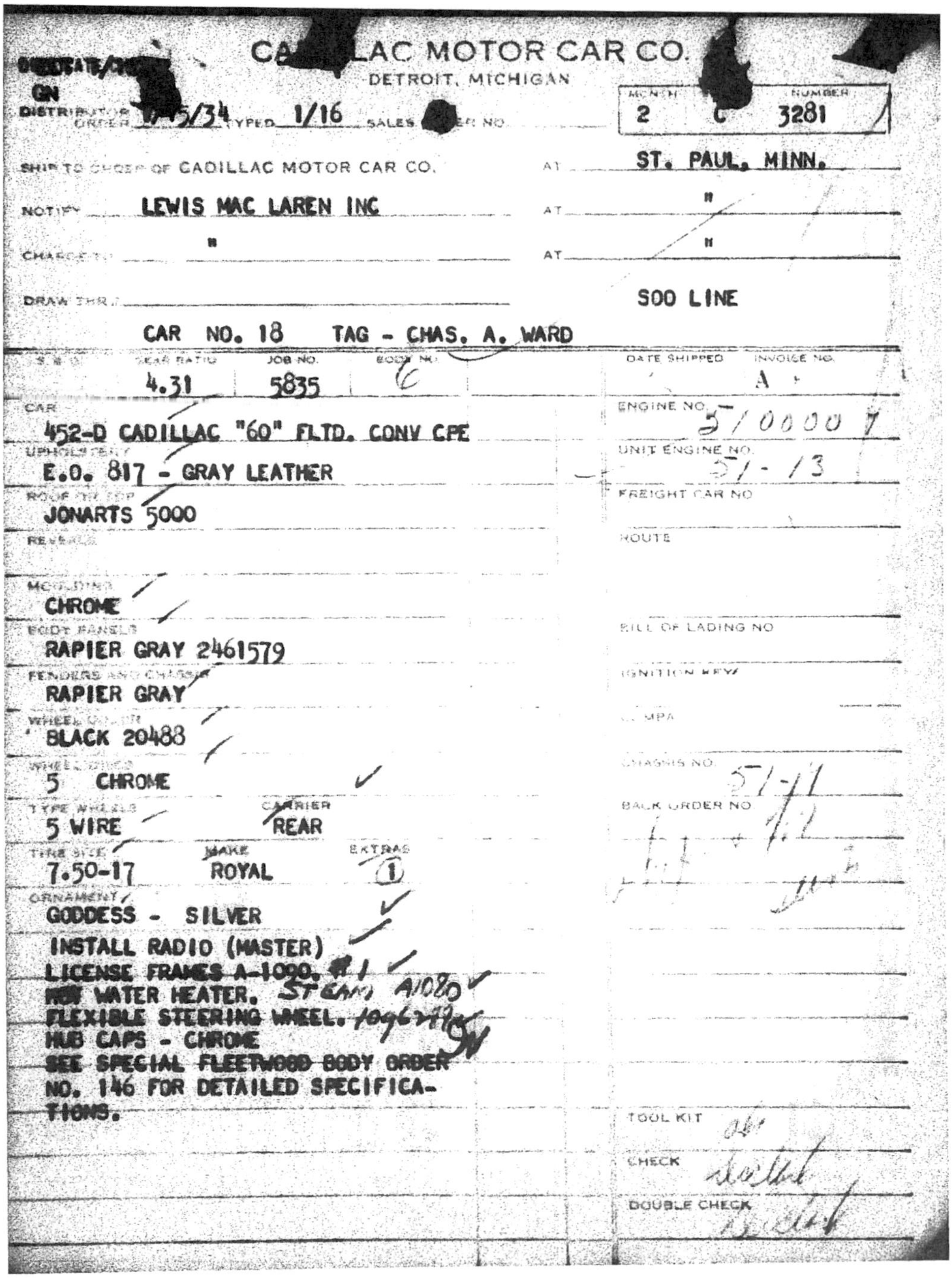

CADILLAC MOTOR CAR CO.
DETROIT, MICHIGAN

DISTRIBUTOR ORDER 1/15/34 TYPED 1/16 SALES ORDER NO.

MONTH 2 C NUMBER 3281

SHIP TO ORDER OF CADILLAC MOTOR CAR CO. AT ST. PAUL, MINN.

NOTIFY LEWIS MAC LAREN INC AT "

CHARGE TO " AT "

DRAW THRU SOO LINE

CAR NO. 18 TAG - CHAS. A. WARD

GEAR RATIO	JOB NO.	BODY NO.	DATE SHIPPED	INVOICE NO.
4.31	5835	6		A

CAR: 452-D CADILLAC "60" FLTD. CONV CPE

ENGINE NO. 5100009

UPHOLSTERY: E.O. 817 - GRAY LEATHER

UNIT ENGINE NO. 51-13

FREIGHT CAR NO.

ROOF OR TOP: JONARTS 5000

ROUTE

MOULDING: CHROME

BILL OF LADING NO.

BODY PANELS: RAPIER GRAY 2461579

IGNITION KEYS

FENDERS AND CHASSIS: RAPIER GRAY

WHEEL COLOR: BLACK 20488

CHASSIS NO. 51-11

WHEEL DISCS: 5 CHROME

TYPE WHEELS: 5 WIRE CARRIER REAR

BACK ORDER NO.

TIRE SIZE 7.50-17 MAKE ROYAL EXTRAS (1)

ORNAMENT: GODDESS - SILVER

INSTALL RADIO (MASTER)
LICENSE FRAMES A-1090.
HOT WATER HEATER. STEAM A1080
FLEXIBLE STEERING WHEEL.
HUB CAPS - CHROME
SEE SPECIAL FLEETWOOD BODY ORDER NO. 146 FOR DETAILED SPECIFICATIONS.

TOOL KIT

CHECK

DOUBLE CHECK

All that's left is a build sheet. **This is the shipping order or "build sheet" for 1934 Cadillac V-16 convertible coupe, engine number 5100009. The car was earmarked for Minnesota businessman Charles A. Ward, and to our best knowledge, it no longer survives. Information on the build sheet identifying the original purchaser is relatively uncommon.**

branded trinkets. Mr. Ward was hired, and by 1932 he was a member of the board and a vice president. When Herbert Bigelow drowned while on a fishing trip, Charles Ward inherited one third of Mr. Bigelow's $3 million estate (1932 dollars). The board of Brown & Bigelow elected Mr. Ward President, and he led the company with a firm and productive hand for the rest of his career, indulging in substantial philanthropy along the way.[50]

In 1934 (notwithstanding that it had sold only 125 V-16 cars in 1933), Cadillac again announced a 400-car ceiling on the year's production. In spite of the persistent economic depression, there was good reason to hope for increased sales. The newly restyled V-16 cars (like the other cars in the Cadillac and LaSalle lines) were dramatically streamlined with pontoon fenders and bodywork that enclosed all the mechanical bits that had previously been visible. Art deco features and ornamental touches abounded. The V-16 cars were now fully twenty feet long, and the 154-inch wheelbase was a half-inch longer than Duesenberg's long-wheelbase chassis. This new design would remain largely unchanged through the 1937 model year. Despite the increased size, the introduction of independent front suspension (newly developed by General Motors engineers) made the new cars much easier to drive and more comfortable. Sadly, fewer than sixty V-16 Cadillacs would be built and shipped for the 1934 model year.

One of the two Series 5835 V-16 convertible coupes that left the Cadillac factory during 1934 was sold to Charles Ward. The build sheet for engine number 5100009, body number 6, bears the instruction "TAG—CHAS. A. WARD" and indicates that the car was shipped to the Lewis MacLaren, Inc. Cadillac dealership in St. Paul, Minnesota. The car was painted Rapier Gray with black wheels and chrome plated wheel discs, and the interior was trimmed with gray leather. The car was equipped with a "Master" radio, a hot-water heater, and a "banjo" style wire-spoke steering wheel. There was only one spare tire (stored under the rear deck), and the goddess atop the radiator shell was silver-plated. A reference to "special Fleetwood Body order No. 146 for detailed specifications" is a frustrating clue, as the special Fleetwood Body orders have not been preserved (the rescue of the Cadillac build sheets by earnest and clear-thinking employees is a coup for which many owners and enthusiasts are immensely grateful).

The two-passenger coupes (convertible and stationary) on the 1934–1937 chassis were striking automobiles. The relatively small passenger compartment was a dramatic contrast to the very long hood and rear deck. The majestic proportions of the cars together with the smooth airfoil-inspired contours give the illusion of forward motion even when the car is standing still.

No one seems to know what became of Mr. Ward's 1934 convertible coupe. In order to survive to the present, each of the big Classics had to survive a number of trials, including the scrap drives of World War II and the Korean War, technological advances that made yesterday's cars seem suddenly old, and just the ordinary depredations of weather, moisture and time. Sad to say, many of these glorious works of art perished over the years, and it's possible that engine number 5100009 is gone. On the other hand, it's

50. A fascinating and thoroughly researched (and illustrated) account of Charles Ward's colorful life written by Shelby Edwards, an associate curator of manuscripts at the Minnesota Historical Society, can be read at the web site of the Society: http://collections.mnhs.org/mnhistorymagazine/articles/64/v64i07p292-300.pdf. Accessed December 9, 2019.

possible that the car will emerge from a private collection, a barn, or a warehouse somewhere.

In the meantime, it's entertaining to imagine a multidimensional fellow like Charles Ward gliding down the road in a sleek and massive 1934 V-16 convertible coupe. The people who owned them are often as fascinating as the cars themselves.

53

Vice Presidential Limousine

John Nance Garner III (1868–1967) was a conservative Texas Democratic politician who served as Franklin Roosevelt's vice president for Roosevelt's first two terms (1933–1941). Championing the prickly pear cactus in the contest to choose Texas's state flower won Mr. Garner the nickname "Cactus Jack." During his service as vice president, he opposed a number of the more assertive aspects of Roosevelt's "New Deal," including its deficit spending and the arbitrary enlargement of the Supreme Court in response to the Court's restriction of some of FDR's programs. In 1893 Mariette Rheiner ran against incumbent Garner for the position of county judge in Uvalde County, Texas. She lost the election, but two years later, the erstwhile opponents were married. They had one son.

In 1934, Cadillac shipped a Series 6275 seven-passenger V-16 imperial sedan with engine number 5100030 and body number 107. Nine such cars were built in 1934 (the high body number reflects the use of the same body shell on V-8 and V-12 chassis). The number 6275 denotes a limousine with a flat, one-piece windshield. There was a divider window between the driver's and passengers' compartments, with two fold-down auxiliary seats to supplement the sofa-like rear seat. The chauffeur's compartment was trimmed in black leather and the passenger compartment in brown wool broadcloth.

Like all 1934 V-16 cars, this one rode on a 154-inch wheelbase and stretched a full twenty feet from the biplane bumper up front to its counterpart in the rear. The body and wheels were painted black, with a chrome molding strip. It was an imposing platform by any standard, but the full-length sedan bodies, like this one, maximized the visual impact. In spite of their great size, innovations like independent front suspension made these automobiles surprisingly easy to drive.

The shipping order or "build sheet" for this car directed that it be charged to Mrs. John N. Garner at "factory." Cars charged to factory accounts in those days are rather unusual—that notation is found, for example, on build sheets for cars ordered by the various Fisher brothers, by General Motors President Alfred P. Sloan, and by Cadillac chief designer Harley Earl, to name several. The wife of the nation's sitting Vice President would certainly be a special customer.

Beginning in 1933 and continuing through the 1937 model year, Cadillac would personalize a V-16 purchaser's car by engraving the owner's name on a plaque in the center of the instrument panel (for 1933 cars) or on the horn button on the steering wheel hub (for 1934 through 1937 cars). The horn button on this particular 1934 Cadillac was engraved at the factory with the name of John Nance Garner (tending to confirm the author's belief that the car was purchased in the name of Mrs. Garner, but was treated as belonging to the Vice President).

It's not known today how the Garners used and enjoyed their limousine. At some

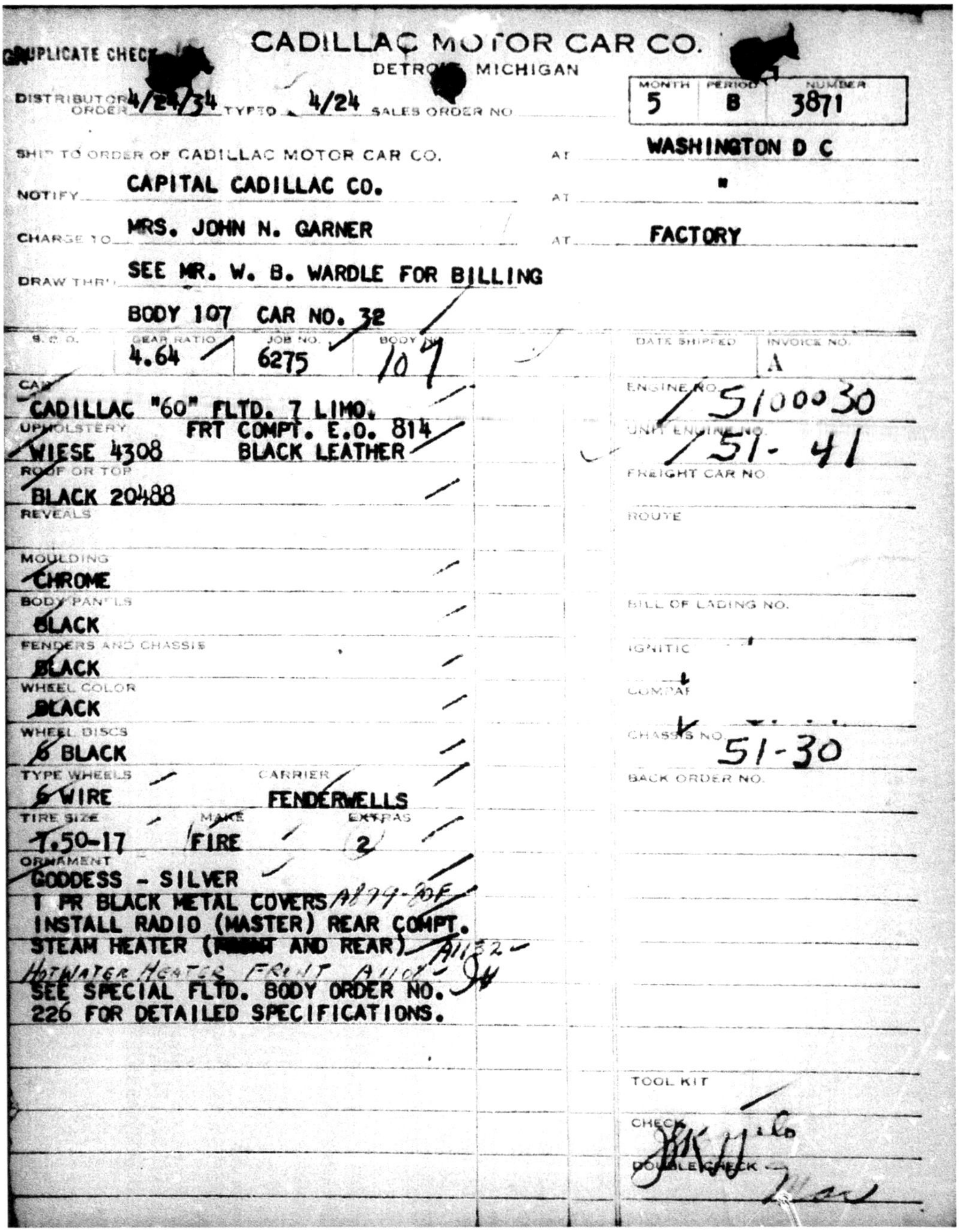

DUPLICATE CHECK

CADILLAC MOTOR CAR CO.
DETROIT MICHIGAN

DISTRIBUTOR ORDER 4/24/34 TYPED 4/24 SALES ORDER NO

MONTH	PERIOD	NUMBER
5	B	3871

SHIP TO ORDER OF CADILLAC MOTOR CAR CO. AT WASHINGTON D C

NOTIFY CAPITAL CADILLAC CO. AT "

CHARGE TO MRS. JOHN N. GARNER AT FACTORY

DRAW THRU SEE MR. W. B. WARDLE FOR BILLING

BODY 107 CAR NO. 32

S. O.	GEAR RATIO	JOB NO.	BODY NO.
	4.64	6275	107

DATE SHIPPED
INVOICE NO. A

CAR
CADILLAC "60" FLTD. 7 LIMO.

ENGINE NO. 5100030

UPHOLSTERY FRT COMPT. E.O. 814
WIESE 4308 BLACK LEATHER

UNIT ENGINE NO. 51-41

ROOF OR TOP
BLACK 20488

FREIGHT CAR NO

REVEALS

ROUTE

MOULDING
CHROME

BODY PANELS
BLACK

BILL OF LADING NO.

FENDERS AND CHASSIS
BLACK

IGNITIC

WHEEL COLOR
BLACK

COMPAF

WHEEL DISCS
6 BLACK

CHASSIS NO. 51-30

TYPE WHEELS CARRIER
6 WIRE FENDERWELLS

BACK ORDER NO.

TIRE SIZE MAKE EXTRAS
7.50-17 FIRE 2

ORNAMENT
GODDESS - SILVER
1 PR BLACK METAL COVERS A879-30F
INSTALL RADIO (MASTER) REAR COMPT.
STEAM HEATER (FRONT AND REAR) A1152
HOTWATER HEATER FRONT A1108-34
SEE SPECIAL FLTD. BODY ORDER NO.
226 FOR DETAILED SPECIFICATIONS.

TOOL KIT

CHECK

DOUBLE CHECK

What the build sheet says. **The shipping order or "build sheet" for this 1934 Cadillac V-16 imperial sedan specifies a black car with brown wool broadcloth for the passenger compartment and black leather for the chauffeur. The goddess mascot on the hood would be silver plated, and there would be different-type heaters for the two compartments. The purchaser appears to have been the wife of the sitting U.S. Vice President, John Nance Garner. Capital Cadillac Company remained in business until late 2020, although it had moved to suburban Maryland.**

point it was purchased by famed polar explorer and pioneering aviator Richard E. Byrd, Jr. Admiral Byrd is reported to have been a collector of fine motor cars, and when he died in 1957, the 1934 V-16 passed to his son (Richard E. Byrd III, who was generally known as Junior rather than III).

In the November-December 1963 issue of the Cadillac-LaSalle Club's monthly publication *The Self-Starter*, an article by CLC member and early V-16 historian Bob Mellin indicated that this flat-windshield limousine was owned at the time by R.E. Byrd.[51] A chart on page 13 of the same publication lists the car as a Series 6075 limousine, body number 107, owned by R.E. Byrd of Boston, Massachusetts, without mention of any modification or conversion into a town car. So at least as late as the end of 1963, the car appears to have been in stock configuration.

Subsequently, perhaps in the late 1960s, Count Johan Otto Raben-Levetzau of Nysted, Denmark, acquired the car from Mr. Byrd. Count Raben was the owner of Aalholm Castle, a fortified estate that dates back to the fourteenth century. Beginning in the 1960s, he had assembled a collection of interesting old automobiles, and had opened the Aalholm Automobile Museum to house and show his cars. Mr. Byrd had written to the museum, asking whether his 1934 Cadillac might be of interest. In his letter he acknowledged that the car was in poor condition, having lain out in the open for fifteen years, and that he was asking a low price for that reason. Count Raben had wanted an open front town car, and he had the seven-passenger limousine converted to fulfill that desire.

It appears that the Count's town car was completed as far as the modifications to the body. The roof was cut away over the driver's compartment, and the tops of the front door window openings were cut out. The vent windows were removed from the front doors, and the door window channels were filled in as though they'd never been there. Some extensive work was done to the cowl of the car, as the stock one-piece windshield and frame were replaced with a center-split, two-pane version that was lower than the split windshields found on some other 1934 V-16 body styles. No provision was made, either at the new windshield header or at the forward edge of the roof, for attachment of a tendelet or cover for the driver's compartment in case of inclement weather.

The rear quarter window openings of the limousine were filled in and covered over to replicate the more formal of the Fleetwood body styles. The upper rear corners of the back doors were rounded, and the body openings were correspondingly modified. The drip moldings that had extended over the now-missing quarter windows were redirected downward once they passed the rear door openings. The car was painted a teal color, and a simulated canework applique was attached to the rear lower quarters of the body and the lower panels of the rear doors.

Count Raben must have spent a substantial amount of money on refashioning his 1934 V-16. The entry in the Museum's catalog that Cadillac historian Yann Saunders read in 2002 stated: "Unfortunately, although the initial cost to acquire the car was low, restoration proved to be very expensive." The work on the car appears to have stopped before the worn upholstery, the weathered chrome trim pieces, the damaged running boards or the missing rear bumper were addressed.

In 2009 the car showed up on the web site of Danish vendor of collector cars Viklit

---

51. Mellin, Bob, "Cadillac V16: 1934–1937 Roster and Summary," *The Self-Starter*, Cadillac-LaSalle Club, Inc., Detroit, MI, Vol. 5, No. 2, November-December 1963: pp. 8–13, 10.

Count Raben's creation. **In the 1960s, Danish Count Johan Otto Raben-Levetzau had the 1934 V-16 limousine (formerly owned by Vice President John Nance Garner and later Admiral Richard Byrd) converted into this town car with canework applique on the lower rear doors and quarter panels. No provision was made for a roof or cover for the driver in the event of inclement weather (courtesy Brian Coffee).**

Graae Jørgensen, with an asking price of €34,500. Not long thereafter, collector and restorer Brian Coffee informed the author that he was the car's new owner. Mr. Coffee reports that Mr. Jørgensen had purchased the Cadillac from one of the children of Richard Byrd III, and included in the deal were all of the parts that had been removed in the course of the modifications. Mr. Coffee and his employees found, inside the door pockets, letters signed by Admiral Byrd and other interesting artifacts consistent with the car's reputed provenance.

According to Brian Coffee, the engine had good compression when he obtained the car, and he and his associates have seen to it that the engine runs well. He has gathered a variety of parts with an eye to proceeding with a full restoration.

A car such as this 1934 Cadillac presents an interesting dilemma to a contemporary owner. It has been extensively altered from its original, factory-fresh configuration in a unique fashion. One could undertake to complete that transformation to have the resulting town car for his own pleasure, or in hopes of interesting another purchaser. Or the modifications could be undone and the car returned to the condition in which it was first sold. Either choice entails a good deal of work and materials to bring the body to the desired style (whether an open-front, V-windshield town car, or a flat-windshield closed limousine) and both pathways entail costs for necessary upholstery, paint and plating. And closed cars, even those with open chauffeur's compartments, generally bring lower sale prices than their open counterparts.

In 2017, the big Cadillac was listed for sale on the web site of Significant Cars, Inc., a dealer in the Indianapolis area, and recently a notation was added indicating that it has been sold. We'll have to wait and see what becomes of this historically significant motor car.

54

A Tale of Two Cars

Alden O. Johnson was one of the charter members of the Cadillac-LaSalle Club. Founded in 1958, the club was formed by old Cadillac enthusiasts who wanted to enjoy the benefits of mutual assistance in restoring, finding parts for, and enjoying their cars. It was such a good idea that it's still going strong well over half a century later. Shortly before the CLC came to be, Mr. Johnson acquired one of the fifty Cadillac V-16s built for the 1935 model year.

While no 1935 V-16 could be called run-of-the-mill, the one Mr. Johnson owned is special. It is a Series 5880 four-door convertible with a divider window between the front and rear compartments—only four were built that year. With the top down, the driver and passengers could experience open-air motoring in style. Put the top up and roll up the divider and door windows, and the pampered privacy of a limousine cossets the rear-seat occupants. Until the previous year, Cadillac had called such a car an "all-weather phaeton." The new designation was simply "convertible sedan."

This Cadillac convertible sedan was shipped new to Indianapolis, Indiana, in June 1935. The build sheet for the car indicates that it was ordered all black with chrome moldings, and with black leather seats and trim. Two spare tires were carried in the front fenders, and a sterling silver goddess perched atop the radiator shell. The optional flexible ("banjo") steering wheel and a "Master" radio in the front compartment were also ordered. To the extent that they could accommodate, Cadillac offered to do whatever a prospective purchaser asked, in order to tailor each V-16 to the owner's preferences. An instruction on the build sheet to "SEE SPECIAL FLTD. BODY ORDER NO. 329 FOR DETAILED SPECIFICATIONS" indicates that the original purchaser of this convertible sedan had made additional requests for this car, but the Fleetwood Body orders have been lost and we have no way of knowing what those requests were.

In the top section of the build sheet are the words "TAG—E.B. LILLY." Such an instruction meant that the car was to be designated and set aside ("tagged") for the indicated person or company. An ad in the September 17, 1921, issue of the "Brooklyn Chamber of Commerce Bulletin" identifies E.B. Lilly as "Manufacturer and Banker and director to several Corporations." Or perhaps the E.B. Lilly who ordered this car was one of the principals of the Eli Lilly and Company pharmaceutical research and manufacturing business. Civil War veteran Col. Eli Lilly established his company in Indianapolis in 1876, and his son Josiah K. Lilly and grandsons (Josiah K. Lilly, Jr., and Eli Lilly) continued it.

The build sheet shows an engine number of 5100143, but the number of the engine in the car is 5100043. Although only one digit is one number different, it is unlikely that a mistake was made. The discrepancy is most likely explained by an engine swap at some point in the car's life. The build sheet for engine number 5100143 is for the right year and

Long and low. **1935 V-16 convertible sedan shows lavish use of streamline design and art deco details. Pontoon fenders, teardrop head- and taillights, and even cigar-shaped door handles offer minimal wind resistance. Dummy vent louvers on the front fender echo the real ones on the hood side panel. Spinner-type hub caps were an extra-cost option (courtesy John Groendyke).**

body style (and body number—86). Number 5100043 is too low an engine number to have been originally installed in a 1935 car.

There is a build sheet for engine number 5100043, and it specifies a Series 5875 seven-passenger limousine, shipped a year before the convertible sedan (in June 1934), and to Cadillac's Chicago branch. The front compartment of this car was trimmed in black leather from the Eagle Ontario company, and the passenger compartment in imported English broadcloth. Like the convertible sedan, this limousine was painted entirely black with a chrome molding. Instead of fender-mounted spare tires, there was a single spare, stowed under the deck lid. Again a silver goddess was ordered, but the "Master" radio was installed in the rear compartment. Detailed specifications were set forth in Fleetwood Body Order No. 323 (unfortunately, no longer extant). In the top part of the build sheet there appears the instruction "TAG—THOMAS HOWELL."

This writer is convinced that the Thomas Howell referred to in the build sheet for engine number 5100043 was none other than infamous grain market speculator (and manipulator) Thomas M. Howell of Chicago. During the 1920s and 1930s this Mr. Howell made a substantial fortune (in millions of pre-war dollars) playing the futures markets at the Chicago Board of Trade, where, according to a 1939 *Chicago Sunday Tribune* article, "his reputation as a plunger made him an almost legendary figure for many years." Plunger was a slang term for one who (alone or in concert with others) would buy up

Inside scoop. **With the front fender removed for service, internal details of this 1935 V-16 convertible sedan are revealed. Battery box next to the frame rail (center foreground) meant that replacing the battery had to be done from underneath the car. Manifolds and air intake tubing largely conceal the engine. Coil spring independent front suspension (r.) was new for 1934, and vastly improved ride and handling (courtesy John Groendyke).**

futures contracts and deliverable supplies of a commodity to force up the market price, and then let the price plunge after he (and his associates) had reaped quick profits.

In January 1935 Mr. Howell was barred for two years from trading on all U.S. grain exchanges for engaging in price manipulation and for other offenses. In 1936, in response to his shenanigans and those of other colorful speculators like Arthur W. Cutten, Congress passed the Commodity Exchange Act. Closing the gate after the horse was gone, that legislation outlawed many of the activities that had so enriched Mr. Howell and other feckless wizards of the trading pits.

As is so often the case, even if the original owner is known (or a likely candidate has been identified), what happened for the early part of the car's existence is shrouded in mist. At some point, perhaps in the 1940s, E.B. Lilly's convertible sedan came into the possession of a U.S. Army captain, who sold it to a St. Paul, Minnesota, used car dealer in the 1950s. The car dealer sold it to the late Dexter Buell, from whom it passed to John Morgan. The next owner was a Mrs. Norval, who sold it in 1957, to Alden O. Johnson, whom we met at the beginning of this story. It was still recorded with Mr. Johnson in 1963, and in a roster of extant V-16s that had been prepared by Stan Squires in the early 1970s, it was said to be "disassembled, with no running boards, but otherwise [in] good condition."

Former President of the Classic Car Club of America Dick Gold, who lived in the Minneapolis area, had arranged with a mailman to pay the man if he found interesting old cars in the garages of the people on his route. The mailman appears to have turned up the 1935 V-16 convertible sedan, and Mr. Gold became an owner. In 1984 Mr. Gold sold the car and it joined the collection of Dr. Barbara Mae Atwood.

Despite the fact that the convertible sedan had survived complete and with very little wear, Dr. Atwood decided to begin a thorough restoration. She placed the car in the capable hands of Steve Babinsky, who recalls that by the time Dr. Atwood had acquired the car, it had been repainted in yellow, but was in good condition. The restoration was completed in 1991, and the car took a first in class at the Pebble Beach Concours d'Elegance (to add to an assortment of awards it garnered from Antique Automobile Club of America events before and after the restoration).

In January of 2009, the car was offered at RM Auctions' "Automobiles of Arizona" event, where it brought $473,000. Distinguished Texas collector Paul Andrews became the new owner, mechanically refreshing and detailing the car so it could be driven. In 2015, Mr. Andrews and his son made a number of cars from their collection (including this one) available for sale through RM Auctions (now partnered with Sotheby's) in a sale that took place on May 2. The sale price was $605,000, and the new owner was Enid, Oklahoma, businessman and collector John Groendyke. On January 16, 2020, Mr. Groendyke's car was sold at the RM Auctions Arizona Auction for $425,000, exclusive of buyer's premium.

Two long, black 16-cylinder Cadillacs were ordered a year apart in the mid–1930s, one by a member of a well-known entrepreneurial family, and the other by a grain market millionaire. The owners' lives don't appear to have intersected, but their cars did—the engine of one survives, and it powers the other. The rest is history.

55

New Life Out of the Ashes

ONE OF THE OLDEST BRANDS in ice cream is Breyers. In 1866, William A. Breyer started making ice cream and selling it out of his home in Philadelphia. Later he hawked his product from a horse-drawn wagon. In 1908, his son Henry incorporated the Breyer Ice Cream Company. By 1918, the company was churning out over a million gallons a year, and in 1926 the family sold the company to National Dairy Products Corporation.

On December 29, 1934, a 1935 Cadillac V-16 convertible sedan was shipped to Cadillac's New York Branch, to be featured at the 1935 New York Auto Show. Engine number 5100104 was the fourth V-16 car, by engine number, for the 1935 model year (1935 V-16 engine numbers began with 5100101). That the body number (64) was not correspondingly low was due to the sharing of the Fleetwood body shells across the V-8, V-12, and V-16 lines, and across the 1934 through 1937 model years. Trim and interior fitments varied as would befit the respective levels of exclusivity.

The car was an impressive presence, painted "Crescendo Green" (including the instrument panel) with a chrome inlay for the body molding. Nearly twenty feet long, this lordly Cadillac sported a silver plated goddess atop the radiator shell, fender-mounted spare tires with painted metal covers, and a "Master" radio. The interior was trimmed in two types of cloth with "Lackawanna Green" leather bolster rolls at the leading edges of the seats. The convertible top and the fabric boot that covered it when folded were piped in leather to match the color used on the seats. There was a special Fleetwood Body Order that provided greater detail regarding the appointments and specifications for the car, but that has been lost.

After its stint at the auto show, the convertible sedan was diverted to Philadelphia where it was sold to Henry W. Breyer, Jr. (1904–1972), son of Henry and grandson of William Breyer. The green color of the car was similar to the hue that the Breyer company used for the packaging of its ice cream. Little is known about how Mr. Breyer may have used and enjoyed his Cadillac, because then as now, the family treasures their privacy. But in 1952, this very green car was sold to William T. Walter of Drexel Hill, Pennsylvania, and two years later he sold it to a man in Wenonah, New Jersey, named Thomas W. Synnott II.

During the early 1960s, an enthusiastic member of the Cadillac-LaSalle Club named Bob Mellin was working on a comprehensive history of the 1934 through 1937 Cadillac V-16 cars, as well as a roster of those that had survived the hazards and depredations of the elements, the wartime scrap drives and the changing tastes of the car-buying public. He was helped greatly in obtaining archival information from General Motors by influential GM designer David Holls. Mr. Holls had been heavily involved in the design of the iconic 1959 Cadillacs, and he would be instrumental in the development of other seminal

THE SELF STARTER

Published monthly by the Cadillac-LaSalle Club, Inc., which has been formed for the express purpose of encouraging automobile enthusiasts to band together for mutual interests in the preservation, restoration and enjoyment of the Cadillac and LaSalle cars built through 1942. This Club is not affiliated in any way with the General Motors Corporation.

VOLUME IV JUNE 1962 NUMBER 9

-IN THIS ISSUE-

DREAM COME TRUE by DAVE HOLLS

1935 V-16 Convertible Sedan

and other interesting subjects

Membership Sec. . . . .William R. Tite
22600 Amherst, St. Clair Shores, Mich.

Editor. . . . . . A. Uhlir
710 Symes, Royal Oak, Mich.

***Cover girl.* This is how the 1935 V-16 convertible sedan that Dave Holls restored appeared when it was featured on the cover of the June 1962 issue of the Cadillac-LaSalle Club's monthly publication *The Self-Starter* (courtesy *The Self-Starter*).**

projects, such as the 1963 Corvette Sting Ray and the 1966 Buick Riviera. His long career at GM Styling would last until he retired in 1991.

In the course of compiling the roster of mid–30s V-16 survivors, Mr. Mellin spoke with Thomas Synnott II about his 1935 convertible sedan and a 1936 V-16 limousine that Mr. Synnott had bought as a back-up car for the convertible. Mr. Mellin wanted to buy the limousine, but Mr. Synnott wouldn't sell the limousine unless he could also sell the

1935 V-16 #104, Dave Holls
(taken Summer 1962)

Top-down elegance. **Posed at the home of GM styling executive Dave Holls, it's easy to see why the big open cars like this 1935 V-16 convertible sedan are so popular. The lines are sleek and graceful for a twenty-foot-long motor car (courtesy *The Self-Starter*).**

convertible. So Mr. Mellin approached Dave Holls about the cars and in 1962, Mr. Holls bought the convertible and Mr. Mellin got the limousine.

In an article entitled "Dream Come True" that he wrote for the June 1962 issue of the Cadillac-LaSalle Club's monthly magazine/newsletter *The Self-Starter*, Dave Holls described his fifteen-year quest to own a Cadillac V-16.[52] He qualified that by acknowledging his "very special craving" for one of the 1934–1937 cars—cars with "[s]tyling so advanced that it was possible for it to remain virtually intact for no less than four years." In the same article, Mr. Holls spoke of driving with his wife from his home in Detroit to New Jersey to retrieve his dream car. Originally he intended to bring the car back with a tow bar hitched to his modern car, but the 7,000-pound weight of the V-16 convertible sedan thwarted his plan. So climbing into the driver's seat with his wife driving their other car, he set off. The morning was a pleasant opportunity to get to know the car as he drove. After lunch, a short circuit in the wiring for the lights caused smoke and some concern, but didn't stop the trip. Later that afternoon, a flat tire in a parking lot was replaced with one of the spares. But when a second tire went flat, they found out that the other spare was soft and that the lights didn't work. Just 160 miles from home, they had to arrange for a tow. But once home, Mr. Holls eagerly set to work on his car and began what he called "the slow process of spit and polish to restore all of its former grandeur."

Dave Holls put many hours into restoring the convertible sedan, but on January 2, 1963, the Holls residence caught fire and although the family escaped unharmed, the V-16 was terribly damaged. Much of the body was burnt and deformed when the structural

52. Holls, David, "Dream Come True," *The Self-Starter*, Cadillac-LaSalle Club, Inc., Royal Oak, MI, June 1962: cover, pp. 2–3.

After the fire. **Partially disassembled, this is how the rear portion of the body looked when Ross Morgan received the burned car (courtesy Ross Morgan).**

wood framing burned away, and there was not much left but the chassis and (undamaged) drive train. The insurance company put the wreckage up for sale as salvage, and Bob Mellin was able to acquire it, intending to use or sell the intact parts.

During the ensuing years, the remains of Henry Breyer, Jr.'s once-proud V-16 Cadillac passed through other hands (including, reportedly, those of Detroit V-16 enthusiast Richard Ancerewicz), always the subject of sad thoughts among collectors about how perishable precious things are. In late 2015, Australian V-16 collector and restorer Ross Morgan acquired the car and he began a long-overdue restoration. With luck and care, this Cadillac will once again command awe and respect, as it once did at the New York Auto Show and on the streets of Philadelphia.

56

Realizing What Never Was

By the mid–1930s, the Great Depression had caught up with the luxury auto makers and had sent a number of storied and revered companies into bankruptcy. Marmon and Peerless went down. Pierce-Arrow and Duesenberg were struggling, but not long for this world. Packard would make it through by dint of its introduction of a lower-priced line. But backed by the financial reserves of General Motors, Cadillac seemed to brush aside the economic gloom (at least in the brand's advertisements), and for 1934 it introduced a bigger, boldly restyled line of V-16 cars.

The new cars rode on a 154-inch wheelbase, and extended a full twenty feet between the tips of the elegant biplane bumpers. Teardrop shaped pontoon fenders merged with streamlined bodywork in an imposing display of art deco futurism. The newly-developed independent front suspension made these cars drive much more like modern automobiles, and gave passengers a much smoother ride.

Fleetwood offered a wide selection of body styles for the 1934 V-16s, both closed and open. Some featured a windshield split vertically at the center with the two panes angled back and to the sides. Others retained the traditional one-piece windshield. In keeping with the theme of aerodynamic design, provision was made for storing the spare tire inside the rear compartment of the car, instead of carrying spares in wells carved out of the front fenders. A buyer could still order fender-mounted spares, but as an option.

The radically streamlined styling theme for the '34 V-16s would be maintained

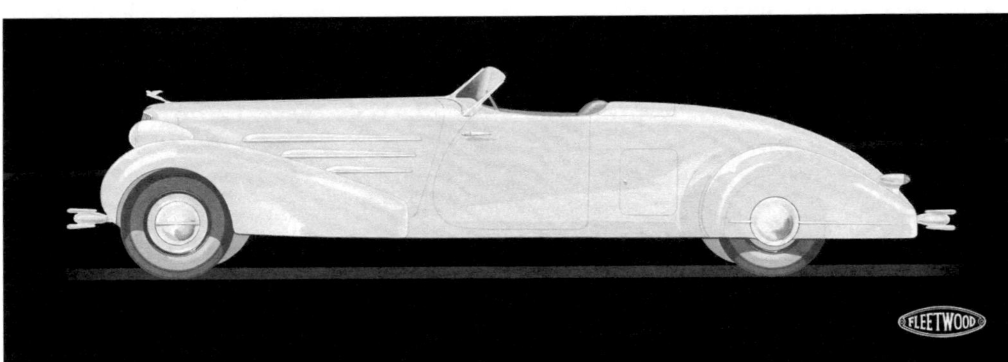

Fleetwood design for a 1934 V-16 roadster. **One of the many styles that Fleetwood created for 1934, this sleek roadster (officially style 5802) was never ordered by a customer, and it never clothed a V-16 chassis when these cars were new. By the mid–1930s, luxury car buyers preferred weather-tight passenger compartments, rendering roadsters largely obsolete (courtesy Jim Schild).**

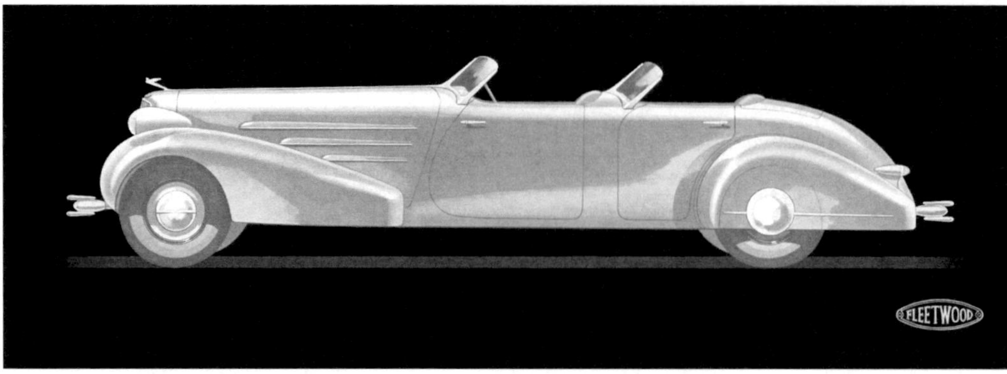

Design drawing for a never-built dual-cowl phaeton. **Largely eclipsed by convertible sedans with roll-up windows, touring cars and phaetons like this style 5859 were becoming less available from fine car makers. With the superb streamlining characteristic of the 1934–1937 V-16 cars, the disappearing top and tonneau windshield make this big car almost racy (courtesy Jim Schild).**

almost unchanged through the 1937 model year, and as before, most purchasers opted for closed sedans, formal or plain. Those who ordered open styles chose the models with roll-up windows. The once-numerous roadster, phaeton and touring car configurations, although offered, were not ordered and remained unbuilt. This was a pity because the Fleetwood drawings for the Series 5802 two-passenger roadster, 5859 five-passenger dual-cowl sport phaeton, and 5857 seven-passenger touring car prove that the new streamlined styling theme was quite amenable to what were by then somewhat archaic structures.

In the early 1980s, noted Classic car restorer Francis Roxas of Alsip, Illinois, had just finished constructing a series of LeBaron-design bodies for Classic-era Lincolns, and he had seen drawings in a Fleetwood book of designs for the 1934 Cadillac line that caught his interest and gave him an idea for his next project. The drawings by Canadian stylist John Hampshire in a section entitled "Special Individual Fleetwood Custom Bodies" near the end of the book were intended to show what Fleetwood was capable of doing for the willing (and well-heeled) customer. The Series 5802 roadster and Series 5859 dual-cowl phaeton were among the designs illustrated. Mr. Roxas decided to bring the dual-cowl phaeton to life.

He enlisted the help of renowned automotive design instructor (and long-time Chief Honorary Judge at the Pebble Beach Concours d'Elegance) Strother MacMinn. "Mac" had worked for Harley Earl in the GM Art & Colour Section during the 1930s, had written extensively on automotive design, and had taught for years in the Industrial Design department of the Art Center School (now known as ArtCenter College of Design) in Los Angeles.[53] Mr. MacMinn used the Fleetwood promotional drawing to create full-size exterior renderings of the Series 5859 phaeton. Former General Motors director of corporate design David Holls was able to obtain full-size factory blueprints for the first-generation V-16 chassis. So prepared, the team went to work on a low-mileage

53. The late Charles Jordan, former GM Vice President for Design, was quoted in Mr. MacMinn's *New York Times* obituary as saying, "Mac never designed a car, but no one influenced car design more than he did."

***1937 Cadillac V-16 dual-cowl phaeton.* Professional attention to detail is apparent in this magnificent realization of a Fleetwood design that was offered but never ordered as a new car. Restorer Fran Roxas started with a 1937 V-16 imperial sedan and built the new body "from scratch," and saw to it that every effort was made to emulate what the Fleetwood craftsmen would have done (courtesy Ronald Verschoor).**

1937 Cadillac V-16 Series 5875 imperial sedan, engine number 5130311 (new for 1937 were hydraulic brakes). The sedan's chassis was retained, along with the grille, hood, floorpan and fenders (with some modifications). The rest of the body was fabricated using the period-correct composite technique in which a wood framework is constructed and steel body panels are formed and then attached to the wood framework. The metal fabrication was done by Scott Knight and the wood structure was crafted by Don Linsley. At every step, great care was taken to ensure that the result was as Fleetwood would have achieved, had they built this particular design.

The finished automobile was, true to the Fleetwood drawing, a dual-cowl phaeton for five passengers with a disappearing top and raked, vee windshields for the front and rear seats. In 1984 car was awarded a First in Class in the New Coachwork Class at the Pebble Beach Concours d'Elegance. In the mid–1990s, it made a return appearance at Pebble Beach and placed second, notwithstanding that the work on the car had been completed ten years earlier. Eventually Mr. Roxas sold the phaeton, and it was acquired in 1998 by the Milhous Collection. In February 2012, it was sold at auction to the Pack Automotive Museum for a price of $962,500.

In the early 1990s, because the dual-cowl phaeton had turned out so well, Mr. Roxas decided to build the Series 5802 roadster. A 1935 Series 5875 imperial sedan (engine number 5100137) served as the donor this time. Enlisting the same team of expert craftsmen,

***1934 V-16 roadster.* A second realization by Fran Roxas of a never-ordered custom style, this car shows just how sporty and flashy a twenty-foot-long automobile could be. Massive proportions of the 1934–1937 V-16 chassis are highlighted by the two-seat passenger compartment. Separate fenders and absence of running boards evoke contemporary race car design. Opening in the raised hood panel accommodates the cowl vent (courtesy Ronald Verschoor).**

Mr. Roxas set them to work. The Fleetwood drawing of this car is a direct side view. Although a rumble seat is not shown in the profile image, the presence of a golf-bag door in the side of the body indicates that there would have been a rumble seat that would fold flush with the rear deck. So Mr. MacMinn designed such a rumble seat, and in order to avoid spoiling the car's lines with a set of steps for the rumble seat passengers, he contrived a door on the right-hand side that would permit ready entry from street level. The challenge of designing those items was matched by the challenge of fabricating them. As with the dual-cowl phaeton, the fenders had to be altered because the donor cars were built with running boards, while the Fleetwood drawings for the roadster and the phaeton showed clean rocker panels and unencumbered fender ends. To complete the roadster's stunning presence, Mr. Roxas installed the iconic "biplane" 1934 bumpers (a one-year-only feature that proved impractically delicate in daily use).

When the roadster was finished and ready to show, it was presented at Pebble Beach in the mid–1990s, along with the dual-cowl phaeton. The roadster took First to the phaeton's Second Place. Like the phaeton, this car entered the Milhous collection and was sold to the Pack Automotive Museum at the same auction as the phaeton, but for a price of $1,001,000.

By 1934, automotive design was in the throes of radical rethinking—streamlining and aerodynamics, longer and lower, rapid technological advance. At the same time, the nation (and the world) were in the grip of the Great Depression. Cadillac V-16 car sales for each of the years 1934 through 1937 never exceeded 60 units. Few of those buyers opted for sporty or flashy models. None opted for the old-fashioned windowless styles—the roadster, the dual-cowl phaeton, or the seven-passenger touring car—notwithstanding the exquisite way Fleetwood envisioned them. Thanks to Fran Roxas's impulse and determination, we are able to see two of those never-ordered special custom designs in solid form and to appreciate a special moment in the progression of automotive history.

A further consideration that bears mentioning is that the willingness of the market to value each of these cars at $1,000,000, more or less, contradicts the conventional wisdom that a big Classic that has been modified (other than custom work done by one of the respected carriage houses during the Classic era) is inevitably less valuable than an unaltered example. Neither of the two donor cars, no matter how well preserved or well restored, would be at all likely to sell for a price close to what this roadster and phaeton brought. That forces an uneasy conflict. On the one hand, something valuable is lost if a solid and original example of one of the great Classic cars that is a special creation in its own right is sacrificed to realize a lost or never-made sister car (even one more unique or special). On the other hand, there's something to be said for the value of bringing to the contemporary world one of the many beautiful Classics that were destroyed over the years or never realized. It would appear that the market, at least, has addressed the question.

57

The Pirate

JOHN B. HAWLEY, JR. (1899–1980), was a Texan who earned a civil engineering degree from Cornell University, moved to the Minneapolis–St. Paul area in 1924, and went to work for Cargill, Inc. In 1929, he was able to purchase Northern Pump Company, newly formed from the combination of two Minneapolis companies, Northern Fire Apparatus Company and the Pagel Pump Company. Northern Pump began as a fifty-employee manufacturer of pumps for fire engines. By the time World War II was over, Mr. Hawley had transformed it into the largest manufacturer of heavy naval guns in the U.S. In the process he became a very wealthy, if controversial, man.

In 1932, Mr. Hawley obtained the company's first contract with the U.S. Navy, to manufacture hydraulic equipment, including submersible pumps. In 1940, the brash entrepreneur convinced the Navy to let his company build anti-aircraft guns under contracts totaling $50 million. The Navy was pleased with the product and the rate of production, but competitors, and his somewhat cavalier business and employment practices, led many to see him as a profiteer. According to Minnesota Historical Society records, Mr. Hawley's salary was the sixth highest personal salary in the U.S. for fiscal year 1944.

After the War, Mr. Hawley turned his company towards the manufacture of oil field drilling machines (notwithstanding he had little previous experience in that business). "Oilmen are a bunch of fuddy-duddies," said he. "I'm a pirate."[54]

It's not known whether John B. Hawley, Jr., acquired his 1936 Cadillac V-16 convertible sedan (bearing engine number 5110222) new or used, but at some time during the 1940s the car underwent something of a makeover or update. The fender-mounted spare tires were eliminated for uninterrupted aerodynamic lines.[55] Modified versions of the sculpted 1942–'47 Cadillac bumpers replaced the simpler originals. The teardrop-shaped headlight pods were discarded and sealed-beam lamps were mounted in the forward curves of the front fenders, with sheet metal fairings and chrome trimrings added to smooth out the new design. The running boards were narrowed between the front and rear doors, and flashy chrome stone guards graced the lower forward surfaces of the rear fenders. The car was painted black with red wheels. Finally, three horizontal louvers were added to each rear fender to match those on the front fenders (much as Cadillac would do with their 1938–1940 V-16 cars). Photos taken in December 1947

54. Kenny, Dave, *Minnesota Goes to War*, St. Paul: Minnesota Historical Society Press, 2005: pp. 111–115.

55. The 1934 Cadillacs for the first time made provision for storing the spare tire inside the car. Many (including the original buyer of this 1936 convertible sedan) still opted for twin spares carried in fenderwells, and Cadillac obliged them through the 1940 model year.

John B. Hawley, Jr.'s updated convertible sedan. **Taken when the car was on exhibit at the Museum of Science and Industry in Chicago, this photograph shows how Mr. Hawley modified his 1936 V-16 convertible sedan. Headlights have been faired into the front fenders. The running boards have been cut away to leave step plates for front and rear passengers. The bumpers are those used for Cadillacs built during 1942–1947. Bright metal stone guards have been fitted to the fronts of the rear fenders (courtesy Museum of Science and Industry, Chicago).**

at the Northern Ordnance, Inc.[56] plant show the car with the modifications, shiny and spotless.

In 1949, Mr. Hawley donated his V-16 Cadillac to the Museum of Science and Industry in Chicago, Illinois. The car was featured in the November–December 1963 issue of the Cadillac-LaSalle Club's monthly newsletter *The Self-Starter*. It would remain in the museum's collection and would be seen there by countless visitors until the museum de-acquisitioned it in 2008. At that time, the car brought a sale price of $194,000 at the Bonhams's Vintage New England Auction held at the Larz Anderson Auto Museum in Brookline, Massachusetts (well below the pre-auction estimate of $300,000–$500,000).

Under new ownership, the decision was made to undertake a full recovery of the car's original as-new configuration, with the services of Stone Barn Automobile Restoration in Hackettstown, New Jersey. The fender-mounted headlights gave way to original

56. Northern Ordnance, Inc. was a subsidiary of Northern Pump Company, formed in 1942 in Fridley, Minnesota.

1936 V-16 separate units meant to flank the radiator shell. Side-mount spare tires once again adorned the front fenders (the spare tire wells had only been covered over during the modifications), and authentic metal covers were again fitted. Plain, straight-edged running boards were fitted with the correct-pattern rubber matting. Correct 1936 V-16 bumpers replaced the 1942 units, and the leading edges of the rear fenders lost the chrome stone guards. Interestingly, the rear fender louvers remained. The car wore Phantom Metallic paint, as per the build sheet specifications, along with Vincennes Red wheels. Although the car was structurally sound and showed little wear (a very believable 16,000 miles showed on the odometer), collecting the necessary parts for the restoration was an arduous process. The result was well worth the efforts.

At the 2015 Pebble Beach Concours d'Elegance, the V-16 that Mr. Hawley had owned was shown, and it was awarded a third-place prize. In October 2017, its private owner offered the 1936 V-16 convertible sedan at the RM Sotheby's Hershey Auction. Once the hammer fell, the selling price was announced as $715,000, and a new owner took possession.

Opposite, top: Restored to original condition. **Mr. Hawley's once-modified 1936 Cadillac V-16 has been returned to "like new" condition, looking the way its build sheet described it. The location is the Hershey Lodge in Hershey, Pennsylvania, in 2017. Only the three louvers on the rear fender remain of the 1940s modifications (courtesy David Kane).** ***Bottom: Leather and fine wood surround the driver.*** **The front compartment of this 1936 V-16 convertible sedan features the available flexible "banjo" steering wheel. The glove box door mirrors the shape of the instrument cluster. An accessory heater can just be seen below the far right end of the instrument panel (courtesy David Kane).**

58

A Parts Car Too Good to Use

Mr. William B. Ruger, Jr., of the Sturm, Ruger & Co. firearms family was an experienced collector of fine motor cars. In the mid–1990s, he was having a 1937 Cadillac V-16 restored by noted Chicago-area restoration expert Fran Roxas. When a 1936 V-16 town sedan became available for purchase, the men decided to buy it for use as a parts car for the 1937. The 1937 Cadillac V-16 cars were nearly unchanged from the 1936 cars, the few changes including hydraulic brakes and a front stabilizer bar. This particular '36 V-16 was being sold from the estate of a fellow who had owned several Cadillacs and other fine old cars. For some reason the man's wife had set fire to his garage. The 1936 town sedan had sustained only slight damage, and according to Mr. Roxas, it was otherwise in great shape. When they saw the state of completion and preservation of the town sedan, he and Mr. Ruger agreed it would be better to restore it than to dissect it as a parts source.

In the 1930s, a town sedan (also known as a club sedan or close-coupled sedan) was generally a less-common configuration than the five- and seven-passenger sedans made

***A big but graceful car.* The wheelbase is the longest of any production American car (154 inches), and the overall length is a hair shy of twenty feet. But the proportions of the town sedan body lend a visual appeal and litheness uncommon to such a large car (courtesy Chad Chambers).**

***Sparkling instruments and steering wheel.* The optional flexible "banjo-style" steering wheel and the art-deco-themed gauge array speak to the driver in the language of luxury. The v-shaped item to the right, just above the ignition switch, is the radio control set, with a key lock just below the dial. Early car radios often had locks to keep the curious from draining the car's battery (courtesy Chad Chambers).**

by the same manufacturers. The usual sedan arrangement had a good deal of extra leg-room between the rear seat and the back of the front seats (with or without folding auxiliary or "jump" seats). Much like the sedans we're familiar with today, a town sedan had the rear seat passengers riding pretty close to the front seats, and a luggage compartment built into the bodywork behind the rear seat back cushions.

The V-16 town sedan that Mr. Ruger purchased bore engine number 5110221 and body number 24. The Fleetwood style designation was 5833-S, and three of that style were built during the 1936 model year. The same body was offered during the years 1934–1937 and a grand total of eleven of these V-16 town sedans were built during that period. (The same body shell was also offered on V-8 and V-12 chassis, and that is how Mr. Ruger's car wound up with a body number higher than 11.)

New for 1936 on the Cadillac V-16 closed cars was General Motors Corporation's "turret top," a one-piece roof design that eliminated the old fabric insert stretched over wood slats and wire mesh. The turret top represented a major improvement in body integrity, torsional strength, and outward appearance.

On Mr. Ruger's behalf, Mr. Roxas undertook a careful restoration of this very solid, original 1936 town sedan, a process that took two years to complete. The car was re-painted in its original color of Tunis Blue. The interior was re-trimmed with

1936 Cadillac V16
TOWN SEDAN
Style No. 5733-S

broadcloth for the doors and headliner, and Bedford cord for the seats (with leather on various high-wear surfaces). The only variance from the original bodywork was replacement of the fender-mounted spare tires with a single spare tire stowed in the trunk. Mr. Ruger preferred the clean lines of the body when not encumbered by external spare tires, and he pointed out that changing a tire on these cars from the trunk is much easier (and less complicated) than retrieving a spare from one of the fender wells. For the sake of drivability on tours, a 3.31 to 1 gear set was fabricated for the rear axle.

Shortly after the restoration was finished, the car was shown at the 1998 Meadow Brook Concours d'Elegance in Rochester Hills, Michigan, where it received a First in Class. Later the same year, it drew another First in Class at the Pebble Beach Concours d'Elegance and performed splendidly on the Tour d'Elegance that's always held in connection with the Pebble Beach show.

In 2012, at the St. John's Auction held by RM Sotheby's, the blue 1936 town sedan was sold for $247,500. The new owner was collector John Groendyke of Enid, Oklahoma. In late 2019, Mr. Groendyke determined to downsize his collection of fine cars and the V-16 town sedan was one of the cars he consigned to the RM Sotheby's Arizona Auction, January 16–17, 2019. At the auction, the car brought a price of $167,500, not including the buyer's premium.

***Opposite, top: Cheating the wind.* Dramatic streamlining of the 1934–1937 V-16 cars presented minimal frontal area to the onrushing air. Teardrop fenders, bullet headlamps, and narrow radiator shell were just as smooth visually as they were aerodynamically (courtesy Chad Chambers). *Bottom: Fine wool and inlaid wood.* Rear compartment of the 1936 town sedan envelopes the passenger in comfort and elegance. Jaeger clock and cigar lighter at the center of the front seatback, as well as a lockable compartment are thoughtful amenities (courtesy Chad Chambers).**

59

The Ambassador's Carriage

During the 1930s, what car would best convey the dignity and authority of the United States Ambassador to Great Britain? If you guessed a new Cadillac V-16 limousine it would be hard to contradict you. According to the lore associated with it, 1937 Cadillac Series 5875 imperial sedan, engine number 5130347 was brought over from New York to London to serve newly-appointed Ambassador Joseph P. Kennedy, Sr., during a fraught and troubled time. It's known for certain that the car arrived in Britain early in its history and stayed there for decades.

Joseph Kennedy had helped Franklin Roosevelt win re-election in the 1936 presidential election, not least by publishing a book *I'm for Roosevelt,* which was credited with significantly increasing support for FDR among business leaders. The ambassadorship to the Court of St. James became vacant, and Roosevelt named Kennedy to fill the post in early December 1937. Kennedy's tour of duty was controversial, to say the least, and he resigned in November 1940.

The 1937 limousine described earlier was shipped first to Cadillac's Detroit Branch, and in August 1937 it was diverted to New York City. Cadillac's shipping ledger shows a shipping date of December 31, 1937. It was a black car with black sidewall tires, and it was trimmed inside with brown pattern cloth from automotive textile supplier William Wiese & Company. Among the optional equipment specified on the car's build sheet are rear compartment radio, two fender-mounted spare tires, flexible steering wheel, frames for the license plates, full spinner wheel discs and a silver radiator goddess. More detailed specifications were set out in a Special Body Order, but those Fleetwood special order documents have not survived.

The car was registered in Britain and equipped with local number plates (FXU-1) and European-regulation turn signals. One can only imagine how tricky it must have been to maneuver a twenty-foot-long, three-ton American car through the London streets and squares on official diplomatic business. Like all 1934–1937 V-16 cars, this one had a wheelbase of 154 inches, the longest of any production U.S. passenger car. But whether or not the limousine was actually used at the American embassy, in due course it came into the possession of a colorful and enthusiastic Scottish polymath by the name of John Cuthill Sword.

Mr. Sword, who lived from 1892 to 1960, was an early aficionado of distinguished

***Opposite, bottom: Spacious and plush.* The passenger area of this 1937 V-16 limousine is as comfortable as it looks. Hidden roll-down silk shades for the rear and quarter windows can provide extra privacy, and the window behind the driver's seat keeps conversations confidential. The seat back cushion and lower cushion adjust separately, fore and aft, and the side armrests sport smoking kits and storage pockets (courtesy Steve Plunkett).**

Twenty feet and then some. The accessory trunk adds to an already impressively long automobile. The effects of the mid–1930s streamlining craze on automotive design are readily apparent on this sleek 1937 Cadillac V-16 sedan. Cigar-shaped door handles, teardrop head and taillights, "speed streak" louvers, pontoon fenders and curves everywhere else make the car look fast standing still (courtesy Steve Plunkett).

***View across the divider.* This formal or "Imperial" division between the driver's and passengers' compartments characterizes a limousine or Imperial sedan. Note the built-in Jaeger Le Coultre clock and twin storage compartments. Full-width auxiliary seats fold out below the crank for the division window. Perforated plate over the driver's head covers the speaker for the intercom so the owner can give instructions to the chauffeur when the division window is up (courtesy Steve Plunkett).**

old cars. He has been described as "an industrialist, farmer, bus operator, airline pioneer and large scale collector—mainly of cars, but many other things as well, including model and miniature steam locomotives."[57] When his extensive estate was auctioned in 1962, the 1937 V-16 was sold. It then came into the hands of U.K collector, restorer and dealer Charles Howard (b. 1936, not to be confused with the California Buick distributor and owner of the famed race horse Seabiscuit). From his ownership, the car was repatriated to the United States in 1994.

One subsequent owner was collector Dennis Gibbs (b. 1944), said to list his occupations as real estate, banking, wind turbines, philanthropy, and early retirement. In 2006, Canadian collector Steve Plunkett acquired the V-16 limousine and added it to his extensive collection of venerable Cadillacs. In 2010, the car appeared in a television miniseries titled *The Kennedys*, filmed at Castle Loma in Toronto, Ontario.

In 2015, the car was consigned for auction at the Hershey Auction conducted by RM Sotheby's in conjunction with the annual car show and swap meet, and was sold at a price of $110,000. At that point in its life, the car had been repainted once, but was otherwise a very well cared-for original car, with the only obvious sign of age being the surface cracking of the leather upholstery in the chauffeur's compartment.

57. Scott, Peter, *A History of the Thames Side Promenade Miniature Railways*, 2015, Appendix Two.

60

The Fixer's Formal Limousine

EDGAR J. "EDDIE" MANNIX (actually christened Joseph Edgar Allen John Mannix) was by any definition a Hollywood mogul. Born in Fort Lee, New Jersey, he got his start in show business working at the Palisades Park amusement park. From there he got into motion pictures, working in, and managing, theaters. From there he moved into the production end of the business, ultimately becoming general manager and vice-president of Metro-Goldwyn-Mayer Studios. He had a well-deserved reputation as a power broker and as someone who could smooth out or resolve potentially embarrassing or tricky situations for the studio and its personalities.[58]

In the Autumn of 1936, Mr. Mannix took delivery of a 1937 Cadillac V-16 Series 5875-FL imperial cabriolet (one of two built for 1937).[59] The original owner's identification card is made out in the name of Bernice Mannix, Edgar's wife, and is dated September 22, 1937. Tragically, not two months after that date, Mrs. Mannix was killed in a car accident (not involving the Cadillac).

The V-16 imperial cabriolet was entirely black, with its top covered in black landau leather. At not quite twenty feet in length, it was as imposing as Mr. Mannix's reputation. This body style was a long sedan with folding jump seats, and it was built to convey seven, including the driver. There were no rear quarter windows, a feature that afforded an extra measure of privacy to the rear seat occupants. The driver's compartment was upholstered in utilitarian leather and separated from the passenger area by a roll-up window. This was a formal car in every sense of the word. The build sheet references a separate Fleetwood Body order with "detailed specifications," but that document is lost to the ages. We do know that the car was ordered with the optional sterling silver goddess ornament (gold was also available), and with a radio for the rear compartment.

Eddie Mannix was a good friend of movie star Clark Gable. An MGM source disclosed that when Gable agreed to work for MGM for what was then an unheard-of sum of money, he declined to sign a contract, saying, "Why do I have to sign it? I shook hands with Eddie Mannix."[60] Part of the lore of Mr. Mannix's 1937 V-16 sedan is the story that he permitted Clark Gable and Vivian Leigh to use it during the filming of the 1939 blockbuster hit *Gone with the Wind.*

---

58. *The Fixers: Eddie Mannix, Howard Strickling and the MGM Publicity Machine*, by E.J. Fleming (Jefferson, NC: McFarland, 2005) tells the colorful story of Eddie Mannix's career and the incidents in which he was involved, implicated, or instrumental in containing.

59. The letter "F" stands for "formal" and indicates filled-in quarter windows. The letter "L" calls for a leather roof covering.

60. May, Walter, "1937 Cadillac V-16 Series 90 Fleetwood Imperial Cabriolet," *Bulletin* (CCCA) October 2007, pp. 17–18.

When Hollywood moguls had style. Art deco details set off the streamlined massiveness of this impressive vehicle. Edgar Mannix was respected (and feared) in the film industry during the 1930s, and this 1937 V-16 limousine was a fitting conveyance. The leather-covered roof and closed rear quarters establish formality and ensure passenger privacy (courtesy Skip Tetz).

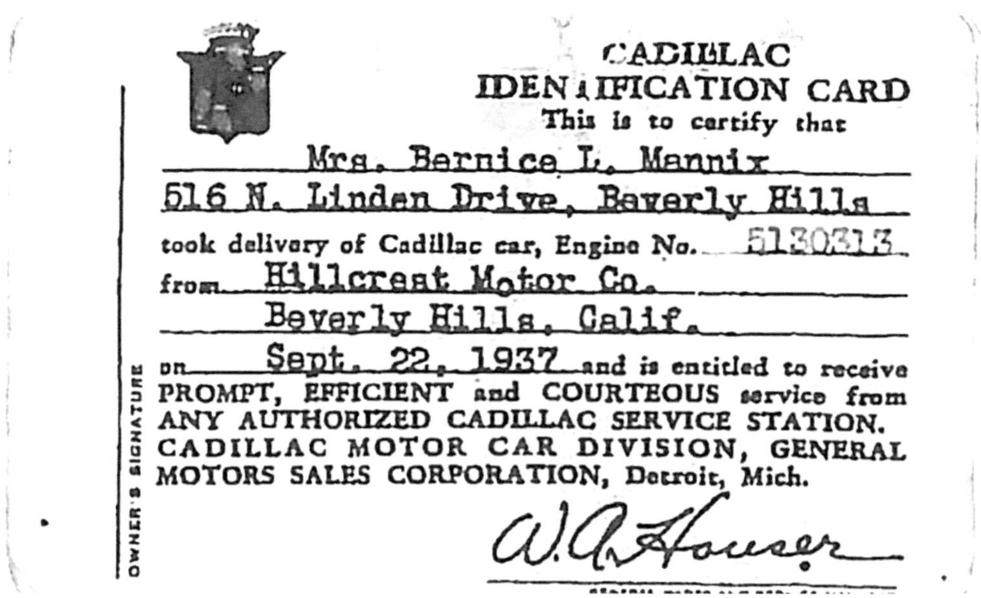

CADILLAC
IDENTIFICATION CARD
This is to certify that
Mrs. Bernice L. Mannix
516 N. Linden Drive, Beverly Hills
took delivery of Cadillac car, Engine No. 5130313
from Hillcrest Motor Co.
Beverly Hills, Calif.
on Sept. 22, 1937 and is entitled to receive PROMPT, EFFICIENT and COURTEOUS service from ANY AUTHORIZED CADILLAC SERVICE STATION.
CADILLAC MOTOR CAR DIVISION, GENERAL MOTORS SALES CORPORATION, Detroit, Mich.
W. A. Houser
OWNER'S SIGNATURE

Mrs. Mannix's owner identification card. Each purchaser of a Cadillac automobile received an owner identification card for use when seeking authorized service. Edgar Mannix had the 1937 Cadillac V-16 formal limousine that he used registered in his wife's name (courtesy Skip Tetz).

Receiving accolades. **Skip Tetz's 1937 V-16 formal limousine takes a bow as it receives a First in Class award at the 2016 Pebble Beach Concours d'Elegance (courtesy Skip Tetz).**

In 1945 the big Cadillac was placed in storage in a studio warehouse. Eddie Mannix died in 1963, but it was not until 1967 that his V-16 was taken out of storage and offered for sale by Russell C. Jackson in Scottsdale, Arizona. The advertisement in *Hemmings Motor News* claimed 22,000 actual miles and sought a price of $10,000. During the 1970s, Tom Barrett (co-founder, with Russell Jackson, of the Barrett-Jackson auction enterprise) purchased the car from a man in Pasadena, California, and undertook some restoration (notwithstanding its still-excellent general condition). He refreshed leather, carpets and woodwork, and touched up areas where the paint had cracked. Mechanical maintenance matters were also addressed.

The late railroad enthusiast and classic car collector Peter Tilp of Union, New Jersey, owned the Cadillac, also during the 1970s. At that time some work was done on the car at Automotive Restorations, Inc., in Lebanon, New Jersey. During the 1980s, it was owned by John Klein of Indianapolis, Indiana, when the car was also featured in the book *The Classic Era* by Beverly Rae Kimes (photograph on page 540). Subsequently, the Mannix Cadillac passed to a collector in Colorado, and then by way of auction to a gentleman in Ontario, Canada.

Somewhere along the line, the body data tag appears to have been replaced with a reproduction that indicates a "VIN. No." of 5130313. Vehicle identification numbers were not known in 1937 (manufacturers used serial numbers or engine numbers to identify individual cars for recording, licensing and insurance purposes). And in the 1930s Cadillac did not put an engine number or serial number on the body data tag.

In August 2008, the car was sold at RM Auctions' "Vintage Cars of Meadow Brook" event, for $192,500. At RM's St. John's Auction in July 2011, it brought a high bid of

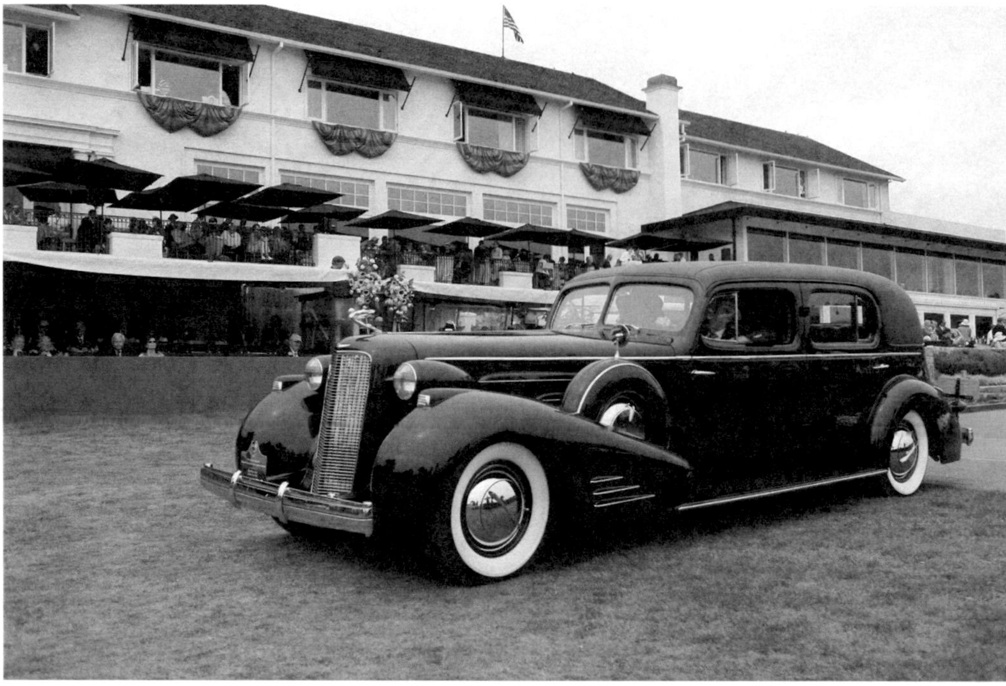

Sleek and imposing. **Mid-1930s aerodynamic contours make this impressive car look fast while standing still. Skip Tetz's 1937 V-16 formal limousine poses in front of the reviewing stand at the prestigious Pebble Beach Concours d'Elegance in August 2016 (courtesy Skip Tetz).**

$130,000 that failed to meet the seller's reserve. In 2012, RM Auto Restoration performed a bare-metal repaint and re-chroming on the car, and in the same year, the Cadillac was awarded Best in Class and Most Elegant Closed Car at the 2012 Ault Park Concours in Cincinnati, Ohio. In late 2014, this imposing limousine again was offered, this time at Auctions America's "Bid Anywhere" sale, with an estimate of $200,000 to $250,000. According to the company's website, the sale price was $206,250.

In August of 2016, current owner Skip Tetz of Goshen, New York, brought this fine formal car to the Pebble Beach Concours d'Elegance, and it was awarded first place in its class.

61

A Formal Town Sedan

SOME OF THE MOST INTERESTING special-order V-16 cars were ordered by Colonel Sam McLaughlin. Born Robert Samuel McLaughlin, he was known as Colonel Sam because he had been awarded an honorary commission in a reserve armored regiment of the Royal Canadian armed forces. In 1907, he started an automobile manufacturing business, making cars with Buick engines. His company later became General Motors of Canada. He served as President of the Canadian company and as Vice President of the parent corporation, and he sat on GM's board of directors into the early 1960s.

Colonel McLaughlin's 1938 V-16 Cadillac was a Series 9039 town sedan. That body style was a four-door, five-passenger design with a shorter passenger compartment (and longer rear deck) than the other sedan styles in the V-16 line for that year. Seen from the side or from a three-quarter rear view, it is surprisingly graceful and appealingly

1938 town sedan in a tuxedo. **With its leather-covered roof and black paint, this Series 9039 V-16 town sedan makes a formal yet graceful statement. Special-ordered as a limousine for GM of Canada executive Col. R.S. McLaughlin, its build sheet called for numerous options (courtesy Tom Hamilton).**

proportioned for such a large car. The absence of rear quarter windows affords passengers in the back seat a feeling of privacy. The town sedan was not a separate body shell, but was hand-modified from one of the full-size sedan bodies. The entire rear of the body was transformed. Even the rear doors, the deck lid, and their respective openings had to be built up specially—the regular sedan parts are not the same.

This particular town sedan, bearing engine number 5270100, was ordered with a large number of special features and modifications. The shipping invoice or "build sheet" is two pages long, highly unusual for the 1938–1940 Cadillacs. Unfortunately, the Fleetwood Special Body Order records no longer exist, and we do not have access to the one that was referenced on this car's build sheet (which would have included more detailed information than appears on the build sheet itself). The roof of the car is covered in black leather, and the driver's area is separated from the rear passenger compartment by a roll-up window. No other V-16 car in this body style was made with a leather roof and division window. Another unique exterior feature is the mounting for the license plate. On the 1938 Cadillacs, the license plate was attached to a bracket above the left-hand tail light assembly. Colonel McLaughlin's car has the license plate mounted in the center of the rear surface of the deck lid, using the 1937 Buick attachment gear and illumination.

As befits a chauffeur-driven conveyance, the front seat area was trimmed in black leather, and the rear compartment was upholstered in cloth (in this case a light tan wool broadcloth). Also typical of a chauffeur-driven car, a locking exterior door handle was specified for the rear compartment. The panel behind the front seat, into which

Attention to detail. **Finely finished wood around the windows was standard in these cars. The door and window handles, however, were color-finished to match the upholstery (courtesy Tom Hamilton).**

the division window would disappear, was to have "two small glove compartments at top with large compartment below" for storage of passengers' personal items. The build sheet also called for "special plush [carpet] mats to match upholstery" and for a sheepskin rug. The interior hardware items—door handles, window cranks, switch plates and the like—were to be "color plated" to match the upholstery color, and they were rendered in light tan with chrome accents that allowed for contrast.

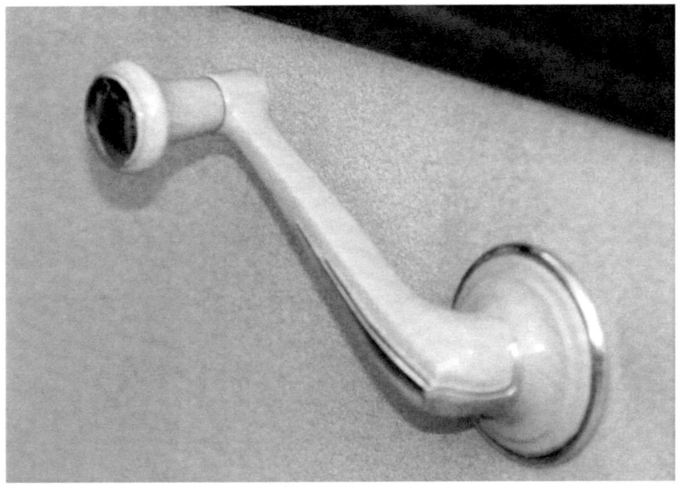

Close-up of specially finished window crank. **Coordinated color and careful attention to detail characterize this individualized custom treatment (courtesy Tom Hamilton).**

Less exotic extra equipment included a rear-seat radio, a "banjo" type steering wheel, a heater-defroster, antifreeze, and "1 qt Duco." The last item would have referred to a can of touch-up paint. What might be the most interesting entry on the build sheet is the phrase "special attention." This would have called for inspection by the Cadillac

Art deco details. **The instrument panel and controls are standard 1938 Cadillac, except for the optional flexible "banjo" steering wheel and the V-16 horn button (courtesy Tom Hamilton).**

General Manager before a car was released to a very important customer or auto show. Colonel McLaughlin certainly qualified as a very important customer, and the car likely got a thorough going-over before he saw it.

In 1939, Colonel McLaughlin's special order V-16 was purchased by a stockbroker named Dorothy Killian who lived in Montreal, Canada, and worked out of New York City. She had her monogram painted on the passenger compartment doors, and she had her own chauffeur. Well, actually she had more than one. Isaac Walten would see to her transportation needs in Montreal and the summer home in Nova Scotia, and Joe Percoco would drive in New York. Ultimately, she decided to have the car garaged in New York.

In the late 1970s, the forty-year-old Cadillac needed service, and a dispute arose with the mechanic, a fellow named Bud Kornoff, over the quality of the work. Mr. Kornoff wasn't paid, and he responded by selling the car without a title to the Roaring 20s Autos and Antique Car Museum in Wall, New Jersey (now long-closed). Someone saw the car there and a court case ensued, and in 1982 an order was issued requiring a proper sale. A fellow named David M. Gallo, Sr., bought the car in the sheriff's sale.

Mr. Gallo showed the unique Cadillac town sedan at a Classic Car Club of America Grand Classic meet in Philadelphia, and a man came up to him, identified himself as Joe Percoco, and said that he had worked as a chauffeur driving the car for Dorothy Killian. He said that she had passed away, but that her other driver, Isaac Walten of Nova Scotia, was still living. Mr. Gallo subsequently tried to get in touch with Mr. Walten, but was not successful.

Not long afterwards, David Gallo sold the car to Seattle, Washington, classic car

***Plush, comfortable and private.* The rear compartment is roomy, luxuriously appointed, and convenient. Holes in the panel where the armrest nestles are for the rear seat radio speaker. A silk shade can be lowered to cover the rear window (courtesy Tom Hamilton).**

A business-like engine compartment. **Where the 1930–1937 engines were designed to be seen and visually appreciated, the 1938–1940 engines were much more subdued in appearance. This one is barely visible, deep in its bay, under the air cleaners, carburetors, and manifolds (courtesy Tom Hamilton).**

dealer Tom Crook. Mr. Crook took the car to Seattle and from there it was sold to Al Sandin in 1983, who would own the Cadillac for something over 30 years.

In early 2015 some classic car fanciers from Scottsdale, Arizona, attended an auction in Palm Springs, California, where a collection of cars was being sold, separate from the auction, including the 1938 V-16 Cadillac town sedan. Tom Hamilton of Allyn, Washington, had purchased a 1966 Cadillac convertible from those same people, and he was intrigued by the V-16. He got as much information about the car as he could, and from that he could tell it was somewhat unique. He went to see the car, drove it and concluded a deal. Then on January 12, 2015, he drove the car home, and continued to do as much research as records and resources would permit. Colonel McLaughlin's 1938 V-16 town sedan was shown at the 2016 Grand National Meet of the Cadillac-LaSalle Club in Las Vegas, Nevada, and drew much admiring attention. Then at the 2019 Annual Meeting of the Classic Car Club of America held in Scottsdale, Arizona, the car was judged "Most Original" of the Classic cars displayed at the meet. To this day, the Cadillac has not been restored, and is a true original car. Its owner continues to get to know the car and to enjoy it.

62

Mr. Wrigley's Limousine

PHILIP K. WRIGLEY (1894–1997) was the taciturn son of the man who founded (and gave his name to) the Wm. Wrigley Jr. Company, an institution still renowned as the maker of Spearmint, Doublemint, and Juicy Fruit gum. When his father died in 1932, Philip Wrigley inherited the chewing gum company and the ownership of the Chicago Cubs baseball team. During his long life, he owned a variety of fine cars including five new Duesenbergs[61] and a 1957 Cadillac Eldorado Brougham. When in the mid–1960s a cousin of Fred and August Duesenberg unsuccessfully attempted to produce a modern version of that big classic, Philip Wrigley was one of the enthusiastic prospects who put down cash for one of the cars. Reportedly, one of the fine cars that Mr. Wrigley bought new was a 1938 Cadillac V-16 limousine, Series 9019-F. The Series 9019-F was a long imperial sedan without any occasional or "jump" seats. The story is that Mr. Wrigley wanted to use this car solely for himself and his wife.

Mr. Wrigley's car bore engine number 5270227 and body number 4 (of a total of 5 1938 V-16s built with this body style). It is somewhat unusual in having spare tire storage in the trunk, instead of in wells in the front fenders with metal covers. Without the fender-mounted spares to break up the line, this car looks longer and more graceful than most of the other late-series V-16 sedans. The driver's compartment is trimmed in leather, as was customary with chauffeur-driven cars in the classic era. The rear compartment is upholstered in gray wool broadcloth. Instead of a fixed foot rail, there are three wedge-shaped, carpeted hassocks that can be placed to suit the passengers' comfort. With the hassocks tucked up against the divider, the expanse of carpeted floor emphasizes the spaciousness of the passenger area of the car.

It's not known how Mr. Wrigley disposed of the car, but it showed up in the early 1960s, when Cadillac-LaSalle Club member Bill Tite was compiling a list of surviving 1938–1940 V-16 Cadillacs. Mr. Tite's list notes that in 1963 the car was owned by E.W. Massey of Kinston, North Carolina. Around 1967, Dale Gabriel of Michigan had acquired title to the car, and in 1971, he signed that title over to John Kosmatka, then living in Milwaukee.

Mr. Kosmatka said that the man who sold him the big Cadillac had been employed by one of the Detroit car companies, but was laid off and living on his savings. Mr. Kosmatka travelled to Detroit to see the car, and he and Mr. Gabriel discussed a price. Mr. Gabriel showed him some paperwork substantiating the claim that Philip Wrigley had been the original purchaser. He stated that he had lowered the price for the car and that

61. Hinckley, James, Hinckley, Jim, and Robinson, Jon G., *The Big Book of Car Culture: The Armchair Guide to Automotive Americana*, Motorbooks, 2005, pg. 138.

It's only original once. **Eighty-plus years after it left the factory, this 1938 imperial sedan remains majestic. Notwithstanding slight surface rust on lower fender edges and hood spears, a dent in the rear fender, and oxidized paint, the car projects a noble presence. Under-the-car radio antenna can be seen stretched under the running board (courtesy Motostalgia LLC).**

he needed money. Mr. Kosmatka said he would think about it, and that's what he did on the trip back to Milwaukee. By the time he got home, he had made a decision and he phoned Mr. Gabriel and they struck a deal. He went back to Detroit, paid for the car and drove it home to Milwaukee.

Dale Gabriel offered to show Mr. Kosmatka the best route out of Detroit, and as he was driving, the engine began to seize up and he pulled over to the side of the road. On examination it became apparent that the water pump seal was the problem. Mr. Gabriel said that his warehouse was nearby, so they brought the car there. The offending water pump was extracted (there are two on a side-valve V-16 engine). Mr. Gabriel disclosed that he knew a man with a lot of parts, and they were able to find a replacement water pump and install it. On the 400 mile trip back home and afterwards, Mr. Kosmatka never had any other trouble with the car.

Of all the cars that Mr. Kosmatka has owned, this 1938 Cadillac "was the most fantastic to drive" because of the weight of the car and the smoothness of the engine and drivetrain. On the road back to Milwaukee, he drove cautiously, keeping his speed at 50 m.p.h. as other cars passed him. He noticed that one modern car ahead of him bobbed up and down over an uneven stretch of road. But the V-16 didn't bob at all when it passed the same spot. Unfortunately, Mr. Kosmatka left behind the documents that Mr. Gabriel had shown him, relating to Philip Wrigley's ownership. He said that he was interested in the car itself, and not so much in its provenance. It was, he said, "the smoothest, nicest driving car I've ever had."

In 1973, he moved to Cedar Park, Texas, for health reasons, and in 2015, Mr.

An engine with patina. **The workaday design of the late-series V-16 engine is emphasized by normal weathering over the years. The coils are aftermarket items and surface rust has colored the crankcase breather cap and the cover for the exhaust crossover (courtesy Motostalgia LLC).**

Kosmatka (then 86 years old) decided to sell the '38 Cadillac and several other cars. They included a 1932 Cadillac V-12 convertible victoria, a 1933 Cadillac V-12 five-passenger coupe, a 1908 Reo Model G Roadster with detachable tonneau, and a 1923 Milburn Electric Model 27L. Mr. Kosmatka had stored the cars on his property in Texas for around forty years, and the vendor he chose to conduct the sale decided to describe the cars as "barn finds," even though that term typically describes cars that have been parked and forgotten, only to be discovered by heirs or investigators snooping into old storage buildings. An auction date of June 12 was set.

In the photos taken for the sale, the V-16 appeared to be a solid original car, nearly complete and showing minimal effects of age and the elements. The original cloth upholstery had some moisture stains in places, and some evidence of moth damage. The leather-trimmed front compartment was in good shape, with some wear but no tears. Outside, some of the brightwork showed some pitting or beginnings of rust haze, and there was some delamination in the window glass. The black paint looked like it might shine up nicely with some rubbing compound and wax, give or take some chips and nicks.

Mr. Kosmatka's V-16 sold for $46,750, and according to him the buyer was a gentleman from Canada. In 2017, the car showed up in a YouTube video[62] visit to an Ontario shop that specializes in motorcycle and automobile customization. According to the

62. https://www.youtube.com/watch?v=3fow7ZssjQE, published February 10, 2017, and accessed December 10, 2019.

conversation on the video, the owner of the Cadillac envisions discarding the car's body aft of the cowl and instrument panel, and fabricating a new body for the car, with a rather large budget in mind for the project. How that ultimately plays out will be interesting to see.

63

For the Governor of Texas

THE 1938–1940 V-16 CADILLACS were massive automobiles, over eighteen feet long, bumper to bumper, and weighing about three tons. They shared their steel body shells with the top-of-the-line V-8 cars (Series 75), and there was a full selection of styles to choose from—sedans, coupes, convertibles (two-door and four-door), limousines and town cars. The wheelbase was long—141 inches on all the models—and visually, the cars were imposing. The four-door models seemed to go on forever, and the deck lids of the two-door styles were enormous.

Among the offered body styles was a town sedan, Series 9039, a style that was also known in earlier days as a close-coupled sedan. Unlike the larger five and seven-passenger sedans in the V-16 line, a town sedan has the rear seat directly behind the front seat, with adequate foot room, but without the expanse of floor space seen in the standard sedans (some of which had folding auxiliary seats between the front and back seats). As a result, the contours of the car body yield a more gently proportionate profile. On the whole, the Series 9039 town sedan is probably the most graceful of these enormous cars.

Town sedans were generally purchased as family cars, as distinguished from corporate vehicles or chauffeur-driven cars. The reduction in rear-seat legroom compared to the other sedans resulted in additional luggage space under the rear deck, making these cars wonderful touring vehicles.

The 1938 town sedan that bore V-16 engine number 5270283 and body number 17 was shipped from the factory to New Bedford, Connecticut, on April 29, 1938. We don't know who purchased it as a new car, but almost twenty-five years later in early 1963, Bill Tite of St. Clair Shores, Michigan (a Cadillac-LaSalle Club member and early expert on the 1938–'40 V-16s), published an article that included names and addresses of the owners of the then-known surviving flathead V-16 cars.[63] Among the cars listed with their respective owners was the one with engine number 5270283, and its owner was shown as L.H. Diamond of Colorado Springs, Colorado. A surviving Texas title certificate for the car indicates that in 1978 Louis H. Diamond of Colorado Springs conveyed the same 1938 Cadillac to Carter B. Christie, of Austin, Texas. Fast-forward to the year 1995, when

***Opposite, bottom: Characteristic face.* This 1938 V-16 town sedan displays the typical front end of the 1938 through 1940 V-16 cars, similar to the Series 75 V-8 cars (excepting the aftermarket driving lights and optional spotlight). Cars with fender-mounted spare tires always have hinged metal covers (courtesy MotoeXotica).**

---

63. Tite, W.R., "The Sweet Sixteen," *The Self-Starter*, Cadillac-LaSalle Club, Inc., Detroit, Michigan Vol. V, Number 4, February, 1963, pp. 10–14.

A graceful profile. The town sedan body on the 1938–1940 V-16 chassis is probably the best proportioned. These are massive cars, and the curves of this style, especially in the rear, ameliorate the visual impression of bulk. Fabrication of the rear door openings and quarter panels required significant hand work (courtesy Leake Auction Company).

Odyssey Restorations, Inc., of Spring Lake Park, Minnesota, handled a consignment sale of the car for Mr. Richard Long of St. Paul Minnesota, after performing miscellaneous repairs and service. That surviving Texas title certificate was one of the documents provided by Mr. Long in connection with that consignment sale.

Eight years later in 2003, the car showed up in California, owned by William Verhulst of San Diego. In late 2005, Rick Tarnutzer purchased the town sedan from Mr. Verhulst who told him that the car had been ordered new by the Governor of Texas. In 1938, the incumbent governor was James V. Allred, known before becoming governor as "the fighting district attorney." Fort Worth businessman and radio personality Wilbert Lee O'Daniel ("Pappy O'Daniel") succeeded him in 1939. Unfortunately, there isn't much information available to demonstrate that either of these gentlemen owned a 1938 V-16 Cadillac.

Mr. Tarnutzer had intended to give the Cadillac a complete restoration, but that didn't happen. On August 17, 2007, the Bonham's auction company sold the car at their Quail Lodge sale for $55,000 to the Sterling McCall Collection in Texas. In 2008, the car was treated to an extensive restoration at Black Knight Automotive in Houston, Texas. When Mecum Auctions sold many of the Sterling McCall Collection vehicles April 13–14, 2012, the V-16 town sedan brought $74,200.

At the April 21–23, 2017, Leake Auction in Dallas, Texas, the sale price was $48,000, reflecting a general softening of the market for some of the big Classics. Later in 2017, the car was offered for sale by MotoeXotica Classic Car Sales at $109,000 (and in an eBay listing that brought a $46,600 high bid but no sale). Most recently the Cadillac was consigned to the January 17, 2018, Worldwide Auctions sale in Scottsdale, Arizona. Although the pre-sale estimate was set at $125,000-$150,000, the sale price was $71,500. This car deserves to find a home, and perhaps it has.

64

A Thoroughbred for a Breeder of Champions

In 1924, William Wright (who had done very well for himself once he established the popular Calumet Baking Powder Company) bought a small Lexington, Kentucky, farm and began raising Standardbred horses for harness racing. When he died in 1931 and his son Warren took over, the emphasis turned to Thoroughbreds. Over the succeeding decades, Calumet Farm would turn out an impressive array of champion race horses, including eight Kentucky Derby winners and two Triple Crown laureates ("Whirlaway" in 1941 and "Citation" in 1948). Shortly before the stock market crash of 1929, Warren Wright had successfully completed a sale of the Calumet Baking Powder Company to the Postum Cereal Company.[64] So, the Wright family escaped the depredations of the Great Depression.

Ordered new in the name of Calumet Farm was a 1939 Cadillac V-16 formal imperial sedan, Series 9033-F with engine number 5290100. Series 9033-F denotes a seven-passenger limousine with a leather covering over the roof and filled-in upper rear quarters (no rear quarter windows). Two full-width auxiliary seats behind the partition with its roll-up window could be deployed in the rear compartment, or they could be folded away for a very roomy, private setting. There were eight such cars built in 1939, out of a total of 133 V-16 cars that year (plus two bare chassis and two separate engines).

Calumet Farm would own the V-16 limousine into the 1970s, and perhaps until the death of Warren Wright's widow Lucille. The car would thereafter find its way into the private collection of Eugene Beardslee of Brookville on New York's Long Island.

Mr. Beardslee had founded and operated Beardslee Transmission Equipment Co., a distributor of industrial equipment. He also assembled an impressive collection of Classic and special interest automobiles. He worked with top restorers, including the late Bob Turnquist of Hibernia Auto Restoration. In 1983, at Mr. Beardslee's request Hibernia performed on his 1939 V-16 a year-long restoration process that the copywriter for the Bonhams auction company called a comprehensive refurbishment. Among other things, the car received new paint in midnight blue with a new matching leather roof covering.

Beginning with his death in 2000, Mr. Beardslee's heirs prepared for sale and found new homes for small groups of the cars from his collection. On June 3, 2012, the 1939 V-16 limousine that Calumet Farm had bought new was offered at Bonhams' Greenwich Concours d'Elegance in Connecticut. Photographs on the Bonhams website show a

64. Shortly thereafter, Postum became General Foods Corporation.

An automotive thoroughbred. Warren Wright, owner of Calumet Farm, ordered this 1939 formal limousine new. The stately presence of the car is amplified by its leather roof covering. The car later became part of the collection of the late Eugene Beardslee (courtesy Tim Stentiford, Motorland Classic Cars).

car looking very much as though it had just left the showroom, and the catalog description said it was "in fine working condition." The auctioneer's estimate was $75,000 to $100,000, but the car was not sold. Afterwards the car was listed for sale by Motorland, LLC in Arundel, Maine, at a price of $89,500. As of this writing, the car resides in a private museum collection in Maine.

Opposite, bottom: Formal to a "t." **The Series 9033F body style featured solid upper rear quarters (no quarter windows) and leather roof covering. With a large, dignified car to start with, these additional attributes accentuated privacy and elegance (courtesy Tim Stentiford, Motorland Classic Cars).**

65

Lazarus

In the Gospel, Lazarus is the dear friend of Jesus who dies, only to be revived and brought out of his tomb by the Lord Himself. Richard Long of Newport, Rhode Island, named his 1939 Cadillac Series 9033 V-16 limousine Lazarus because it, too, was led out of the grave and back into life.

The build sheet says that Mr. Long's Cadillac (engine number 5290061 and body number 26) was shipped new to New York City, but there's no way to know at this time who the original owner was. Equipped with a window between the front seat and the rear compartment, this could have been a wealthy person's formal transportation, driven by a full-time chauffeur. Or it might have served corporate V.I.P.s, or a movie star. In any event, what we know of its history begins after the Second World War.

In the mid-1940s, a funeral director bought this car and made it part of his business. At some point, the man's son tried to help out by changing the car's oil. But the son forgot to replace the oil he had drained from the engine. Of course, the next time the car was started, things went rapidly wrong. The funeral director took the wounded car to his mechanic and asked him to get it running well enough to sell, and that's what the mechanic did.

The next owner was a man with a large family who reckoned that this large car with many seats would work well for his needs. But it was only a few days before the temporarily fixed engine gave out once again, whereupon the repairman that this fellow consulted said, "No problem! I can put a V-8 engine in there and you'll be all set."

And so the big V-16 limousine received a smaller replacement engine and went on to rack up more miles. Ultimately, though, that engine wore out, and the owner solemnly consigned the car to a salvage yard. There it rested until Richard Long wandered by in 1980, browsing through the yard. The unusual profile of the car caught his eye and he headed for the office to ask about it. It was in sad shape with no wheels or headlight lenses, but most of the car was still there, and it looked like a good candidate for restoration.

The yard owner was almost a caricature of a stereotype—sitting in a dilapidated chair in a filthy office, with a ferocious cigar hanging from his lips. Mr. Long asked about the 1939 Cadillac limousine, and the yard owner said that the group of cars was going to be cut up for scrap in a few days. Mr. Long asked how much he wanted for it, and he responded by asking how much Mr. Long was offering. He said he'd pay $75 if the car were delivered to his home, and a deal was struck.

The scrape of metal on metal rang out as the car slid from the transport vehicle. Any misgivings Mr. Long may have had about his acquisition were overcome, and over the ensuing years, he brought the sad motor car back to its original regal presence. He located another side valve V-16 engine to replace the V-8 that had been installed after the

***As found in a junkyard.* This is the 1939 Cadillac V-16 imperial sedan as Richard Long found it. Plenty of missing parts, exposure to the elements, and a substituted V-8 engine posed plenty of challenges to Mr. Long's project to restore the car (courtesy *The Self-Starter*).**

oil-starved original engine failed. The replacement engine had been removed from a Series 9023 seven-passenger sedan and used to run a speedboat on the St. Lawrence River. It had been severely used, and the warehouse in which it was stored had burned to the ground. When Mr. Long got it, the V-16 engine was missing many of its external components, including manifolds, carburetors and generator. Finding those missing items "took forever." Rebuilding the engine took three years, but it was successful.

The original black exterior paint color has been replaced with a deep maroon, and because the beige upholstery that came with the car required replacement, Mr. Long selected a gray color that better sets off the warm wood trim pieces on the doors and windows. When he asked the supplier why the cloth was so expensive, he was told that the letters "RR" in the catalog number indicated that this material was a Rolls-Royce fabric selection.

In its first outing involving a judged car show, Mr. Long's V-16 imperial sedan received a second-place award at the 2013 Cadillac-LaSalle Club Grand National Meet in Quincy, Massachusetts. His goal was to be able to drive the car regularly to help the recently-rebuilt engine sort itself out and settle in. There were still a few things needed for the car, such as the "lull straps" for the rear seat passengers and some final mechanical adjustments. But most of the work had been completed, and the result was stunning. The big Cadillac was featured in a lavishly illustrated article in the March 2014 issue of the

Luxurious rear compartment. **Seen through the leather-lined opening of the imperial division window, the wood-trimmed interior shows off the careful re-upholstering job. The cloth material used for the rear compartment turned out to be a Rolls-Royce fabric selection (courtesy *The Self-Starter*).**

Cadillac-LaSalle Club's monthly periodical *The Self-Starter*. Congratulations to Mr. Long and to everyone who helped him bring back this fine motor car.

Sadly, Richard Long passed away in February of 2017. In December of the same year, his 1939 V-16 Cadillac imperial sedan was offered for sale in *Hemmings Motor News* for $80,000. This author fondly hopes that this beautiful beast finds a worthy home.

Opposite, bottom: Massive presence. **Mr. Long put a lot of time and work into transforming a junked old car into a gleaming classic. He chose a warm deep maroon paint color instead of the original black. Sixty Series 9033 seven-passenger imperial sedans were built in 1939 (courtesy *The Self-Starter*).**

66

The Roebling Cadillac

THE NAME ROEBLING IS FOREVER linked with the design and construction of an ingenious suspension bridge across the East River between Manhattan and Brooklyn. The Brooklyn Bridge was an engineering breakthrough in its day and still carries a steady flow of vehicular and pedestrian traffic. John Augustus Roebling, the German immigrant who conceived and, in 1867, began building the bridge, died before its completion (victim of tetanus that resulted when his foot was crushed by a ferry boat colliding with a dock).

Ruth Metcalf Roebling's formal limousine. **Widow of one of the bridge-building Roeblings, Ruth purchased a very distinguished car. Chauffeur driven, it offered maximum privacy for the owner. The rear compartment had a separate lock, and the owner could share that key with the driver—or not (courtesy Darin Schnabel and RM Sotheby's).**

The soul of gravitas. **Leather roof covering and closed rear quarters of this car combine elegance and discretion. 1940 was the last year for the V-16s, and the last year for this stately body (which was shared with the Series 75 V-8 cars).**

But he left five sons and four daughters, and a family business that would figure largely in American industry well into the twentieth century.

Washington Augustus Roebling, eldest son of John Augustus, completed the Brooklyn Bridge and served as president of John A. Roebling's Sons Company until his death in 1926. He was succeeded as president by his nephew Ferdinand William Roebling, Jr. Among the work that Ferdinand Roebling, Jr., had done for the company had been drawing the plans for the Williamsburg Bridge, another East River suspension bridge upstream from the Brooklyn Bridge. During his tenure as president, the company erected the George Washington Bridge across the Hudson River, and he devoted great energy to a variety of business, civic and philanthropic activities.

Ruth Metcalf Roebling (whom Ferdinand William Roebling, Jr., had married in 1905) was left a widow in 1936. In 1940, she purchased a new Cadillac V-16 limousine, engine number 5320019. The car was a Series 9033-F formal sedan with a leather-covered roof and without rear quarter windows, and it was one of five such cars built that year. It's a very traditional car in black lacquer with side-mount spare tires. The driver's compartment is trimmed in the black leather that was typical of chauffeur-driven sedans in the pre-war era. Mrs. Roebling would keep the car until her death in 1960.

In 1962, ownership of the Cadillac passed to Holt Apgar Murray of Princeton, New Jersey. An old car enthusiast and member of several antique and classic car clubs, Mr. Murray distinguished himself flying B-17 bomber missions in Europe during the Second World War. After the war, he joined Crescent Insulated Wire and Cable Co., Inc., the business his grandfather had founded, where he became vice-president. After he passed away in 2005, the 1940 V-16 passed to his grandson. Shortly thereafter it was sold

Chauffeur's office. Leather, then seen as more utilitarian, was the traditional trimming for a chauffeur's compartment. Fine cloth was for the owner. The 1940 Cadillac dash favored simplicity and broad expanses of walnut burl applique.

***Plenty of accessories but where's the engine?* The 1938 through 1940 side-valve V-16 engine was designed from a far more pragmatic direction. Open the hood and see two air cleaners, two coils, two distributors, two carburetors, some manifolds and a generator. If you look hard, you can just see the engine itself. There were half as many moving parts, and the same power with less weight and less displacement, but the engine was not as visually attractive as its predecessor.**

at auction, purchased by Athens, Georgia, businessman and long-time Cadillac enthusiast Jimmy Wilfong.

On March 8, 2008, at the Amelia Island Auction run by RM Auctions[65] the car was sold for $82,500. It became part of the collection of William B. Ruger, Jr., retired Chairman and CEO of the firearms manufacturing company Sturm, Ruger & Co., Inc. In 2012, RM Auctions again offered the venerable V-16 formal limousine, this time at its St. Johns Auction, July 28, 2012, in Plymouth, Michigan.

Judging from the photographs and the auction materials, this proud Cadillac is in very good condition. The exterior paint has been redone, and the engine has been rebuilt, but the interior is excellently maintained and some nominal wear can be discerned in places like the driver's floor and the engine compartment. Unless a new owner insisted on competing in the regular judged classes with the car, it could be left and enjoyed and conserved exactly the way it is.

***Opposite, bottom: A drawing room on wheels.* A tufted, sumptuous couch is surrounded by inlaid wood window frames, occasional seating for guests, radio controls on the right-hand wall, and a clock. The comforts of a well-to-do home.**

65. In 2015, RM Auctions entered a strategic partnership with Sotheby's and has since been known as RM Sotheby's.

After the auction, RM Auctions reported that the car was sold for $55,000. Later in the Fall, the car and its particulars appeared in the catalog for the December 7–8, 2012, Raleigh Classic Car Auction at the North Carolina State Fair Grounds. Estimated price was given as $63,000 to $67,000.

67

The Derham Coupe

THE DERHAM CUSTOM BODY COMPANY of Rosemont, Pennsylvania, was one of the custom coachbuilding firms that made the Classic Era an artistic and stylistic high point in automotive history. In a carryover from the days of horse-drawn carriages, people who had the means and an appreciation of finer things would contract with a specialty firm to have the exterior design, trimmings, and interior appointments of their carriage (or later, their motor car) carried out to their personal tastes and preferences. The purchasers of many of the more prestigious automotive brands would buy a bare chassis—engine, frame, running gear, and perhaps the fenders and front clip—and the chosen coachbuilder would either design a body for the car from scratch, or offer the client one of a series of styles in the firm's catalog, subject to the client's desires as to minor changes in the design, choice of cloth type, surface finishes, and decorative touches. The finished product was a personalized, rolling work of art.

The ranks of custom coachbuilding companies were thinned brutally during the 1930s. The Great Depression reduced the number of motor car buyers who could afford the expense of a custom "job," and many of those who still had the means no longer felt comfortable in a vehicle that might be considered ostentatious. As well, the development of automobile construction, moving away from separate body and fenders towards a more integrated whole, made it increasingly difficult to really individualize a car in a way that would stand out in an esthetically pleasing way. After the Second World War, the craft of taking a bare chassis off a manufacturer's assembly line and fashioning a complete and custom-made body for it would largely be left to the builders of ambulances and hearses.

Derham was one of the fortunate few firms that survived both the Depression and the changing tastes and preferences of buyers of prestige automobiles. It would continue personalizing the products of America's car companies for individual and corporate clients well into the second half of the twentieth century, and undertaking projects such as a convertible version for Ford's Lincoln Continental Mark II in the mid 1950s.

Harry G. Haskell (1870–1951) was a vice-president, director and executive committee member of E.I. du Pont de Nemours & Company. In the autumn of 1939, through Delaware Motor Sales Company (Cadillac's dealer in Wilmington) Mr. Haskell entered into discussions with Derham for a five-passenger coupe that would be tailored to his (very particular) preferences. He wanted something that would improve upon his existing 1936 V-12 Cadillac five-passenger coupe, which he would trade in as part of the deal. Unlike many purchasers of bespoke custom motor cars in the 1920s and early 1930s, his aim in contracting with a custom coachbuilder was not to obtain a flamboyant or eye-catching vehicle—rather, he wanted a discreet but fine automobile with much more refinement in the area of interior comfort and personalization.

***Derham factory drawing.* This is the rendering shown to Harry Haskell for his approval before the car was built. A 1940 V-16 chassis was purchased with complete cowl and windshield. Derham Custom Body Company constructed the rest of the body from the cowl back. Faint handwritten notes call for removal of chrome strips on fenders, simplification of chrome belt molding, and installation of fender-mounted spare tires (courtesy Classic Car Club of America Museum archives).**

Mr. Haskell settled on a V-16 drivetrain, and the drawing prepared by Derham in response to his expressed desires resembled a Cadillac Series 9057-B coupe, with an "almost fastback" roofline. But from the cowl back, the body of the car would be fabricated entirely by Derham. A 1938 V-16 chassis with complete closed-car cowl and windshield was purchased from Cadillac, equipped with a standard heater and a radio, and the project was begun.

The regular Series 9057-B body is a gentle "notchback" style, with a crease where the roof meets the rear deck. Derham smoothed the back of Mr. Haskell's car, almost completely, and replaced the stock rear window with one shaped like an elongated semicircle.[66] A padded leather roof covering maintained the visual separation between the roof and rear deck, and front sections of the rear quarter windows became pivoting vent panes. The car was finished in black lacquer with black leather on the roof. The three chrome fender spears that decorate each fender of a 1940 V-16 car were removed along with the V-16 emblems from the spare tire covers, and the stock door handles were replaced with smaller, straight grips. A folding luggage rack was to have been mounted at the rear, but Mr. Haskell decided against it.

---

66. The profile of the finished car would look like something of a cross between Cadillac's 1934–1937 aerodynamic coupes and the outline of the Series 9057-B coupe.

The completed car. This photograph was taken by the Derham Custom Body Company to document the car upon completion of the project. Painted black with a black leather roof covering, with the fender trim spears omitted, the car is anything but ostentatious. Discreet diamond-shaped monogram with the owner's initials graces the door (courtesy Classic Car Club of America Museum archives).

Sleek roofline. This is another documentation photograph taken by Derham before the car was delivered to the purchaser. Not quite a fastback, the car is dramatically streamlined. The luggage rack was deleted at the purchaser's request, and the purchase price reduced by $75 on that account. Cadillac script has been removed from rear bumper (courtesy Classic Car Club of America Museum archives).

The specifications for the interior and exterior appointments and fittings go on for a page and a half of single-spaced type. They include numerous details for the dimensions, shapes, and firmness of the seats and armrests, frequently referencing his existing car for comparison. A hat rack was to be taken from the existing car and installed in the new one. A vanity unit (no ashtrays) was to be placed below the left rear quarter window

Distinctive lines. **The smooth, swooping curve from the roof backward, the leather roof covering, and the formal backlight are some of the modifications made by the Derham Company to create a unique V-16 coupe (courtesy The Nethercutt Collection).**

and a cigarette lighter on the right rear armrest. Ingenious footrests on the back of the front seat bases would fold up to provide additional toe room for rear seat passengers. A silver-leaf monogram was to be applied to the driver's door, same as the one on Mr. Haskell's previous car. Several versions of the specification list, along with extensive correspondence and related documents are preserved in the Derham records at the Classic Car Club of America Museum archives.

As noted, the car was to be painted black, with a black leather roof covering. The instrument panel was to be black, as was the steering wheel and steering column. Even the vent window frames were black, and external ornamentation was minimal. This was a car that was meant to be different and personal, but subtle. And that reflects the general mood of those who could still afford a hand-crafted, coachbuilt motorcar.

Harry Haskell took delivery of his custom V-16 coupe in the summer of 1940, and the price was $10,251.30 in pre–War dollars (less $600 for his 1936 V-12 coupe trade-in and $75 for the luggage rack he decided not to keep). (According to the web site www.saving.org, $10,000 in 1940 is roughly equivalent to $176,000 today.)

After Mr. Haskell's death, the car passed to Herbert Becker of Long Island, New York. David Ficken of Babylon, New York, had been a fan of the 1938–1940 side-valve Cadillac V-16 cars, and he had been looking for this particular car. He found it in a barn on Long Island, having last been registered to a John Kaasik of 3 West 103rd Street in New York City. When Mr. Ficken purchased the car, he found it in complete condition, but in need of attention. In 1970, he traded the Derham V-16 coupe to John Linhardt of Queens, New York, for a 1941 Cadillac convertible coupe in good condition. Mr. Linhardt

***Mild custom.* From the front, the Derham Company's custom bodywork on the 1940 V-16 chassis is subtle—the car looks a lot like a standard Series 9057-B five-passenger coupe. Giveaways include the missing trim spears from the fender sides, the leather top covering, and the slightly lowered roof (courtesy The Nethercutt Collection).**

had spotted Mr. Ficken's ad in the enthusiast publication *Car Tips*, in which the car was priced at "[b]est offer or $3,500 on a first come first served basis." The ad described the car as "basically very solid and complete" but the seller disclaimed any knowledge about the internal condition of the engine.

According to Mr. Linhardt, when he took possession of the Derham coupe, it was missing both water pumps and distributors. But it did come with all of the paperwork related to Mr. Haskell's ordering of the custom work by the Derham firm. Unsure how he could obtain the missing components and get the car running, Mr. Linhardt offered it for sale. Very soon he received a phone call from J.B. Nethercutt, heir to the Merle Norman cosmetics fortune and a respected collector of fine automobiles. Mr. Nethercutt asked Mr. Linhardt for the engine number of the car, and the next day a gentleman appeared on Mr. Linhardt's doorstep and purchased the unique Cadillac coupe for $3,250 on behalf of Mr. Nethercutt. That was March 9, 1970.

J.B. Nethercutt had water pumps and distributors removed from another Cadillac V-16 car he owned and had them installed on the Derham coupe. He got the car running and freshened, and within a month of buying it, entered it in a Grand Classic meet of the Classic Car Club of America. Mr. Nethercutt commenced a complete restoration, and had the car painted red. The original leather top was replaced with tan leather. The spare tire covers now have "V-16" badges and rearview mirrors. The upholstery was re-done in a vivid flame-stitch pattern using French mohair fabric that was reportedly obtained from American race car driver Phil Hill. Curiously, the radio pre-set buttons have call letters for Los Angeles-area radio stations, which may indicate that another car's radio found its way into the instrument panel.

After the restoration was complete, the car was shown at a Classic Car Club of America meet in Buck Hill Falls, Pennsylvania. When the Nethercutt collection sold the car at the Pebble Beach auction of Gooding & Company in 2010, the sale price was $176,000. Less than three years later, it crossed the auction block again. This time the occasion was Gooding's 2013 Amelia Island sale, and there the price was $156,750.

During its time with the Nethercutt Collection, the 1940 Cadillac Derham coupe was frequently photographed and featured in magazine articles and books. Fewer than five hundred of the side-valve, second series Cadillac V-16 cars were built during the 1938–1940 production run. Out of those, this Derham-bodied coupe stands alone in terms of the aerodynamic treatment of the rear half of the body (as well as Mr. Nethercutt's color and fabric choices). Consequently, it's impossible to ignore.

Bibliography

Ackerson, Robert C. "Cadillac V-16: Worth its weight in prestige." Reprinted in *Standard Catalog of Cadillac 1903–2000,* 2nd Edition, Edited by Lenzke, James T., Iola, Wisconsin: Kraus Publications, 2000: pp. 217–221.

Albert, Ken. *For the Love of Old Cars—The Jack Passey Story.* Evansville, IN: M.T. Publishing Company, Inc., 2008.

Amelia Island sales catalogue, RM Auctions, Inc., March 14, 2015.

Artzberger, Bill. "The 16 cylinder Cadillac: Smoothness, silence, acceleration and hill-climbing ability," *Standard Catalog of Cadillac 1903–2000,* 2nd Edition, Edited by Lenzke, James T. Iola, WI: Krause Publications, 2000: pp. 222–223.

Bachelor, Dean. *Dry Lakes and Drag Strips—The American Hot Rod.* St. Paul: MBI Publishing Company, 1995, 2002.

Borgeson, Griffith. "The Engine of Engines to Power the Car of Cars—The OHV Cadillac V-16 Engine," *Automobile Quarterly,* Fourth Quarter 1984, Kutztown, PA: Vol. 22, No. 4: pp. 340–365.

Brown, T.C. "1931 Cadillac V-16 Pinin Farina Boattailed Speedster," *Motor Trend,* Petersen Publishing, Los Angeles, Vol. 37, No. 3, March, 1985: pp. 111–118.

Cadillac Communications. "Cadillac & Pininfarina, an Enduring Relationship," commemorative brochure for the 1999 Concorso Italiano, Monterey, CA, as excerpted in *The Self-Starter,* Cadillac-LaSalle Club, Inc., Detroit, MI, Vol. 43, No. 4, April 2000, Detroit, MI: pp. 14–15.

Cole, Nick. "The Pursuit of Elegance, The Elegance of Pursuit: 1931 Cadillac V-16 Roadster by Pininfarina," *Automobile Quarterly,* Vol. 20, No. 4, 1982, Kutztown, PA: pp. 418–425.

DeMars, Robert. "World's Fair Cadillac: The Fleetwood Aerodynamic Coupe 1933–1937," *The Self-Starter,* Cadillac-LaSalle Club, Inc., Detroit, MI, 1974 Annual Edition: pp. 2–9.

Donnelly, Jim. "Automotive Pioneers—Sam McLaughlin," *Hemmings Classic Car* #82, July 2011: pg. 74.

Driggs, Frank and Lewine, Harris. *Black Beauty, White Heat: A Pictorial History of Classic Jazz.* New York: William Morrow and Company, Inc., 1982.

Edwards, Shelby. "Brown & Bigelow's Charles Allen Ward," *Minnesota History,* Minnesota Historical Society, Vol. 64, Issue 7, Fall, 2015, St. Paul, MN: pp. 292–300.

Ferguson, Clark. "1930 Cadillac V-16, Series 452A Roadster by Fleetwood, Style 4302," *Torque,* Michigan Region Classic Car Club of America, September-October 2002: 5–9.

"Fire Wagon Returns to Cadillac" in *The Self-Starter,* 1974 annual edition, The Cadillac-LaSalle Club, Inc.: pp. 9–10.

Fleming, E.J. *The Fixers: Eddie Mannix, Howard Strickling and the MGM Publicity Machine,* Jefferson, NC: McFarland, 2005.

Franzen, Elmer. "If at First You Don't Succeed, Try, Try Again," *The Self-Starter,* Cadillac-LaSalle Club, Inc., Bloomfield Hills, MI, Vol. VIII, No. 4, February 1966: pp. 12–13.

Goad, Tom. "1930 Cadillac, 16 Model 452 Cabriolet Sedan by Fleetwood," *Torque,* Michigan Region Classic Car Club of America, Ferndale, MI, No. 371, March-April 2004: pp. 5–11.

Hendry, Maurice A. *Cadillac: Standard of the World—The Complete Seventy-Five Year History.* Princeton: Automobile Quarterly Publications, 1973.

Hendry, Maurice A. *Cadillac at 100—Legacy of Leadership.* New Albany, IN: Automobile Quarterly Publications, 2008.

Hinckley, James; Hinckley, Jim; and Robinson, Jon G. *The Big Book of Car Culture: The Armchair Guide to Automotive Americana.* Motorbooks, 2005, pg. 138.

Holls. David. "Dream Come True," *The Self-Starter,* Cadillac-LaSalle Club, Inc., Royal Oak, MI, June, 1962: cover, pp. 2–3.

Holls, David. Letter to the Editor, *The Self-Starter,* Cadillac-LaSalle Club, Inc., Detroit, MI, Vol. 34, No.7, July 1991: pg. 11.

Holls, David. "Salon Picture of the Month," *The Self-Starter,* Cadillac-LaSalle Club, Inc., Detroit, MI, Vol. 7, No. 8, June 1965: pg. 13.

"John Arthur Moir, Jr.," obituary (Dec. 1, 2018). *Antique Automobile,* Antique Automobile Club of America, Vol. 83, No. 1, Jan./Feb. 2019, Hershey, PA: pg. 82.

Kear, Lynn, and Rossman, John. *Kay Francis: A Passionate Life and Career.* Jefferson, NC: McFarland, 2006.

Kenny, Dave. *Minnesota Goes to War.* St. Paul, MN. Minnesota Historical Society Press, 2005:

Kimes, Beverly Rae. *The Classic Car,* Des Plaines, IL: Classic Car Club of America, 1990.

Kimes, Beverly Rae. *The Classic Era,* Des Plaines, IL: Classic Car Club of America, 2001.

Koch, Jeff. "Colossal Cadillac," *Hemmings Classic Car* #147, Vol. 13, Issue 3, December 2016: pp. 48–51.

LeForge, Rick. "Happiness is a Sixteen Cylinder Cadillac," *The Self-Starter,* Cadillac-LaSalle Club, Inc., Detroit, MI, Vol. V, No. 6, April 1963: pg. 11.

LeForge, Rick. "Turn Left at Tucumcari," *The Self-Starter,* Cadillac-LaSalle Club, Inc., Detroit, MI, Vol. VII, No. 11, September 1965: pp. 4–10.

Litwin, Matthew, and Conwill, David, "Worldwide Auctioneers, Pacific Grove," *Hemmings Motor News,* Bennington, VT, Vol. 66, No. 11, November 2019: pp. 78–83.

May, Walter. "1937 Cadillac V-16 Series 90 Fleetwood Imperial Cabriolet," *Bulletin* (CCCA) October 2007: pp. 17–18.

Mellin, Bob. "Cadillac V16: 1934–1937 Roster and Summary" The Self-Starter, Cadillac-LaSalle Club, Inc., Detroit, MI, Vol. 5, No. 2, November-December 1963: pp. 8–13.

Mellin, Bob. "Cadillac V-16 Introduction," *The Self-Starter,* Cadillac-LaSalle Club, Inc., Detroit, MI, Vol. IV, No. 12, September 1962: pp.3–7.

Melton, James, with Ken Purdy. *Bright Wheels Rolling.* Philadelphia: Macrae Smith Company, 1954.

Merkel, Alan. "A Rewarding Restoration," *The Self-Starter,* Cadillac-LaSalle Club, Inc., Detroit, MI, Vol. 54, No. 7, July, 2011: pp. 6–11.

Merkel, Alan. "Where did all the 16s go? A documentary study of the 1930–31 Cadillac V-16s," *Standard Catalog of Cadillac 1903–2000,* 2nd Edition. Edited by Lenzke, James T. Iola, WI: Kraus Publications, 2000: pp. 225–229.

Milici, Chris. "The Dimmittmobile," *The Self-Starter,* Cadillac-LaSalle Club, Inc., Detroit, MI, Vol. 55, No. 2, February, 2012: pp. 18–22.

Milici, Chris. "'Hot Rodding' Cadillac Style—Cadillac action on the dry lakes," *The Self-Starter,* Cadillac-LaSalle Club, Inc., Detroit, MI, Vol. 55, No. 3, March, 2012: pp. 11–15.

Mukhtar, Sheikh. Letter to the Editor, *The Classic Car,* Classic Car Club of America, Schiller Park, IL, Vol XVIII, No. 2, Jun. 1980, cover story.

Oddo, Frank. *The Street Rodder's Handbook.* New York: HP Books, 2003.

"Picture Restoration of a Madam X." *The Self-Starter,* Cadillac-LaSalle Club, Inc., Detroit, MI, Vol.VI, No. 9, July 1964: pp. 10–11.

Saunders, Yann. *The (New) Cadillac Database.* Internet website accessible at http://www.car-nection.com/yann/Dbas_txt/indx2001.htm.

Schapiro, Amy. *Millicent Fenwick: Her Way.* New Brunswick, NJ: Rutgers University Press, 2003.

Schild, James. *Fleetwood—The Company & the Coachcraft.* Columbia, IL: The Auto Review, 2001. Revised second edition published June 2011.

Schinnerer, Paul. "Cadillac Safari," *The Self-Starter,* Cadillac-LaSalle Club, Inc., Detroit, MI, Vol. VII, No. 3, Jan. 1965: pp. 10–11.

Schneider, Roy A. *Sixteen Cylinder Motorcars—An Illustrated History.* Arcadia, CA: Heritage House, 1974.

Scott, Peter. *A History of the Thames Side Promenade Miniature Railways.* Reading, UK: Peter Scott, 2005, Appendix Two.

Smith, LeRoi, and Tony Hossain. *Classic Cars—Cadillac.* New York: Crescent Books, 1983.

Tite, W.R. "The Sweet Sixteen," *The Self-Starter,* Cadillac-LaSalle Club, Inc., Detroit, MI, Vol. V, Number 4, February, 1963: pp. 10–14.

Tomaine, Bob. "Back in a Cadillac: V-16 fan tracks down a coupe like his grandfather had." *Old Cars Weekly News and Marketplace,* Vol. 40, No. 39, October 13, 2011, Palm Coast, FL: pp. 76–78.

Towell, Ann. "—Moving East," *The Self-Starter,* Cadillac-LaSalle Club, Inc., Bloomfield Hills, MI, Vol. VIII, No. 9, July 1966: pp. 7–13.

Uhlir, Agnes. "1930 Cadillac V-16 'Fleetdowns' Roadster by Fleetwood," *The Self-Starter,* Cadillac-LaSalle Club, Inc., Detroit, MI, Vol. VI, Number 6, April, 1964: pp. 111–14.

Uhlir, Agnes. "WOW! V-16 452 Cadillac Landaulet," *The Self-Starter,* Cadillac-LaSalle Club, Inc., Detroit, MI, Vol. VIII, No. 2—Nov.-Dec. 1965: pg. 10.

Van Gelderen, R.E. and Juhring, J. "Upper Midwest Grand Classic—Minneapolis, MN," *The Self-Starter,* Cadillac-LaSalle Club, Inc., Detroit, MI, Vol. VIII, No. 8—Aug. 1966: pp. 18–19.

Verschoor, Ron and Hamilton, Tom. "1938 Cadillac 90 Series Town Sedan by Fleetwood—The Most Original Classic at this Year's Annual Meeting," The Classic Car, Classic Car Club of America, Rolling Meadows, IL, Vol. LXVII, No. 1, Spring 2019: pp. 46–48.

Wenger, Terry and Mellin, Robert C. "The 1934–'37 Cadillac V-16s," *The Self-Starter,* Cadillac-LaSalle Club, Inc., Detroit, MI, Vol. 49, No. 11—Nov.-Dec. 2006: 17–22 and Vol. 50, No. 1—Jan. 2007: pp. 17–20.

Zeiger, Rick. "Cadillac at Concorso Italiano," *The Self-Starter,* Cadillac-LaSalle Club, Inc., Detroit, MI, Vol. 43, No. 4, April 2000, Detroit, MI: pp. 15–18.

Zeiger, Rick. "A Worldly Cadillac," *The Self-Starter,* Cadillac-LaSalle Club, Inc., Detroit, MI, Vol. 44, No. 7, July 2001, Detroit, MI: pp. 14–16.

Index

Numbers in ***bold italics*** indicate pages with illustrations